THE OTHER EMPTINESS

Entering Wisdom
Beyond Emptiness of Self

BY TONY DUFF

PADMA KARPO TRANSLATION COMMITTEE

First edition, November 2011
ISBN paper: 978-9937-572-67-5
ISBN e-book: 978-9937-572-68-2
Janson typeface with diacritical marks and
Tibetan Classic typeface
Designed and created by Tony Duff

Produced, Printed, and Published by
Padma Karpo Translation Committee
P.O. Box 4957
Kathmandu
NEPAL

Committee members for this book: translation and composition, Lama Tony Duff; editorial, Tom Anderson, Jason Watkin; cover design George Romvari.

Web-site and e-mail contact through:
http://www.pktc.org/pktc
or search Padma Karpo Translation Committee on the web.

CONTENTS

PART 1: EXPLANATIONS BY THE AUTHOR

PART 2: EXPLANATIONS BY DOLPOPA

PART 3: EXPLANATIONS BY
KHENPO TSULTRIM GYATSO

PART 4: EXPLANATIONS BY
JAMGON KONGTRUL THE GREAT

IMPORTANT BACKGROUND

History, Background, and Sources

The Buddha made it clear that the teaching on emptiness is the most fundamental of all his teachings. He taught it in various ways and at increasing levels of profundity during his life. In the centuries since then, his followers have looked at his teaching again and again, trying to discover the meaning intended in his various levels of teaching on emptiness. As a result, many schools of thought about emptiness and many ways of practice to go with them have appeared. That has also been true in Tibet, where Buddhism began with the uptake of the various views and practices of emptiness present in India at the time and went on to develop its own ways of expressing the view and practice of emptiness. "Other Emptiness" or "zhan-tong" as it is called in Tibetan,[1] is a name that originated in Tibet during the development of Tibetan Buddhist thought. Other Emptiness, which refers to a particular view and practice of emptiness, is the subject of this book.

---

[1] When these teachings were first being given to Westerners, it was popular to use the Tibetan term "zhantong" to name them. By the time of publication, the direct and truly exact English translations "other emptiness" and "other empty" have been accepted as the standard translations for the term, so they are used in this book. The term is explained at length in subsequent chapters.

1

Four main traditions of Buddhism arose in Tibet: Nyingma, Kagyu, Sakya, and Gelug. There were also some smaller, though no less important ones, such as the Jonang. Their view and practice of emptiness were not the same. However, they fell into two very distinct groups: those whose view and practice of emptiness was consistent with and not consistent with Other Emptiness. The Nyingma, Kagyu, one faction within the Sakya, and Jonang traditions comprise the group whose view and practice of emptiness was consistent with Other Emptiness. The Gelug tradition and the rest of the Sakya tradition comprise the other group.

Unfortunately, one amongst all of those traditions did not agree to disagree with those who did not follow their view of emptiness. Followers of the Gelug tradition have, since the tradition began with its founder Tsongkhapa [1357–1419], taken the stance that they are the only ones in Tibet who truly understand and propagate the Buddha's teaching on emptiness. Historically, they have behaved very aggressively towards the traditions whose view and practice is consistent with Other Emptiness, even going so far as to shut down monasteries of that group in order to destroy the teaching on Other Emptiness. This history is told later in the book as an unfortunate but necessary part of understanding the story of Other Emptiness.

From the above you can see that the majority of Tibetan Buddhists follow the view of Other Emptiness and do not accept the Gelug understanding of emptiness. However, the Gelug tradition became very powerful within Tibet because of being intimately linked with the Tibetan government in central Tibet. As a result, their ways and views often overshadowed those of the other traditions. This happened yet again when Tibetan Buddhism first came to the West in the very late 1960's. At that time, it was the view of the Gelugpa tradition, with its strong emphasis on the Consequence Middle Way[2] understood according to the Prajñāpāramitā teachings in the Buddha's second turning of the wheel of dharma, that became prevalent in the West. I was present at the time and remember the degree to which we all—academics and Buddhists alike—believed that what we were being told by the Gelug masters was the Buddha's teaching on emptiness, nothing more to be said! We all thought—and there are many who still do think—that their view of emptiness was and is the accepted view of emptiness across the whole of Tibetan Buddhism. This situation became further entrenched when Westerners who had become expert in it, people for example like the very knowledgeable Professor Jeffrey Hopkins, wrote about it extensively and in depth so that the view and practice of emptiness of the majority of Tibetan traditions, Other Emptiness, was overshadowed and did not come to light.

The above situation was exacerbated by the fact that Other Emptiness is a very profound teaching that goes beyond logic. It has taken time for Westerners to become sufficiently expert in it that they could start to write authoritatively about it. However, in very recent years a few publications have started to appear, written by students who have become expert in the teachings of Nyingma, Kagyu, and Sakya traditions. The publications and in some cases the teachings of these Westerners have started to present the other side of the view and practice of emptiness as it was understood in Tibet, and there is, at the time of writing, a knowledge just beginning to develop that the Gelug presentation of emptiness is not the universally accepted one within Buddhist thought. In fact, it is starting to be understood that the Gelug view is not even the majority view. I have been part of this effort, having already published several books on Other Emptiness that present texts and teachings primarily of Nyingma and Kagyu masters. A short history of my involvement is presented next so that readers can have confidence in the presentations made in this

---

[2] Skt. Prāsaṅgika Madhyamaka.

book. It mentions authors and source texts which are important and which have been translated. This will assist readers in the development of a sense of who is who in the world of Other Emptiness teaching and literature.

During the 1970's, I studied extensively with the Gelug tradition and received many explanations long and short on their view and practice of the Middle Way—Madhyamaka—from Lamas Yeshe and Zopa of FPMT fame, and from Geshe Lodan and Zasep Tulku who were my monastic preceptors at the Australian monastery Chenrezig Institute, of which I was one of the founding members, during that time. In addition, I was fortunate enough to practise their instructions during extensive retreats in the forests of Australia. In short, during this phase of my journey, I gained a detailed theoretical and practical knowledge of the Gelug teachings on emptiness.

In 1980, I shifted to the United States where I studied intensively for eight years with the vidyādhara Chogyam Trungpa and immersed myself in the Other Emptiness view and meditation of his Kagyu lineage. As a member of his Nālandā Translation Committee, I was especially fortunate to hear very extensive sets of teachings on Other Emptiness from the outstanding Nyingma khenpo Palden Sherab and the outstanding Karma Kagyu khenpo Thrangu Rinpoche. I also heard smaller teachings on the subject from the Karma Kagyu tulkus Jamgon Kongtrul and Traleg Rinpoches. At that time, Khenpo Palden Sherab encouraged me to translate Mipham's excellent work on Other Emptiness from the Nyingma perspective called *Lion's Roar Proclaiming Other Emptiness*[3], which I did under that title. Thrangu Rinpoche pointed me to a practical text on Other Emptiness by Jamgon Kongtrul the Great called *Instructions for Practising the View of the Other Emptiness Great Middle Way, "Light Rays of Stainless Vajra Moon"*, provided me with the reading transmission, then asked me

---

[3] Published by Padma Karpo Translation Committee, authored by Tony Duff, revised edition February 2011, ISBN: 978-9937-8244-6-0.

to translate it. The translated text has been published under the title *Instructions for Practising the View of the Other Emptiness Great Middle Way, A Text of Oral Instructions by Jamgon Kongtrul*[4]. During this period I received extensive, detailed instruction from Khenpo Tsultrim Gyatso on the chapters in Jamgon Kongtrul's very famous *Treasury which is an Encyclopædia of Knowledge* that deal with Other Emptiness and its place within all of the Buddhist philosophical schools. That chapter has been translated based on his teachings and included in this book. ✓

✓ During that time, my knowledge of Tibetan grammar learned from Western sources was proving to be a serious impediment to understanding fine points of argument in these texts, so Traleg Rinpoche strongly encouraged me to learn Tibetan grammar on its own terms, provided me with a textbook used in the Karma Kagyu tradition, and suggested I translate that, too. I later learned Tibetan grammar in depth at a Tibetan university in a Tibetan-only environment and translated not only that text but several others as well[5]. I understood then what Traleg Rinpoche had seen, that Western versions of Tibetan grammar which are being taught to most Westerners in the name of being Tibetan grammar are not correct presentations of Tibetan grammar. This really does hold back the greater translation effort. All the translations in here have benefited from having learned Tibetan grammar not only in depth but on its

---

[4] Published by Padma Karpo Translation Committee, authored by Tony Duff, 2011, ISBN: 978-9937-572-03-3.

[5] These translations of grammar texts, with their extensive introductions and notes are available from the Padma Karpo Translation Committee web-site. They include the root texts of Tibetan grammar by Thumi Saṃbhoṭa, *The Root of Grammar, the Thirty Verses* and *Application of Gender Signs*, the two *Great Living Tree* grammars by Yangchen Druppay Dorje for beginners, *Situ's Words* by Ngulchu Dharmabhadra for medium-to-advanced studies, and *Application of Gender Signs Clarified* by Ngulchu Dharmabhadra and Yangchen Druppay Dorje for very advanced studies. There are others, too.

own terms directly in Tibetan from Tibetans rather than through Westerners and their incorrect ideas of it.

In 1995, I was fortunate to meet and translate for the head of the Tibetan Jonang lineage who, with his chief khenpo, was visiting the United States for the first time. The early masters of the Jonang lineage played a crucial role in the development of the Other Emptiness teaching in Tibet and I found that my understanding of it was broadened and deepened considerably through the extensive discussions I had with them privately, not to mention the translations done for them in public. He encouraged me to practice the quintessential text presenting the Jonang view of Other Emptiness, called *Mountain Dharma: An Ocean of Definitive Meaning* by Dolpopa Sherab Gyaltsen, the greatest of the Jonang authors. I have not had time to complete the work, but a portion of the first chapter on the crucial subject of buddha nature has been done and has been included in this book.

In 1996 and 1997, Other Emptiness appeared in front of me again, this time in the form of four days of private teachings and several weeks of group teachings on the subject provided by the great Karma Kagyu Khenpo, Tsultrim Gyatso. This khenpo is a principal lineage holder of the more recent champion of the Other Emptiness system, Jamgon Kongtrul the Great. The khenpo asked me to translate all of the teachings mentioned above, organize them nicely within a framework of other material of my own choosing, and publish them. Originally, they were to form the backbone of this book, but space considerations meant that they had to be

Figure 1. Milarepa

divided up and published in more than one book. I took all of the material that presented Other Emptiness in conjunction with Milarepa's songs and combined them into a book titled *The Theory and Practice of Other Emptiness Taught Through Milarepa's Songs, Including Teachings of Khenpo Tsultrim Gyatso*[6]. Some of the remainder found their home in this book and some found their way into other books. His teachings in the Milarepa book and this book complement each other and should be read together.

Figure 2. Gyalwang Je

My work during the 1990's as the director of the Drukpa Kagyu Heritage Project brought yet more Other Emptiness materials to my attention. I found a Drukpa Kagyu text by the second Drukchen, Gyalwang Je, called *"Chariot of Establishment"*, *Treasure Trove of a Mind Absorbed in the Profound Meaning* to be especially interesting. Gyalwang Je was famous for his realization combined with scholarship. His text contained a complete exposition of the Kagyu view and showed the Other Emptiness view in several ways, including within the non-dual approach of the *Kālachakra Tantra*. I translated and published it, together with an extensive introduction, under the title *A Juggernaut of the Non-Dual View, Teachings of the Second Drukchen, Gyalwang Je*[7].

---

[6] Published by Padma Karpo Translation Committee, authored by Tony Duff, 2011, ISBN: 978-9937-572-10-1.

[7] Published by Padma Karpo Translation Committee, authored by Tony Duff, 2011, ISBN: paper book 978-9937-572-07-1.

In the year 2000, I completed translations of the important texts of the Indian master Maitrīpa, who generally speaking was one of the

main figures in the transmission of the Other Emptiness teaching into Tibet. He was also the source of the view of the entire Tibetan Kagyu lineage. One feature of his writings is that they unequivocally demonstrate that the Other Emptiness view was very much alive and well in India, despite the strong denials of that by its later Tibetan opponents. I taught one of his texts to Westerners in Bodhgaya during the

Figure 3. Master Maitripa

annual prayer gatherings in 2002 and saw that it was time to publish the important ones in English. They were published together with ample explanations, under the title *Maitripa's Writings on the View, The Main Indian Source of the Tibetan Views of Other Emptiness*[8]. It too makes excellent companion reading for this book.

From 2000 onwards, I focussed on study and practice in the Nyingma tradition. With that, I became very familiar with the writings of the most important figures in that tradition—Guru Rinpoche, Longchen Rabjam, Jigmey Lingpa, Mipham, and others—and received many teachings from masters of the tradition, especially during extensive teachings and retreats received and done in Tibet, that only served to increase my knowledge of Other Emptiness. Finally, I gained certainty that the Kagyu and Nyingma traditions do indeed share the same Other Emptiness view, something which has been questioned by Western practitioners of these traditions. That understanding has also been incorporated into this book.

---

[8] Published by Padma Karpo Translation Committee, authored by Tony Duff, second edition 2010, ISBN: 938-9937-9031-7-2.

The practices of the Nyingma tradition led to gaining deep certainty in the view of Other Emptiness, and I began to teach it widely, starting in 2012. I found it very helpful for Western audiences in this particular time. It provides a way to introduce people to the non-conceptual, non-dual approach which is the deep teaching of Buddhism, without having to expose them to the highly secret Mahāmudrā and Dzogchen before they are ready. It has the happy feature of drawing together all of the Buddha's teachings of sūtra and paving the way for instruction in tantra, especially of Mahāmudrā and Dzogchen. So, after that long personal journey, which in retrospect was more than necessary, I have put together this book, a compendium of explanations, teachings, and writings that will help illuminate the darkness surrounding the view and meditation—or theory and practice—of the Other Empty approach.

Those who are expecting hard-headed philosophy and a great deal of logic as is seen in the Middle Way approach of the second turning of the wheel of Buddha's dharma will not find it here. This book has an overall tone of making precise distinctions—this is, this is not— rather than one of attempting to prove that something does not exist. That is exactly as it should be, for the hallmark of the third turning of the wheel of Buddha's dharma, in which the Other Emptiness view is taught, is summed up as being "a wheel in which fine distinctions are taught"; such and such is shown to be so or not so, and so on. This might make those who are strongly habituated to Middle Way syllogistic reasoning uncomfortable but that is to be expected. This is a different approach which has a different feeling to it, as will be explained in more detail further on in this book.

Arrangement of the Book

The book is in four parts, with each part comprised of the explanations of a specific author. The material is arranged in order of increasing difficulty, with the last two chapters on theory requiring an extensive knowledge of technical Buddhist teaching. Furthermore, the chapters of theory culminate in the final chapter which shows the actual practice.

Part one consists of my own writings which explain the subject in plain English and delve into many issues that need clarification using a Westerner's voice. These clarifications made directly in English ease the necessary work of understanding the explanations of Tibetan masters whose works have been translated into English. Therefore, part one is followed by parts two to four which contain the explanations of Tibetan teachers, translated from Tibetan.

Anyone who is approaching the Other Emptiness teaching must understand to begin with that it is actually a very profound thread of the entire tathāgatagarbha teaching found in the third turning of the wheel of dharma. Therefore, it is appropriate to begin the explanations of Tibetan authors with an exposition on tathāgatagarbha.

Dolpopa Sherab Gyaltsen was the greatest exponent of the Other Emptiness teaching in the Jonang tradition and one of the greatest exponents of Other Emptiness in Tibet. His most important composition was the famous *Mountain Dharma: An Ocean of Definitive Meaning* that he composed in order to show that the Other Emptiness teaching was part of the Buddhas teaching. Therefore, it is appropriate to present the opening section of that in which shows how the Buddha and his followers in India gave the tathāgatagarbha teaching. To give you a little more feel for the *Mountain Dharma: An Ocean of Definitive Meaning* text, the text is divided into three parts: "the ground, path, and fruition phases" as Dolpopa refers to them. The ground phase is longer than the other sections and deals with many aspects of the ground in individual sections. Its first two sections simply set out what tathāgatagarbha is and provide scriptural suppot for it. Those two sections are presented in part two.

Part three consists of various teachings given by Khenpo Tsultrim Gyatso on Other Emptiness, arranged so that the reader is led into a deepening understanding of Other Emptiness not merely as a philosophical matter but as a practical way to go to enlightenment. It starts with a short but very clear history of the Other Emptiness teaching, then delves into the view and meditation of Other Emptiness. It includes a very handy chapter in which the khenpo presents and explains the main scriptural passages used to support Other Emptiness. Some of the more difficult philosophical points are touched on in a chapter on key points but, on the whole, his teachings avoid much of the difficult philosophical argument usually associated with the teachings on Other Emptiness.

Part four, the final part of the book, contains three selections from key treatises on Other Emptiness written by Jamgon Kongtrul the Great. The first two are rigorous philosophical texts and the third is instruction on how actually to practice Other Emptiness.

The two philosophical texts fit in like this. Other Emptiness is based on the teaching of the Buddha given in the third turning of the wheel of dharma. The Buddha appointed his regent Maitreya as the care-taker of this dharma. Maitreya taught it to the Indian master Asaṅga, who wrote it down in a set of five texts called *The Five Dharmas of Maitreya*. Of them, the one called *Great Vehicle Highest Continuum Treatise* expounds the Other Emptiness view very clearly. Jamgon Kongtrul the Great wrote a major commentary to that treatise from the Other Emptiness perspective called *The Lion's Roar of the Non-Regressing Commentary to the Highest Continuum*. The treatise has a lengthy introduction, which has been presented as the first selection in this part. It was included specifically because it contains a wealth of background material to the subject of Other Emptiness.

The second selection comes from his very famous *Treasury which is an Encyclopædia of Knowledge*. This selection contains two sections of the chapter on the higher training of prajñā that are crucial to the development of a correct understanding of the Other Emptiness view. The first is called "ascertainment of provisional and definitive meaning within the three wheels and within the two truths". The

second is called "ascertainment of the view" in which the view of each
of the main tenet systems of Buddhism is presented, culminating in
the view of the Other Emptiness Middle Way.

The third selection comes from his *Instructions for Practising the View
of the Other Emptiness Great Middle Way, "Light Rays of Stainless Vajra
Moon"*[9]. Given that one of the aims of this book is to show once and
for all that Other Emptiness is not merely a philosophical endeavour,
this final selection is a fitting conclusion to the whole book because
it unequivocally shows that Other Emptiness is not intended for
academic pursuit but, like all Buddhist theory, is intended as a basis
for practice done to dispel confusion so that we can return to our
original, enlightened condition.

Translation Sources

I would like to note that all the translations in this book are mine.
Other translations of the selections from *The Lion's Roar of the Non-
Regressing* and *The Treasury which is an Encyclopædia of Knowledge*
included have been published elsewhere but with major errors of
translation; I felt there was no choice but to translate them afresh.
All of Khenpo Tsultrim's teachings were translated by myself and
have been published here and elsewhere at his personal command.

Style of Other Emptiness Presentation

There is no question amongst Tibetan experts that the Kagyu and
Nyingma traditions are based in the view of Other Emptiness. The
Gelug tradition does not subscribe to the view at all and does not
mention it in its own teaching. The Sakya tradition does not
generally subscribe to the view, though there is one segment of Sakya

---

[9] As mentioned earlier, the complete text with much more information
about Other Emptiness and a substantial and very useful introduction
has been published in a separate book under the title *Instructions for
Practising the View of Other Emptiness, A Text of Oral Instructions by
Jamgon Kongtrul.*

followers who do understand and follow it. Then there is the small but all-important tradition called the Jonang school whose founder coined the phrase that eventually became the term "other empty" and whose whole tradition of teaching and practice is proclaimed to be nothing but Other Emptiness.

Anyone well-versed in Other Emptiness usually will not draw on only one of these traditions when discussing the teaching, but will draw on several if not all of them. I have seen that each does have its own emphasis and differing way of presenting the Other Emptiness, but have also seen that, when Other Emptiness is understood, they all are saying the same. For example, Dolpopa Sherab Gyaltsen of the Jonang tradition emphasized the Yogāchāra view very strongly in his teachings, to the point of almost solidifying wisdom. For that reason Jigmey Lingpa of the Nyingma tradition later chided the Jonangs for seeming to fall into the view of permanence. Jigmey Lingpa presented his understanding of Other Emptiness in connection with Consequence Middle Way, in which wisdom is not solidified in the slightest. Dolpopa was not making a mistake—it is very clear that he understood the emptiness of a self-nature in true Middle Way fashion, but by emphasizing the Yogāchāra point of view he made sure that his followers did not lose sight of the fact that non-existent wisdom has to be said to exist. And so on and so on. I have found after exhaustive study that, when you follow through with their respective ways of presenting Other Emptiness, they are using different approaches as skilful ways of getting to the same, direct experience of wisdom. That said, although this book apparently presents many explanations from the Karma Kagyu tradition, it also presents substantial amounts of Other Emptiness teaching from Nyingma, Jonang, and other sources, but does so with the thought that, fundamentally speaking, they do not contradict each other, even though it seems at times that they do. All in all, this book aims to present a view of Other Emptiness that is generally accepted amongst all the schools that follow Other Emptiness and which will be of practical use rather than a highly philosophical dissertation that simply catalogues the subtle differences belonging to one stream of Other Emptiness thought or another.

To conclude this introduction, I must say that I am pleased with this book; it shows that good scholarship can go hand in hand with Buddhist practice but that, in the end, practice is still the point! Having said that, to those scholars who are not practitioners of Buddhism, I could remind you that the Buddha repeatedly said that there was no point to what he was teaching unless it was used for practice. With that, I could quote Nāgārjuna who said that the Buddhist view when used merely to support further development of conceptual views is a case of medicine turning into poison. Unfortunately, experience tells me that the warnings are correct but not frequently heard.

I do remember the story of the exceptionally learned and accomplished Hindu yogin called Āchārya Aśhvaghoṣha who challenged the monks of a major Buddhist institution in India to a debate. Āryadeva was sent by Nāgārjuna to represent the Buddhists because of well-founded fears that Aśhvagoṣha would win and with that insist that the whole monastery reject Buddhism and become Hindu— which was how debates worked at the time. Āryadeva was able to win with the result that, by the rules of debate, Aśhvagoṣha had to become Buddhist. He did so, but it was depressing for him and he could not really accept it. The monks cleverly locked him in the library of the monastery. After a while he became curious. Curiosity led him to extensive reading. That in turn led to deep amazement at and faith in the Buddha's teaching. And he did become a practitioner!

Finally, I need to say that there is repetitiveness in the first part of this book. That is deliberate. It is part of the overall presentation in this book. The book starts slowly, with the first chapters repeating key ideas from various perspectives. Then, the first part of the book as a whole is presented in the style of oral teaching, which is the way that the other emptiness, as a very practical teaching, is presented.

The remaining parts of the book become increasingly less repetitive as the various technical aspects of other emptiness are introduced. The book ends with very technical writings from Tibetan authors which are packed with information and themselves need an explanation if most people are to understand them.

There is nothing haphazard about this book. From beginning to end there is a progression of thought and style which is the heart of how the teaching of other emptiness is presented.

Tony Duff,
Padma Karpo Translation Committee,
Swayambunath, Nepal,
February, 2014

Part 1

Explanations by the Author

Figure 4. Lama Tony Duff teaching Mahāmudrā in retreat
with a statue of Karmapa behind

OTHER EMPTINESS, WISDOM, AND THE TATHAGATAGARBHA TEACHING

If we boil it right down, Other Emptiness is part of the teaching of being in wisdom, which in itself is the final or ultimate teaching of the Buddha. This is fundamental, so it is taken up in many places in this part of the book, for instance in the chapter "Wisdom is the Key Point".

Wisdom is mentioned in all levels of the Buddha's teachings, which is to be expected given that wisdom is what a buddha actually is. However, the Buddha did not give the actual teachings on wisdom to begin with. He taught in a gradual way so that beings could be brought along in the best way possible and did not give the actual teachings on wisdom until the final phase of his teachings. His teachings on wisdom appear in the third or final phase of presenting the sūtra teachings and within the tantra teaching which is thought of as a fourth phase of the teachings. Correspondingly, the teachings on other emptiness are found in those two locations.

Because of the two locations it is sometimes said that there is "sūtra Other Emptiness" and "tantra Other Emptiness". That is a division into two types of other emptiness made from the standpoint of the place where the teaching is situated. However, it is important to understand that the other emptiness aspect is the same in each case. Some would say that there was a difference in the quality of the teaching in each case, but I prefer to say that the view of emptiness

19

in each case is essentially the same and can be understood through the headline of other emptiness. It is true that there is a difference between how directly the sūtra teachings and tantra teachings show wisdom to the followers, with the former showing it a little indirectly and the latter showing it very directly, but the basic meaning of other emptiness is the same in each case. To give a concrete example of that, I asked the khenpo in charge of teaching at the retreat centre of Dzogchen Monastery in Tibet whether Dzogchen itself is other emptiness. He replied, "Yes indeed! The Dzogchen teaching itself does not mention other emptiness but, from the straightforward perspective of what other emptiness is about, there is no question that Dzogchen is an other-empty type of view." And that is my point.

You can understand then that an absolutely complete presentation of Other Emptiness would include lengthy presentations from the perspectives of both sūtra and tantra. I could have composed a book like that and it would have been very interesting, but it also would have made the presentation of Other Emptiness very long and complicated, something that I specifically wanted to avoid. Therefore, this book rarely mentions Other Emptiness in relation to the tantras, but focusses on it in relation to the sūtras.

Leaving aside Other Emptiness in relation to the tantras, where exactly is other emptiness taught in the sūtras? The Buddha taught the sūtras in three distinct presentations, which will be explained at length later in this book. Experts claim that the third presentation has a mixture of themes. From a more general standpoint, that seems to be true. However, a close look shows that it has a single theme of making very clear distinctions about mind, leading to presentations of wisdom. Within that, there are two different types of teaching. One is called Mind Only. In it, everything is reduced to being an aspect of mind and a wisdom-type mind at that, which is a step towards the actual teaching on wisdom. The other is called the tathāgatagarbha teaching. In it, the Buddha shows that every being with a mind has an element or seed of buddha within the mind. That teaching functions as a goad to practise the path because it proves that everyone can become a tathāgata or truly complete buddha. However, it also contains other threads of teaching, including the very profound teachings on the nature of tathāgatagarbha which are none other than teachings on wisdom and are where the other emptiness approach is found.

The other-emptiness type of teaching presents a view of emptiness that is consistent with actually being in wisdom. It is not uncommon for beginners to think that "other emptiness" means the whole teaching on wisdom, but it is not, it is one important aspect of it. It is the aspect which helps followers to have a correct understanding of how wisdom actually sits and thereby to sit in wisdom themselves. Other emptiness has become thought of in some quarters as a kind of mysterious, deep, and very complicated philosophy which is generally beyond the reach even of very intelligent people. However, it is not. It is part of the overall wisdom teaching given by the Buddha to show his followers how to understand their own wisdom so that they could step into a direct experience of that non-dual, non-conceptual wisdom themselves.

An important point connected with this is that people who know a little about the Other Emptiness view usually understand that it is connected with the tathāgatagarbha teaching, but usually do not realize how complete and encompassing the tathāgatagarbha teaching is in its own right. The tathāgatagarbha teaching is not just another part of the third turning of the wheel, one that most people think of as the teaching on "buddha nature". It is a complete teaching in its own right that covers the entire Great Vehicle journey and even has a door for admitting followers of the Lesser Vehicle. Jamgon Kongtrul explains this point in the introduction to his commentary on one of the main texts explaining the tathāgatagarbha teaching called the *Great Vehicle Highest Continuum Treatise*. The introduction has been included in this book in part four, starting on page 191 and the point being made here can be more fully understood from it.

Because the tathāgatagarbha teaching has connections with everything taught in the Lesser and Great Vehicles, discussions of it can lead into very vast and complicated discussions of the Buddha's teaching. Similarly, discussions centred on other emptiness also can become very vast and complicated, something which happened in Tibet, with discussions and debates about other emptiness delving into many aspects of the Buddha's teaching. That in turn laid the foundation for other emptiness becoming known as a very complicated philosophical teaching, one which contained seemingly unending and often very difficult topics. That happened, but, as explained above, it is not the intention behind the Other Emptiness teaching.

There was a book published recently by a Western expert in the tathāgatagarbha teachings. His book on matters connected with other emptiness was over 1200 pages in length. I read it and found that it was well-done and that the author's mastery of his subject was very evident. However, despite being a scholar myself, I became bored with it after the first few hundred pages. It was just too much. Besides, it seemed to be more of the same—a very long exposition about the topics related to Other Emptiness which in the end was just scholarship and did nothing to show the reader the practical aspect nor to encourage the reader to practise. In this book, I want to keep you, the reader, focussed on unravelling the Other Emptiness teaching while understanding that, even though it can become very complicated, it is not meant to be a complicated philosophy but a very practical teaching, taught by the Buddha for the one purpose of entering wisdom.

TOPICS OF OTHER EMPTINESS

OTHER EMPTINESS AS A SCHOOL OF BUDDHIST PHILOSOPHY

Other Emptiness might be intended as a practical teaching on wisdom, but it can be placed within the various schools of Buddhist philosophy. There are four main schools of Buddhist philosophical thought. In order from lowest to highest they are: Vaibhaśhika, Sautantrika, Cittamātra, and Madhyamaka or Particularist, Sūtra Followers, Mind Only, and Middle Way schools respectively. The first two are connected with the teachings of the Lesser Vehicle and the last two with those of the Great Vehicle.

There are sub-schools of the Middle Way school. The main ones are the Yogāchāra Madhyamaka, Svatāntrika Madhyamaka and Prāsaṅgika Madhyamaka or the Yoga Practice Middle Way, Autonomy Middle Way, and Consequence Middle Way schools. Of them, the Consequence Middle Way school was generally accepted in Indian and Tibet as the one with the ultimate presentation of the view.

Other Emptiness as a philosophical school is regarded as a sub-school of the Middle Way and became known in Tibet as the Other Emptiness Middle Way. However, the advocates of the Other Emptiness school have positioned their view within the Middle Way school in various ways according to their own ideas about how the

23

view should be explained. For example, there is a great similarity between the Yogāchāra Cittamātra or Yoga Practice Mind Only presentation and the Other Emptiness presentation, so some advocates, notably Dolpopa Sherab Gyaltsen, have put Other Emptiness as a Yoga Practice kind of Middle Way. His doing so brings a great deal of complexity to considerations over where Other Emptiness should be positioned, because most scholars consider that anything that is Mind Only will be a lesser view than that of the Middle Way. Generally speaking, followers of Other Emptiness accept that the Consequence Middle Way is the highest view and position Other Empty Middle Way as a special, very profound form of that.

This was just a sketch for readers not familiar with the various philosophical schools and how they are positioned. The main point is that when Other Emptiness is being discussed, it should be understood that it is Middle Way view and meditation under discussion, even if the name "Middle Way" is not applied after every mention of Other Emptiness.

ORIGIN OF THE NAME

The Buddhist dharma vocabulary of Tibet includes the word, "zhan-tong"[10]. Most words in the Tibetan Buddhist vocabulary are

---

[10] Tib. gzhan stong. Note that the Tibetan alphabet has two consonants which are similar but not the same in their pronunciation. One of them corresponds exactly to the English "sh" and therefore should be transliterated that way. The other one cannot be properly represented in English because its sound is formed using a positioning of the mouth and tongue that is not used at all in English. However, in the past it has been represented with "zh" and for various reasons I think that is workable. Now it is very common these days to see the word here written in English as "shentong", but this is incorrect because the consonant involved is not "sh" but "zh". This mistaken transliteration

(continued...)

equivalents of Indian Buddhist words but this one is not. It is a word that came into the Buddhist language some time after Buddhism had been introduced into Tibet. In fact, it was not even coined as a word to start with; it started as a turn of phrase containing the separate words "zhan" and "tong"[11] which later was condensed into a new term "zhantong" for convenience.

The phrase containing the two words "zhan" and "tong" was coined by Yumowa Mikyo Dorje, a Tibetan yogin who lived in the 12th to 13th centuries C.E. and who became highly accomplished in Kālachakra practice. He had a profound experience of reality while practising on Mt. Kailash and expressed his experience using the phrase "what reality actually is is empty of something other than itself"[12]. His phrase was later shortened by his followers to the phrase "empty of other"[13]. Later still, his disciples shortened the phrase further to "other empty"[14] and this word entered the Buddhist vocabulary of Tibet at that time.

It was understood that the new term conveyed the full meaning of the original phrase but in a very condensed form that translates

---

[10](...continued)
results in an incorrect understanding of the actual Tibetan spelling, an incorrect understanding of what the word means, and also an incorrect pronunciation of it. A full treatment of the correct pronunciation of all the letters of the Tibetan alphabet is given in my *Standard Tibetan Grammar Volume I, The Thirty Verses of Minister Thumi*, published by Padma Karpo Translation Committee, ISBN Paper: 978-9937-572-35-4.

[11] Tib. gzhan, Tib. stong respectively.

[12] Tib. gnas lugs kyi ngo bo gzhan gyis stong pa.

[13] Tib. gzhan gyis stong pa.

[14] Tib. gzhan stong. Phonetics: "zhantong".

literally as "other empty" meaning "empty of other". It is important to understand and remember that at this point.

Even though Yumowa Mikyo Dorje coined the original phrase and used it later to explain the view of Kālachakra practice to his disciples, he did not write extensive commentaries that explained it, nor did he compose commentaries that would provide the necessary scriptural support for it.

In the latter half of the thirteenth century, a follower of the lineage called Kunpang Thugje Tsondru [1243–1313] started a monastery in a location in Tsang, south of Lhasa, called Jomo in order to give the lineage a home. After that, the tradition became known as the Jonang lineage because they were, literally, "the ones in Jo". Following that, news began to spread of unusually large numbers of people gaining high realization through practising with the Jonang lineage and their view which they were calling "other empty". The Jonangs quickly became famous for their style of meditation done with this view.

A little later, Dolpopa Sherab Gyaltsen [1292–1361] came to the throne of the Jonang lineage. By this time, the term "other empty" had become a core part of the terminology of the Jonang lineage but there was no written explanation that clearly laid out the lineage's other empty view with full scriptural support. Dolpopa, who was exceptionally learned in both sūtra and tantra, took on the task of composing a set of works that would explain its view and meditation with full scriptural support included. Of them, the most famous is *Mountain Dharma: An Ocean of Definitive Meaning* which puts quotations from sūtra and Secret Mantra together with explanations of the view.

Mountain Dharma: An Ocean of Definitive Meaning is regarded within the Jonang lineage as the foundation stone of the establishment of their Other Empty system. The text is filled with quotations from scripture which collectively show that there is a perfectly sound foundation in the Buddha's teaching for the concept of "other empty" and for the view and practice that go with it. Because of this, the lineage holds that the really important feature of the text is the scripture cited in it. The first chapter of the text looks at tathā-gatagarbha and gives many citations from the sūtras and other authoritative sources in support of it, setting the basis for the whole of Dolpopa's exposition of Other Emptiness that follows in the text. As described in the Important Background chapter, an excerpt of the chapter has been included in this book.

A second text by Dolpopa Sherab Gyaltsen that is noteworthy is *The Fourth Council*. This text essentially states that the Other Empty teaching was a piece of the Buddhist teaching that had been missed in the official compilations of it in the first three councils in India and that Dolpopa himself was now amending the loss with his text. The Other Empty view was already out of favour with the Gelug tradition who viewed themselves as the established church of Tibet, protectors of the Buddha's teaching. *The Fourth Council* brought matters to a head and, it is often thought, precipitated the shutdown of Jonang monasteries by the established church that followed shortly after.

In short, because of Yumo Mikyo Dorje and his followers, the word "other empty" was created and came into use in Tibetan Buddhist vocabulary. A tradition of their view and meditation was established that became known as the Jonang lineage. Heads of the lineage, and Dolpopa Sherab Gyaltsen in particular, wrote texts that established the use of the term "other empty" and proved that the Other Empty view and meditation was an authentic part of the Buddhist teaching. Thus, the term "other empty" came to have two meanings: the general name for the view and meditation characterized as being empty of other, and the proper name for any tradition that upheld and advocated that view and meditation.

OVER HALF OF TIBETAN BUDDHISM IS OTHER EMPTY IN STYLE

The third Karmapa, Rangjung Dorje, was a contemporary of
Dolpopa Sherab Gyaltsen. The Karmapa met Dolpopa Sherab
Gyaltsen and, it is said, was very appreciative of the other-empty
approach. Simply stated, it fitted perfectly with the understanding
that had come into the Tibetan Kagyu lineage through the Indian
master Maitrīpa and the Tibetan translator Marpa. From that time
onwards, Rangjung Dorje and all the followers of his Karma Kagyu
lineage openly declared that the view of their lineage was the other
empty view. The histories found in this book trace the main
upholders of the Other Empty view of the Kagyu from the third
Karmapa down through the seventh Karmapa, Karma Thrinlaypa,
the ninth Karmapa Chokyi Dondrup, and the eighth Situ known as
both Chokyi Jungnay and Tenpa'i Nyinje, all of whom were important figures in the Karma Kagyu. After them comes Jamgon
Kongtrul the Great, who was a champion of that view in the nineteenth century C.E. His subsequent incarnations were important
upholders of the view and, in these times, Khenpo Tsultrim Gyatso,
who is a disciple of the previous incarnation of Jamgon Kongtrul, has
become famed as the holder of Jamgon Kongtrul's lineage. Thus,
the Karma Kagyu school had direct contact with Dolpopa Sherab
Gyaltsen and there is no question that they declared themselves to
be Other Empty followers after that.

What then of the rest of the Kagyu? The real point is that the
concept of other empty applies to the whole Kagyu transmission, not
just to the Karma Kagyu because of Rangjung Dorje's meeting with
Dolpopa Sherab Gyaltsen. In fact, the Jonangs gave voice to a
particular approach to view and meditation that already existed within
Tibetan Buddhism and provided a name that became a convenience
for describing that approach. Thus, you can read the works of any
of the Kagyu schools, earlier and later, and, even though you might
not see the term "other empty", you will see the view and meditation

corresponding to it clearly expressed in all of their writings. The very root of this is that Nāropa sent Marpa, the founder of the Tibetan Kagyu lineage, to the Indian master Maitrīpa for teachings on the view. It was from Maitrīpa that Marpa and the Kagyu tradition following him obtained the teachings that embody the other empty approach, even if they did not have that name at the time.

An example of a Kagyu lineage that does not use the word "other empty" in its descriptions of view and meditation but which does express exactly the same view and meditation that the Karma Kagyu calls "other empty" is the Drukpa Kagyu. As the founder and director of the Drukpa Kagyu Heritage Project in Kathmandu, a project that preserved and re-published over 100 volumes of Drukpa Kagyu works during the 1990's, I read Drukpa Kagyu literature widely and had extensive discussions with Drukpa Kagyu masters. There is no question that, while the school does not use the term "other empty", it does present its view and meditation according to its Kagyu roots and that view and meditation is indeed "other empty" in style. This can be seen clearly in the book already mentioned, *A Juggernaut of the Non-Dual View, Teachings of the Second Drukchen, Gyalwang Je*, which contains a text by the second Drukchen about the matter.

The Other Empty style of presentation not only fits with the sūtra view expressed in the Kagyu but is also clearly found in the tantric works and songs of Kagyu siddhas, Indian and Tibetan. Again, they spoke in a way that fully accords with the Other Empty teaching, even though they did not use the term "other empty" themselves. Again, Maitrīpa is a pivotal point in the transmission of this view to the Tibetan Kagyu lineage. He wrote many texts on both sūtra and tantra that show the presence of the other empty view and he transmitted the fullness of that meaning to Marpa who then carried it back to Tibet where it became the view of the whole of the Kagyu. Maitrīpa's writings on the view are essential reading for anyone interested in the subject. For that reason we have, as mentioned in the Important Background chapter, translated many of them and published them together with clear explanations showing their "other empty" approach so that his connections with Other Emptiness can be researched.

Historically, it is obvious that the Kagyu has a special connection with the teaching called Other Emptiness. I could add that every expert Kagyu teacher that I have ever had teachings from—and that includes masters from nearly all the Kagyu lineages—clearly state in person that it really is true, this is the style of the Kagyu lineage, and that it is one of the very special features of the transmission of the Kagyu. In other words, it is not merely that the Kagyu are Other Emptiness followers and that some of the greater figures have cared to state it that way, but that the lineage really is based on this style of teaching and upholds that teaching as its core view.

What about the Nyingma tradition? The history presented here in the introduction to the *Lion's Roar of the Non-Regressing Commentary to the Highest Continuum* points out that they too obtained the view of other emptiness from the Indian tradition. That is true and it is one reason, in my mind, for differences in the way that the Kagyu and Nyingma schools attach importance to the Other Empty presentation. Nonetheless, the view of the Nyingma is as much Other Empty as is the Kagyu. One reason for this can be found in the fact that Śhāntarakṣhita, with his emphasis on what would be called an Other Empty style of presentation, was one of the major teachers in Tibet at the time of the establishment of the Nyingma tradition. A second reason is that the tantras are Other Empty in style and that is how they were always presented by Padmasaṃbhava who, together with Śhāntarakṣhita and his followers, was the main source of the Nyingma teaching.

A further proof that the Nyingma tradition follows the view of other emptiness can be seen in the fact that Nyingma masters who came after Dolpopa Sherab Gyaltsen used the term "other empty" in their writings and proclaimed that view as the ultimate view of the Buddhist teaching. For example, there is Longchen Rabjam who is widely regarded as the most knowledgeable of all Tibetan masters and who earned the title Greatest of All-Knowing Ones because of it. His dharma writings are widely held to be among the greatest in Tibetan literature. He was a contemporary of Dolpopa and clearly states in his works that the Nyingma teaching is Other Empty in style. Then there was the greatest Nyingma scholar in the nineteenth century, Ju Mipham Namgyal, who wrote many texts that explicitly presented and upheld the other emptiness view. Two of his texts that have become famous are *The Lion's Roar that Proclaims Other Emptiness* and *The Lion's Roar that is One Thousand Doses of Sugatagarbha*. The former hammers the point that Other Emptiness is the correct view. In it, Mipham conducts a boxing match in which he thumps away at the detractors of Other Emptiness—who were well known by that time as the followers of Tsongkhapa—repeatedly knocking mistakes in their self-empty-only presentation of the view and repeatedly showing how the other-empty view is the ultimate expression of the Buddhist view. The latter text shows tathāgatagarbha clearly and how it has to be understood to be other empty.

With that history understood, it can be understood why Jamgon Kongtrul the Great writes in various places that the greatest of Other Empty advocates in Tibet were Dolpopa, Rangjung Dorje, and Longchenpa. For example, see his statements in the introductory section from *The Lion's Roar of the Non-Regressing Commentary* which starts on page 191.

The Sakya tradition has mainly followed a view which is not other emptiness. However, there have been a couple of champions of the system within the Sakya school. The most well-known is Sakya Chogden, also known as Serdog Panchen.

All in all, it cannot be ignored that the great masters of Kagyu and Nyingma lineages who appeared after the term "other empty" became established have repeatedly stated that their view is Other Emptiness or is totally consistent with it. In addition, there have been some Sakya masters who also felt that this was the ultimate way to express the view.

The teachings of the established church of Tibet—the Gelugpa school—appeared in the West ahead of the teachings of other Tibetan schools. As a result, it has often been thought, especially amongst academics, that the view of that school is the one view accepted by everyone in Tibet. In fact, as has just been established, the situation is the other way around—the Gelug tradition which appears to be the central, established church of Tibet, is actually the minority in Tibet, with more than half of Tibetan Buddhists following the view of Other Emptiness!

DISAGREEMENTS OVER THE VIEW

The understanding of the view that the Tibetans named "other empty" was present in India from the time of the Buddha and was certainly known in the Indian tradition before the Tibetans attached the name "other empty" to it. This can be verified by looking at histories of the Other Empty system. The next chapter, The History and Lineage of Other Emptiness, was put there specifically to assist with that.

Despite the fact that the authenticity of the Other Empty view can be readily demonstrated in that way, when the Jonangs first coined and explained the term "other empty", the newness of the term coupled with certain expressions of the view upset some powerful groups in Lhasa who could not believe that it was part of Buddha's teaching. This situation was worsened when Dolpopa wrote the text in support of Other Emptiness called *The Fourth Council*, mentioned earlier. The view was already out of favour with the established church of central Tibet, the Gelugpa school, and this *The Fourth Council* with its assertion that the Jonangs could highlight something in the Buddhist canon that the Indian masters following the Buddha had not highlighted brought matters to a head.

For many in Tibet the other-empty view was a perfectly correct understanding and expression of the Buddha's view. However for the established church of central Tibet, the Gelug tradition, and all of the Sakyas at that time, it was not. The Gelug tradition saw it as a singular perversion of the Buddhist view and did everything in their power to eliminate it from Tibet, even to the point of closing down the Jonang and related monasteries. They went so far as to wall up all of the Jonang Other Emptiness texts up in a guarded cave, preventing further publication of the same, and so on. For the record, the history of what these detractors of Other Emptiness did whilst attempting to quash a movement that ran counter to their own ideas was at times breathtakingly wicked. There is a whole history of excesses of bigotry and power that exists in relation to the suppression of the presentation of the view of Other Emptiness by the Gelugpa hierarchy. It is noteworthy that all the villains in these stories appear amongst the detractors of Other Emptiness—there is no record that I can find of proponents of Other Emptiness retaliating with any of the nastiness that was so often directed at them. Recently someone said to me, "Ah yes, that was back in the dark ages of Europe times, wasn't it?" He was surprised when I pointed out that the problem was still alive and strong in the later parts of the twentieth century.

So, now we have a view and a tradition of proponents who uphold a view, both called Other Emptiness. We also have opponents who have worked hard over many centuries and still are working to eliminate them. What then is the Other Emptiness view and how does it differ from the view of its detractors?

OTHER EMPTINESS: A MORE PROFOUND TAKE, SIMPLY STATED

Very briefly, the advocates of Other Emptiness find that the ultimate expression of the Buddha's view is contained in the third turning of the wheel of dharma, primarily in the teachings on tathāgatagarbha—popularly called buddha nature—and also in the fourth turning of the wheel of dharma, in the teachings of Secret Mantra. The detractors of Other Emptiness find that the ultimate expression of the Buddhist view is contained in the second turning of the wheel of dharma, where it is expressed in the teachings called Prajñā-pāramitā, and usually take exception to all other ideas.

It is generally accepted that the third turning of the wheel contains a mixture of teachings. There are many teachings which are the basis for the Mind Only view, there are teachings on tathāgatagarbha in general, and there are some teachings on tathāgatagarbha which in particular are the basis for the Other Emptiness view. The Mind Only and tathāgatagarbha teachings are not the same but they share the approach that there is a core of mind that consists either of a buddha's wisdom or something directly related to it. The overall quality of these third turning teachings is that they are not concerned with looking outwards at the object of mind's cognitive process but with looking inwards at the mind that is doing the cognizing. They do not negate the fictional objects appearing as though they are external to the mind, but present the presence of enlightenment internal to the mind.

The tathāgatagarbha teachings can be taken merely to mean that, because mind has a core which is the same type of thing as the mind of a buddha and because all sentient beings have a mind with that core, all sentient beings can become a buddha. Or, to put it another way, these teachings can be taken simply as proof of the fact that enlightenment is possible. In that case, they have to be seen as a goad that was gently applied after the second turning teachings to enforce the idea that it really is possible to become a truly complete buddha. That would make the third turning teachings provisionally or at least partially provisional, rather than definitive, and that is how the Gelug tradition takes them.

However, the tathāgatagarbha teachings can also be understood in a much more profound way—they can also be understood to be teaching the nature of enlightenment very directly, even more directly than the teachings of the second turning of the wheel. When understood that way, a sub-set of the third turning sūtras are identified as ones that specifically teach this most essential of all Buddha's teachings. The advocates of Other Emptiness have identified them and named them the "snying pa'i don mdo" meaning "sūtras containing the heart or most essential meaning". These sūtras and the profound view contained in them are considered by Other Emptiness followers to contain the ultimate definitive meaning of all of the Buddha's sūtra teachings, so are also called "sūtras containing the heart definitive meaning".[15]

The Buddha entrusted this heart meaning teaching of the third turning to his regent, Maitreya. Much later, Maitreya taught it to the Indian master Asaṅga, who published the teachings Maitreya gave him in a set of five texts called *The Five Dharmas of Maitreya*. Those who do not follow Other Emptiness have taken the five dharmas of Maitreya in the first way described above, as primarily provisional in meaning. Other Emptiness followers see it differently; for example, this is how Jamgon Kongtrul describes them in his *Complete Commentary to the Highest Continuum*:

> Invincible Guardian Maitreya[16] ... first composed the
> *Ornament of Manifest Realizations*. With that text, he
> showed the dharma talk of the definitive-meaning Great
> Middle Way, just bringing out the main points. Then, he
> explained it clearly and extensively in the *Ornament of the
> Sūtras, Distinguishing the Middle from Extremes*, and *Distin-*

---

[15] The Gelug tradition finds it very hard to hear this because their founder, Tsongkhapa, determined that the third turning was not the definitive meaning teaching of the Buddha. It puts them in a bind so-to-speak because, even if they were willing to listen to this other proposition, the founder of their whole system has already declared his position on it unequivocally, and they have no choice but to follow that.

[16] Invincible is one of Maitreya's names, given that there is nothing can stop him from becoming the next world-leading buddha.

guishing the Dharmata. Finally, in the *Highest Continuum*,
he pinpointed the most subtle tenet involved, the one that
is the extraordinary meaning found in the heart sūtras.

For them, that last treatise contains the most important scripture for
explaining the Other Empty view and they use many quotations from
it to support that view. Moreover, there is a system of meditation
that goes with it that the Other Empty followers find in the Buddha's
"heart meaning" sūtras and in Maitreya's treatises, which they refer
to as "The Profound Meditation System of Maitreya". In other
words, there is not only an Other Empty view, but a meditative
practice for it, too.

In sum, those who follow the Middle Way according to the Other
Empty system follow the same second turning of the wheel Prajñāpāramitā teachings that all Great Vehicle followers accept, but
they find the ultimate presentation of view and meditation in the
third turning of the wheel tathāgatagarbha teachings. This approach
of two levels of the view of emptiness was well-known in Indian
Buddhist circles from the beginning. Therefore, when you think
"other empty", you should not think "unusual, oddity, minority" and
the like, which is how its opponents have cast it. To the contrary,
you should think "mainstream Buddhist thought that went from India
into Tibet which had a very subtle take on the third turning teachings
of the Buddha".

In terms of history alone, if you read the story of the transmission
of the Buddha's teachings into Tibet, you will see these two different
takes on the meaning of the teachings of the second and third
turnings of the wheel and how they led to the existence of two
factions in Tibet—those who believed that the tathāgatagarbha
teachings were more general in nature and those who believed that
they were more subtle. For instance, the selection from Jamgon
Kongtrul's commentary to the *Highest Continuum* in part four gives
a very good sense of these two different takes on the teachings of the
third turning of the wheel and how they developed.

Unravelling the Disagreement

The average Tibetan Buddhist might not even think that there could be a disagreement about how the Buddha taught his teaching. He would probably think that, if the Buddha taught things a certain way, it would be obvious to all and any disagreement over it would be easy to resolve. However, the other emptiness view seen within the tathāgatagarbha teachings is particularly subtle, so much so that even very smart people do not always see or accept it. The result in Tibet was a major difference of understanding over what the Buddha taught and why he taught it.

In order to get a clear view of the disagreement and where it comes from, it is necessary to look at each of the three wheels of dharma taught by the Buddha and determine which one teaches what. There are two steps involved: firstly, we have to investigate the three wheels with a view to settling the issue of which order they were taught in and why; secondly, we have to determine whether each wheel of dharma teaches the dharma in a provisional or definitive way. This is taken up extensively in a subsequent chapter in this part of the book.

As clarified in the Important Background chapter, the Gelug view became prevalent in the West, to the point that it has been very common for Westerners simply to assume that what they say is what the Buddha intended and that all Tibetan schools accept the same. However, all Tibetan schools do not accept that, so we need to go back to the beginning so-to-speak and look at various matters for ourselves. Fortunately, Jamgon Kongtrul the Great wrote an entire section of the *Treasury which is an Encyclopædia of Knowledge* in the middle of the nineteenth century that clarified these matters, so that has been included in this book to provide an authoritative source for our own investigations.

The Treasury of Knowledge is an encyclopaedic treatment of the Buddhist tradition. Its seventh chapter is concerned with the higher
training of prajñā. The second section of that chapter is concerned
with issues leading up to the treatment of the view that comes in the
third section following it. The second section dissects the three
turnings of the wheel of dharma both in terms of the rationale behind
their order of presentation and their status as being provisional or
definitive teaching. The dissection is very telling—what emerges
from it is a very different view from the view of those who do not
accept the Other Empty system. Fortunately for us, it provides
exactly what is needed to understand the issues being discussed just
now. Moreover, the second section presents an overview of all the
tenets of all the main philosophical schools of Buddhism, Other
Emptiness included, laying this out for us clearly. Therefore, the
second section has been included in part three of this book[17].

Here is some assistance with studying the excerpt from *The Treasury
of Knowledge*. The original consists of four, densely-written Tibetan
volumes. The first volume starts with root verses, which are the main
exposition put into verse for easy memorization. They are given in
both condensed and highly condensed versions. The main exposition
expands on and clarifies the meaning of those verses. It follows the
root verses and continues on to the end of the volumes. It always
gives a topic heading followed by the relevant line or lines of the
condensed root verses which is then followed by a commentary to
clarify the lines of verse. Now the root verses are very terse and often
do not make sense on their own, so some translators have added
many words in order that the root verses make sense. However, that
changes the original text, so I have translated the root verses just as
they are in the Tibetan: terse, often minus required grammatical

---

[17] An electronic edition of the Tibetan of *The Treasury of Knowledge* is
available from Padma Karpo Translation Committee. It has several
advantages over the paper edition, not the least of which is that it is fully
searchable. The electronic text and a reader for it are available free on
the PKTC web-site.

structure, and often unclear in meaning. Nothing is lost in doing so because the commentary provided immediately following the root verse unravels the meaning. The commentary by Jamgon Kongtrul is of the "bitwise" type in which all words or phrases of the root verse are woven into an explanation whose word order follows that of the root verse. Thus, the key to reading the text is to note the root verses of the text, then to unravel their meaning by reading them in conjunction with the commentary, all the while looking for the words or phrases of the root verse in the commentary.

The section of *The Treasury of Knowledge* we have been talking about goes on to examine the two truths, so translations of it to date include frequent use of these terms for the two truths: "relative" and "absolute" truth. Despite the fact that these two terms are in almost universal use amongst English-speaking Buddhists, they are particularly bad translations which not only do not convey the meaning of the originals but give the entirely wrong idea of what is meant. It has also been popular to translate them with "relative" and "ultimate" truth, but this is no improvement. These terms have been replaced throughout all of our translations by the very accurate terms "fictional" and "superfactual" respectively. A full explanation of why they are accurate translations of the original Sanskrit terms has been provided in the glossary. Moreover, the etymology of both terms is explained in the section of *The Treasury of Knowledge* text included in this book; if you read that carefully, you will be able to understand that these terms "fictional" and "superfactual" are not merely my strange way of doing things, but are what the terms actually mean. There is a tremendous amount of meaning in these terms, which really do mean "fictional" and "superfactual", and it is singularly lost by using "relative" and "absolute" or "ultimate" instead. I should note that what I am saying comes from extensive study of the terms, including long discussions of the original Sanskrit terms with Sanskrit experts in India.

To continue with the issue at hand, as Jamgon Kongtrul says, the Other Emptiness advocates see that the three wheels were taught in a simple linear sequence of increasing profundity. Their detractors do not agree with that, seeing the second turning as the pinnacle teaching and the third as a mixture of teaching that does not take things a step further. Then, the Other Emptiness advocates mark the second and third wheels as the place where the definitive teachings of the Buddha are found, with the second turning being a less profound version and the third turning being the most profound and hence ultimate version. Their detractors see the second turning as definitive with the third turning being a mixture of definitive and non-definitive; for them, the second turning is the ultimate teaching.

Jamgon Kongtrul's presentation includes the Buddha's own statement that the three wheels were taught in a simple linear sequence of increasing profundity, which in itself should be sufficient to prove which is the right way to understand this matter. His presentation backed with the Buddha's own words on which of the turnings of the wheel is definitive and which is not makes a compelling argument for the Other Emptiness approach being the correct one.

THE MIS-UNDERSTANDING THAT OTHER EMPTINESS IS COMPLICATED

The complexities that are churned up by the opponents of Other Emptiness have led most Westerners to believe that Other Emptiness philosophy is extremely complicated. This is unfortunate because Other Emptiness philosophy taken on its own terms, away from the need to prove itself in hard argument, is not complicated.

Examples of the simplicity of Other Emptiness philosophy can be seen in many places in this book. Its presentations are relatively straightforward and not hard to understand if the reader has a reasonable grounding in Buddhist philosophy and has developed far enough to be able to understand the subtlety of the view being expressed. If these presentations were expanded to include the objections that the detractors would raise and the counter-argument that would follow, the result would be a massive book filled with extremely difficult-to-follow argument. If you want to see an example of this type of argument, look at Ju Mipham's *Lion's Roar that Proclaims Other Emptiness* which shows it at length.

Then again, although the Other Emptiness teaching is not complicated, it is, as the teaching itself says, very profound and not meant for everyone. Because of the profundity involved, people who are not so advanced spiritually can find it very hard to grasp. Rather than reject that sort of person, teachers of the system will try to help them to understand it, although many, very subtle distinctions have to be made in order to do that. For example, Jamgon Kongtrul speaking in *The Lion's Roar of the Non-Regressing Commentary to the Highest Continuum* says:

> We hold that, therefore, those less fortunate ones of dull
> faculty are taken into care and then, in order to prevent
> them from becoming obscured by lack of comprehension
> or a wrong way of understanding, this *Highest Continuum*
> treatise was made to show clearly the entirety of what
> those sūtras of the profound sūtra section are attempting
> to express by condensing it down into seven vajra topics.

The seven vajra topics in the *Higher Continuum* summarize many profound points and make many, very subtle distinctions. Once again then, though for a different reason this time, it can seem as though Other Emptiness is a complicated view. Nonetheless, for those whose level of development matches with the profound view of Other Emptiness, the view and meditation of Other Emptiness is simple, straightforward, and, as the Buddha always intended with his teaching, very rewarding.

TWO STYLES OF EMPTINESS: A CRUCIAL POINT OF THE OVERALL OTHER EMPTINESS DEFINITION

The Other Emptiness advocates do not see the second turning of the wheel of dharma as the ultimate teaching. Rather, they see both the second and third wheels as definitive and within that see certain parts of the third turning teachings as ultimate. For them, there is a progression of increasing subtlety, with the teaching of the profound view in the second wheel as a way station to the ultimate teaching of the profound view contained in the third wheel.

Most people who know about Tibetan Buddhism know that the second turning of the wheel teaches emptiness and all experts know and agree that it teaches a particular style of emptiness called "empty of self nature". It is less well known that there is a second type of emptiness which the Other Emptiness advocates say was taught in the third turning of the wheel and which they called "empty of other".

In Tibet, the Other Emptiness advocates came up with a name for each of these two types of emptiness: they said "rangtong"[18] literally meaning "empty of self" for the first and "zhantong" literally meaning "empty of other" for the second. The very basis of the Other Empty teaching is that there are two parts to the teaching—teachings on the self-empty and other empty modes of emptiness—and that both are required and, moreover, required in that order. Essentially, the Other Emptiness teaching as a whole says that the empty-of-self style of emptiness corresponds to the view of emptiness laid out in the Prajñāpāramitā teachings of the second wheel and has to be attended to first, and that only then can the empty-of-other style of emptiness, which corresponds to the view of emptiness laid out in

---

[18] Tib. rang tong or "self-empty", which is the condensation of Tib. rang gis stong pa or "empty of self".

the third wheel, be approached. The Other Emptiness advocates clearly state that the emptiness of other without emptiness of self is not possible. They state that, without it, the Other Emptiness teaching as a whole is missing a necessary piece.

An interesting proof of this lies in the writings of the third Dodrup-chen, a great master of the Dzogchen tradition who was known for his writings elucidating the meaning of Dzogchen. He points out in his *"A Lamp's Illumination", Condensed Advice on Great Completion Thorough Cut*[19] that the root tantra *Sound Breakthrough* of the seventeen tantras, when defining the Thorough Cut practice of innermost unsurpassed Dzogchen, says that it is practised by starting with the view of Prajñāpāramitā:

> The meaning of the name "Thorough Cut" is stated in the Sound Breakthrough to be that, using the power of the meditation of Prajñāpāramitā, the appearances of grasped and grasping are directly cut.

In other words, he is saying that the self-empty view taught in the Prajñāpāramitā is necessary for the practice of Dzogchen. He continues by saying that the self-empty view alone is insufficient and that the other-empty view is needed to meet directly with the wisdom of Great Completion.

In short, this definition that the Other Empty view includes pres-entations of both rangtong or self-empty emptiness and zhantong or other-empty emptiness is a fundamental part of the Other Emptiness teaching that all followers of other emptiness, sūtra and tantra alike, understand and follow. This has to be understood from the outset if the other emptiness teaching is to be properly under-stood.

---

[19] Published by Padma Karpo Translation Committee, authored by Tony Duff, revised edition January 2014, ISBN: 978-9937-8244-6-0.

HOW SELF-EMPTY AND OTHER EMPTY FIT INTO
THE FOUR BUDDHIST PHILOSOPHICAL SCHOOLS

This chapter started out with a synopsis of the Buddhist philosophical schools, to make the point that Other Emptiness as a school of thought is a Middle Way school. Now that we have explained that it includes two approaches to emptiness, one called "self-empty" and one called "other empty", it might be helpful to go back and expand a little on how the Other Emptiness system fits into the four main schools of Buddhist philosophy. Khenpo Palden Sherab's explanation might be helpful here. He said:

> The name "Self Emptiness" was originally coined by followers of the Other Emptiness school to refer to a step in the overall Other Emptiness approach.
>
> Later on it was also used by them to refer to schools that did not follow the Other Emptiness approach but whose approach was consistent with what they, the Other Emptiness followers, called "self emptiness". This meant that they began to use the term "Self Emptiness" to refer to all followers of the Middle Way school except for those who accepted the Other Emptiness Middle Way.
>
> Now, it is important to understand that the schools who do not follow the Other Emptiness Middle Way do not even use the names Self Emptiness and Other Emptiness[20]. For them, there would be the Middle Way and it would be divided only into the two sub-schools of Svatāntrika and Prāsaṅgika Madhyamaka or the Autonomous and Consequence Middle Way schools.
>
> In ancient India, the Autonomous and Consequence Middle Way schools were very well known. The names

---

[20] This point is taken up later in the chapter on terminology. Here you have it clearly stated by a senior Tibetan master of the system.

Self Emptiness and Other Emptiness Middle Way did not appear till later, when they appeared in Tibet. The seed of the ideas connected with these Tibetan names existed in Indian Buddhism, of course, but did not become an issue until later.

At the time of the early spread of dharma in Tibet, at the time of the Dharma King Trisong Deutsen around the 8th century C.E., the Tibetans would say "Middle Way" and not even bother with the distinction of it into Autonomous and Consequence schools. Later, in the 12th to 13th centuries, people such as the great scholar Chokyi Sengge of Tsal and others made a strong distinction between the two. Sometime after that, a further distinction of the Middle Way into Self Emptiness and Other Emptiness schools became known. In that way, you can see that the Self Emptiness and Other Emptiness Middle Way schools are something that arose in Tibet, with most followers considering them to be distinctions of the Consequence Middle Way school. That is how most people would understand it and it is a good way to think about it.

Two Approaches to Reality, One of Them Very Profound

"Mipham -Text Lamp that Dispels Darkness"

The two types of emptiness are not mere philosophy. It is a fact that they were taught because there are two ways in which humans can and do approach reality. One way is to start out by saying, "I am in a deluded state of existence. Within that state and using the deluded, logical mind that is still part of that state, I will formulate what is undeluded existence and will practise to get to it." In other words, one way to look at the Buddhist journey is from the perspective of the person in cyclic existence who is seeking to transcend that unenlightened type of existence and go to enlightenment. That person goes about it with a reference point of being within cyclic existence.

He tries to get to non-dualistic wisdom by developing a correctly-operating aspect of dualistic mind which Indian culture called prajñā. His journey is being conducted within the un-enlightened side, which Indian culture called saṃsāra, meaning, cyclic existence.

A second way is to approach reality from the enlightened side. One says "I am, at root, the undeluded state of wisdom. I will let that wisdom come forth using the special instructions of my teacher and without using any of the apparatus of dualistic mind. When I formulate the view, it will be from this enlightened perspective." This person will conduct his journey by simply bypassing the dualistic mind of cyclic existence in favour of wisdom. All of his expressions of the view and path will be made from the perspective of having or being in wisdom already. He will not want to use the processes of dualistic logic to find the undeluded state of wisdom because that in itself would be a recall of the deluded state he is trying to leave behind.

Simply stated, the detractors of Other Emptiness follow the first approach and its advocates follow the second. When Other Emptiness is given as a practical instruction, it goes straight to the heart. It is a wisdom teaching. It does indeed say that all things are empty of a self, but then shows that the way to live that is to go directly to the fact of wisdom that exists within. Although the Prajñāpāramitā teachings of the first approach get to the same point, applying them involves the much longer journey of using dualistic logic to get to the wisdom within.

It is said within the Other Emptiness teaching that it is more difficult to understand than the Prajñāpāramitā teaching because of its greater profundity. The teaching itself says that, therefore, it is not for everyone. And it is true that there are people who are, for the time being, deep enough in cyclic existence that this kind of teaching, which requires dropping intellect in favour of wisdom, is too fearsome to acknowledge. These people usually cannot encompass

Other Emptiness when they first hear about it. Sometimes, they would even like to eliminate it because of the fear that it induces.

DEEP INTELLECTUAL DISHONESTY AMONGST THE DETRACTORS

The detractors of Other Emptiness believe that the second wheel, with its teaching of empty-of-self emptiness is the ultimate teaching of the emptiness view and that its teaching cannot be rejected. They also believe that this empty-of-self emptiness is the only type of emptiness authentically taught by the Buddha. They also believe that logic is the ultimate way of arriving at a direct perception of reality. Therefore, when they hear the Other Emptiness advocates assert empty-of-other emptiness and when they hear them speaking of something that does not require the use of hard logic for realization, they accuse the Other Emptiness advocates of losing the Middle Way view and even accuse them of spreading heretical teaching because of not staying within the meaning of the second turning teachings.

However, while it is true that the Other Emptiness advocates do assert the empty-of-other view, it is equally true that they assert the empty-of-self view that their detractors claim that they have lost. Historically, the Other Emptiness advocates have always replied patiently to their detractors that the empty-of-self emptiness found in the Prajñāpāramitā teachings is a necessary precursor to the empty-of-other emptiness and that it is an essential part of the overall Other Emptiness teaching.

Amazingly, the detractors have simply turned a deaf ear to this reply, a reply which is both honest and helpful. The detractors seem to have become so stuck on the idea that their own understanding of the Buddha's teaching is correct that they do not hear what the Other Emptiness advocates are saying and keep up their attacks on the Other Emptiness system.

When you understand both sides fully, the apparent blindness of the detractors seems odd. However, there is again the point that the Other Emptiness advocates make, which is that its teaching is exceptionally profound, much more than that found in the second wheel. They say, kindly enough, that this level of profundity is not something that everyone can understand and point out that it is therefore not suitable for everyone to hear. Apparently their detractors, given their closed approach to the issue, fall into the category of those who are not ready yet for this kind of teaching.

Again, the advocates of Other Emptiness say that, if a person does not understand the presentation of reality given in the Prajñā-pāramitā, he will not be able to correctly understand the presentation of reality expressed through Other Emptiness. Throughout all of this, the detractors will argue that the Other Emptiness expression of the view rejects the Prajñāpāramitā teachings even though a cursory examination shows that it does not. The Other Emptiness advocates usually reply with a full explanation that clearly shows that the Prajñāpāramitā understanding has been fully and correctly included. Strangely, their detractors continue to reply by just repeating themselves, without having made any attempt to follow what the Other Emptiness advocates have been saying.

Over a period of time, it became apparent within Tibet that this very self-possessed and dishonest approach of the detractors really was deeply entrenched in their traditions, and especially within the Gelug tradition of Tsongkhapa's followers. This led Kagyu and Nyingma authors in particular to throw up their hands, so to speak, when trying to discuss these matters. Later, some Kagyu and Nyingma authors would just pass off their detractors with a range of derogatory though accurately thrown remarks about them such as "intellectually dishonest" and "mere spouters of their view who have no interest or capacity even for honest debate" and "stuck in spouting tenets and not able to get past what they have been made to learn by rote", and so on. Those all were direct quotes from one text or another that I have read myself. I have read many other such things, too, and note that the writers involved—usually really great masters within the traditions—are not particularly angry. They are just using the words of their own culture to say in the end, "Look you people, you argue up and down and you hide in every corner possible, but it seems as though you are either not interested in or not capable of honest argument. You seem to be capable only of spouting what you have been told is true then arguing to maintain that position, without being willing to apply critical reasoning to the matter at all. You seem to be incapable of an honest and interested look into what the Buddha actually said for the purpose of getting on with the practise of it."

I am not making this up. You will see Jamgon Kongtrul talking like this in *Instructions for Practising the View of the Other Emptiness Great Middle Way* in part three of this book when he says: "The group with the pretentiousness of taking the emptiness experiences belonging to generic examination and analysis as being the dharmatā who say, 'The Great Middle Way is like our presentation of the Middle Way alone, every one else is mistaken!' are lost regarding the path."[21]

Then, the Nyingma master Jigmey Lingpa says of them in his *Highest Wisdom*[22] text, "And, then there are those who have learned a biassed tradition, who make their assertions through a combination of lack of proper examination and their arrogance of thinking that they are full of brilliant qualities due to their path which, consisting of many

---

[21] Generic examination and analysis occur only in dualistic mind. "Generic" here means "generic image" which is the name for one of the many concept structures of dualistic mind. The implication is that they never get out of intellect into wisdom because all their analysis is concept-based. Dharmatā here means "directly experienced wisdom-reality".

[22] By Tony Duff, published by Padma Karpo Translation Committee, October 2010, ISBN: 978-9937-8386-0-3.

facsimiles,[23] has become a condition for speaking ill of others and broadcasting others' faults."

There are many other condemnations like this in Tibetan literature. Some authors openly specify who they are talking about and others, as in the above examples, speak in a way that any well-read or well-taught person will know to whom they are referring. As mentioned earlier, this sort of complaint is usually understood to refer to the followers of Tsongkhapa; most Sakyas hold a tenet that is similar to Tsongkhapa's followers, but have not exhibited the same self-possessed pride and have not fought with others in the same, acrimonious way.

Moreover, there is mention of this in Khenpo Tsultrim's text *The Music of Talk on the Definitive Meaning*, which has been included in this book:

> The subject matter of this tenet system is clearly present in both of the two charioteer's textual systems, yet there are still some who say, "There was no such naming convention in use." I consider this tiresome debate to be meaningless[24].

---

[23] "Facsimiles" here has the sense of conceptually-known truths which are mere likenesses of the actual, directly-experienced truths that the Buddha taught his followers should reach.

[24] Tib. tha snyad. The term "other empty" was invented in Tibet so is not seen in Indian Buddhist literature and the opponents of Other Emptiness use this to say that it could not have been a Buddhist teaching. However, the absence of that particular naming convention for it at the time does not mean that the teaching itself did not exist then.

He is saying that the subject matter of this Other Emptiness tenet system is clearly present in both Nāgārjuna and Asaṅga's texts[25], yet even in the face of that undeniable fact, these opponents of Other Emptiness, primarily the Gelugpa followers, have the effrontery to say, "There is no such thing as Other Emptiness in the Buddhist teaching because the term other empty used to name it is not visible in Indian Buddhist literature. Our presentation of emptiness based solely on the Prajñāpāramitā teaching is correct." I would have to agree with the khenpo that the feeling you get in the end is that any argument with these people is just tiresome and meaningless, both.

This disagreement has raged for centuries in Tibet and, unfortunately, continues in the present, though it has been muted in recent times because Tibetans have been so busy rebuilding after the Communist Chinese invasion. ⟋

✓ THE PROBLEM GOES DEEP

Anyone who sits down and looks into the arguments of both sides will have to be amazed at times at the unwillingness of the detractors to listen to the advocates of Other Emptiness and, as a counterpoint, the unwillingness of the advocates of Other Emptiness to fall into returning any of the nastiness being directed at them. As mentioned just above, you will frequently find places in the literature where the detractors claim that the advocates are failing to do this, that, and the other, when in fact the advocates have already clearly stated that they are doing that—and obviously are doing so. Ju Mipham's *Lion's Roar that Proclaims Other Emptiness* goes through many points of disagreement and repeatedly says something like, "You people who are constantly criticizing us for not doing such and such have not only

---

[25] The systems of Nāgārjuna on the one hand and Asaṅga on the other. There is an extensive consideration of this point of the two charioteers and their systems and how the Other Emptiness view is affected by their systems in our *Juggernaut of the Non-Dual View*.

ignored what we have just said, but even in your own assertions seem
to be making the very mistake that you are accusing us of doing!"

There have been tremendous problems like this in Tibetan culture.
It has to be mentioned because it might help non-Tibetans to
understand Tibetan Buddhism better and especially might help them
not to fall into some of these traps. I know from long experience that
this sort of observation is largely irrelevant to Tibetans within their
traditional milieu; their culture is so bound up with cultural forms
and power plays that this kind of observation is meaningless. For
example, at the Tibetan University at Sarnath, I once sat in on a class
for graduate students of all four lineages. The Gelugpa geshe
teaching the class was explaining the view of the Middle Way
according to his own tradition. He could have given a straightforward presentation of the view according to his own tradition for us
and left it at that, but he could not refrain from making very cutting
remarks about how any other expression of the view, such as the
Other Emptiness one, would have to be wrong! He even singled me
out and gave me a diatribe, in Tibetan, about how his presentation
was the only one that was correct and implied strongly that anyone
following any other presentation was very stupid. His diatribe might
have been effective if I were a Tibetan within the system, but it only
served to convince me of his narrow-mindedness. It was unfortunate
really; his presentation of the Gelug view was very clear and
penetrating and I appreciated it very much. His unwillingness to be
intellectually open and honest was preventing his Tibetan students
in the class from exploring very interesting avenues of the view. In
short, his style, which I found to be fundamentally dishonest, was
deliberately directed at keeping his students in the mould that he
wanted and preventing any possibility that they might explore and
possibly be enormously helped by that exploration. The problem,
it seems, continues on.

STORY OF A SUCCESSFUL JOURNEY FROM THE DETRACTOR'S VIEW TO THE OTHER EMPTINESS VIEW

It does happen that non-Tibetan followers of the detractors' lineages get filled with a view that becomes a blockage to understanding what Other Emptiness is about. I have been through this myself; my early years as a monk doing nothing but studying and practising the Middle Way according to the Gelug presentations that I was being taught certainly were very helpful. After all, it is the Buddha's teaching and when practised, does lead to the removal of obscuration. And I would like to say clearly here that I have only the greatest respect for all of my teachers of the time. However, it is true that there were aspects to the presentation that caused blockages that were very difficult to overcome later when I went to study with the Kagyu tradition and tried to comprehend their Other Emptiness style view.

It took me some years of studying and practising with the Kagyus to get past the blocks that I had inherited and to be able to accept the very profound Other Emptiness style presentation. It took a while longer to come to the point where I could see the validity and goodness of both sides. In the end, after an amount of study and practice of the Other Emptiness that matched the Consequence Middle Way practice I had done earlier with the Gelug tradition, I developed that kind of overview where you see the validity of both sides and you also clearly see how people can go wrong on both sides, then engage in all kinds of mistaken argument.

Part of arriving at that point was coming to an acceptance that not everything I had been told was so cast-iron true as my Gelug teachers had presented. I have friends who started out with me years ago and have remained Gelug followers ever since. I have seen first-hand how exceptionally difficult it can be for them to get through some wrong-headed notions that they hold onto dearly, because of the way that the Gelug tradition presents its own view as being the only way that the Buddhist view could be.

This problem has been far-reaching in its effect. As mentioned earlier, the Gelug way of presenting emptiness came to the West well ahead of others and has for a long time been the accepted understanding amongst academics as the correct presentation of Middle Way view. Often the academics have not even known that there is another possibility, let alone how to look into it. Why? Well, in part it comes down to this Tibetan problem that is being discussed of different factions believing that they are the only true possessors of the teaching. In terms of my own, rather unique experience of both sides, I think it fair to say that, if you have only been exposed to the Gelug view of the Middle Way, you are probably going to have to work quite hard to understand what Other Emptiness is really all about. The effort is worthwhile though; in the end, even if you do not accept the Other Emptiness view, it is almost certain that you will understand your own view and how it sits much better than you did before.

To sum this up, there has been a problem in Tibetan Buddhist culture. This problem is being transmitted to the West, though the problem is not as severe because the cultures are different. Non-Tibetans have a willingness to look further than Tibetans have historically been willing to do. Therefore, I am making the point here that, if you do decide to look into the arguments surrounding Other Emptiness, you have to pay attention to all of it, not just the actual arguments on the view. You might find that the advocates of the view that you yourself have been revering are corrupt in their arguments or at least highly unwilling to listen. If you do find these things—and they are a hallmark of the detractors who tried to eliminate the Other Emptiness teaching—then it should at least give you pause for thought.

Now we have a view, proponents and opponents of that view, acrid debate, and some problems with power, corruption, and so on that have to be worked through. We also have the situation that you, the reader, might have unwittingly inherited some of the problems. I have suggested, essentially, that you might have to clear the slate a little and not only have a fresh mind but also be open to acknowledging corrupt argument when it does appear.

OTHER EMPTINESS IS ABOUT PRACTICE NOT ABOUT POLEMIC OR ACADEMIC ARGUMENT

That said, I would like to raise a distinction that I made earlier and re-state it as clearly as possible. On the one hand, there is Other Emptiness view and meditation; it involves the study and the practice, too, of Other Emptiness. On the other hand, there are the huge and complicated philosophical arguments that developed when some Tibetan figures decided that Other Emptiness was wrong or worse, heretical, and should be eliminated from Tibet. The latter is what many non-Tibetans think Other Emptiness is all about. In fact, it is not. Other Emptiness is a statement of reality which can be taken as is and used as a path without any polemic or academic endeavours. It can be studied and then practised according to your guru's oral instructions with the result that you can gain attainment all the way up to enlightenment. It is very important not to confuse Other Emptiness, a practical teaching for the attainment of enlightenment, with the polemic and complicated philosophical argument that arose around Other Emptiness in Tibet.

Therefore, and as a matter of deliberate choice, this book is not an academic investigation of the complicated arguments that have appeared because some people in Tibet wanted to get rid of the Other Emptiness approach. Rather, it is primarily for people who are interested in Other Emptiness and how it might be the view that informs profound meditation. It is for those who would like to find out about the Other Emptiness view and practice as passed down by the Tibetan lineages who regard themselves as Other Emptiness in approach—the Kagyu, Nyingma, and Jonang schools and a segment of the Sakya school.

Certainly, the writings included in this book look into the points of debate that occurred and certainly they look into the details of the very profound view of Other Emptiness. However, this book is not intended to be a handbook of the difficult argument that happens when the detractors of Other Emptiness get started with their vitriole. Rather, it is a careful compilation of selections that builds a coherent picture of the view first and then the actual practise of Other Emptiness. As such, it clearly presents the living tradition of Other Emptiness view and practice.

Now we have a view, the proponents and opponents of that view, presentations of the view, pitfalls that have to be avoided when approaching that view, and the possibility of a practitioner's approach to the view. The rest of the book attempts to expose the view and a practitioner's approach to it as clearly as possible.

THE HISTORY AND LINEAGE
OF OTHER EMPTINESS

A study of the history involved is a good place to start when trying to understand Other Emptiness. It begins the process of becoming familiar with the system. It provides important background knowledge about the system, such as introducing which scripture is important to the system. Most importantly, it confirms that there is a valid lineage to the teaching of the system, which is a key point in Buddhist practice.

One of the big objections made by the detractors of Other Emptiness is that Other Emptiness is not a genuine teaching of the Buddha but an invention made up later. However, its history shows that it is a teaching that originated with the Buddha, was passed down to his regent Maitreya, then to the Indian master Asaṅga prophesied by the Buddha as a proponent of the teaching, to Maitrīpa, and on into Tibet. Its history also shows that, while it is true that there was no teaching in India named "other empty" or its Sanskrit equivalent, the Tibetan name "other empty" does refer to teachings that came from India, both the sūtra teaching coming through Maitreya just mentioned and the tantras taught by the Buddha himself and his appointees.

The history also shows the importance of the Indian master Maitrīpa to the transmission of the Other Emptiness view into Tibet. Maitrīpa lived in the 9th century C.E. and was famous for rediscovering the *Great Vehicle Highest Continuum Treatise*, one of the five treatises of Maitreya which is particularly important to the Other Emptiness teaching. The treatise had been lost and unavailable for a long time when Maitrīpa re-discovered it, received the reading transmission for it directly from Maitreya who appeared before him, and re-established the teaching of its profound meaning. After that, Maitrīpa became a central figure in the transmission of the sūtra teachings of the Profound Meditation System of Maitreya in India and Tibet. For instance, Nāropa, who was a contemporary of Maitrīpa, told his Tibetan disciple Marpa the Translator to go to Maitrīpa for the view, saying that Maitrīpa was most expert in the view of anyone in India at the time. Marpa did that and Maitrīpa's Other Emptiness-style teaching became the source of the Kagyu view.

Two texts in this book give good histories of Other Emptiness. First there is one by Khenpo Tsultrim Gyatso, which has not been seen in English until now. It started as a talk given at the Karmapa Buddhist Institute in Delhi, India by Khenpo Tsultrim Gyatso which was transcribed and put into a textbook for studies produced at the Karmapa's seat in Rumtek in the 1980's. It is the best history of Other Emptiness I have seen so far. Next there is the introduction from the *Commentary to the Highest Continuum* by Jamgon Kongtrul whose several sections collectively give a very clear picture of how the third turning teaching came into Tibet. There is also a section on the source of the teaching at the beginning of the text *Instructions for Practising the View of the Other Emptiness Great Middle Way* which provides another, useful view of the history involved, and which, as mentioned in the Important Background chapter, we have made available in a separate publication.

That the Other Emptiness view did exist in India can also be verified by looking at the dohās and writings of the Indian tantric masters who were the source of many of the tantric teachings that came into Tibet. This could be done for instance by looking at the teachings of Tilopa and Saraha in *Drukchen Padma Karpo's Collected Works on Mahamudra* and the tantric writings of Maitrīpa, especially the text on Chakrasaṃvara, in *Maitrīpa's Writings on the View*.

THE FOUR TURNINGS OF
THE WHEEL OF DHARMA

The next step towards understanding Other Emptiness is to become familiar with what the Buddha taught and why. This is necessary in general because discussions of Other Emptiness range across all four steps of the Buddha's teaching and cannot be followed without a working knowledge of them. There is also the specific point, mentioned in the last chapter, that Other Emptiness is based on the understanding that the teaching was taught in a sequence of increasing profundity; some argue that they were not, imposing a need to understand the four steps of the teaching in sufficient depth that the matter can be settled with certainty.

The Buddha started his teaching with the proclamation that normal human existence is unsatisfactory. He used the word "duḥkha" for this, which has often been translated as "suffering". However, "duḥkha" means much more than just suffering; it literally means "not all right in any way at all", "unsatisfactory from beginning to end". When speaking of human existence, the vernacular "a bad ride" describes the situation exactly. There is nothing about human or any other type of existence based on ignorance of the enlightened condition that is satisfactory. Having pointed out that truth, the Buddha spent the rest of his life teaching the path to the end of unsatisfactoriness.

He taught the path in both exoteric and esoteric ways. The former were called the teachings of sūtra and the latter the teachings of tantra. The Buddha himself pointed out that he taught the sūtra teachings in three steps, in what he called "the three turnings of the wheel of dharma". Buddhist followers of tantra—and that includes all Tibetan Buddhist followers—agree that the teaching of tantra is a fourth step in his teachings which can be called a fourth turning of the wheel. These four turnings of the wheel of dharma encompass the whole of the Buddha's teaching. Most accept that they were taught in a linear progression of increasing profundity, given that the Buddha himself said that they were and explained why it was so. Some, notably Tsongkhapa and his followers, do not accept this.

As a matter of interest, each turning of the four turnings of the wheel of dharma was a world-shattering event. The truths the Buddha exposed in each had been lost from the human world and were being presented again. In ancient Indian culture, anything that was a complete, self-contained situation was called a "wheel", much as we would say "sphere" in English. In this case, the phrase "turned the wheel of dharma" does not only mean that he "set the wheel of dharma in motion" but that he started up afresh on this earth a whole sphere of dharma.

First Turning of the Wheel of Dharma

When the Buddha turned the wheel of dharma for the first time, he taught the basics. He gave his first teaching near a location which in those days was called "Ṛiṣhipartana" meaning "Rishis Dropping". In the history of the area dating back long before the Buddha, it is said that a group of five hundred highly accomplished ṛishis[26] of a Hindu tradition, upon understanding reality flew up into the sky and merged their minds with God. Because they had merged with reality, their corporeal existence was finished and their cast off bodies simply

---

[26] For ṛishi see the glossary.

fell to the ground. Thus it was called Ṛiṣhis Dropping! The place is off to one side of the actual place where the Buddha turned the wheel of dharma for the first time. At the time of writing, the place could still be seen; it is not marked but is right inside the north-west corner gate of the entire area named the Deer Park.

His very first teaching was called "the Four Truths of the Noble Ones". In it he proclaimed four truths which are known to be true by those who have gone beyond the world to a level of spiritual development that makes them noble compared to the ordinary beings of the world. They were therefore called "the four truths of the noble ones"[27]. He proclaimed: that the existence of sentient beings is unsatisfactory from top to bottom, that there is a cause of that, an end to it, and a path that will lead to the end of it.

After the initial teaching of the first wheel, the Buddha spent some time teaching its details. In general, he encouraged sentient beings to turn away from the unsatisfactoriness involved in being a sentient being and go towards a type of being that would be a final solution to the unsatisfactoriness. This has often been referred to as the teaching of renunciation but the words of the Buddha were more positive than that. He did speak of renunciation in the sense of being revolted by sentient existence which is just unsatisfactory, but he mostly spoke of turning towards the authentic, of going towards a reliable, different kind of existence altogether.

In particular, he taught a path called "personal emancipation". This path can take a practitioner just far enough so that he is out of the worst of the unsatisfactoriness, to a level of personal emancipation from saṃsāra. It is a relatively easy path that leads to a quick emancipation from the burning house of saṃsāra for the practitioner but not for anyone else. The level of emancipation gained is called

---

[27] The Buddha explained that this, not "the four noble truths", is the name.

buddhahood but it is not a truly complete buddhahood. In other words, the result of this path is buddhahood but it is a buddhahood that has only solved the person's immediate problems. It is also called "arhat buddhahood" to distinguish it from the truly complete buddhahood of someone like Śhākyamuni Buddha.

The view connected with the path of personal emancipation is based on understanding that the idea an ordinary person has of himself is a falsehood, that the self he thinks he is does not really exist. Doing the meditations connected with this view leads to the collapse of the falsehood of a personal self and to the discovery of an absence of the falsehood. In Buddhist philosophy, the false personal self is called "the personal self" and its absence is called "lack of a personal self".

In fact, phenomena other than a person do not exist any more than the personal self that an ordinary person believes he has. However, the Buddha did not expose that greater level of truth at this point. Instead, he explicitly taught that the external phenomena are existent. He did this as a matter of skilful means. He allowed his followers to accept that external phenomena exist and had them focus on their most immediate problem of ridding themselves of their belief in a personal self. Together with that, he constantly urged them to get out of the unsatisfactoriness caused by that mistaken belief. Thus, he was able to get them onto a path that would at least get them out of samsaric existence, even if it was not a complete path to unsurpassed enlightenment.

Overall, the Buddha taught the dharma step by step in a process that has been likened to the process of leading children through the stages of growing up. In the analogy, this first turning of the wheel is likened to the necessary step of spoon-feeding babies. It is noted in the scriptures that the Buddha did not teach everything directly in the first turning and even said things that were apparently untrue, for example that all phenomena exist. He did this for sake of leading his disciples along, just as children are not always told the truth directly and are sometimes even told things that are apparently untrue in order to guide them along. Therefore, the teachings of the first turning of the wheel are provisional in meaning.

SECOND OR MIDDLE TURNING OF THE WHEEL OF DHARMA

Once the Buddha had established the basics, he took the next step and turned the wheel of dharma a second time.

As with the first turning of the wheel of dharma, the second or middle turning as it is most often called, was enacted at a specific place and time. The Buddha enacted it at the place called Vulture's Peak Mountain within the country of one of his benefactors, King Bimbisāra. The teachings began with the Prajñāpāramitā Sūtra and were fleshed out during a distinct period of time.

This turning of the wheel of dharma revealed what is called "the bodhisatva's[28] path". The bodhisatva's path literally means "the path of the person who is brave enough (satva) to undertake the journey to the state of truly complete enlightenment (bodhi)". The practitioner of the first turning of the wheel is only concerned with emancipation for himself and, except for keeping a general mind of love and compassion for others, does not have the thought of treading a spiritual path for the benefit of all other sentient beings. The bodhisatva on the other hand understands that the only way to truly benefit all other sentient beings is to get them to truly complete buddhahood and that the only way to do that is to become a truly complete buddha himself. Heroically, he takes it upon himself to do just that.

In this turning of the wheel, the Buddha gave teachings for beings who had progressed and were sufficiently mature that they could hear the truth directly. The Buddha had already pointed out in the first turning of the wheel that the root cause of all unsatisfactoriness is

---

[28] For bodhisatva and its spelling, see the glossary.

having a mind that functions in a way that is out of touch with reality.
The task at hand then for everyone who wants to make the journey
to the end of unsatisfactoriness is to undo the knots that constrict
mind into a wrong mode of operation and prevent it from seeing
things as they really are. In the first turning of the wheel, the Buddha
only exposed the truth about reality partially; he exposed it just
enough so that beings could see through their false notion of a
personal self and free themselves from it. In this second set of
teachings, the Buddha taught the actual situation with regard to
persons and phenomena, which is that both are devoid or empty of
a self, hence the teachings of the second turning of the wheel are
definitive in meaning. ↓ VITAL ↓

In particular, the view that the Buddha taught in this second turning
is that all persons and all dharmas, that is, all phenomena, are empty
of a self-nature. This means that phenomena are empty of, that is,
do not have, the nature of a self that the ignorant, samsaric mind sees
in them. In the first turning of the wheel, the term "emptiness" was
not used. In this second turning of the wheel, where the actual
situation with persons and phenomena was fully and directly exposed,
the term was used to indicate the actual, total absence of self in
persons and phenomena.

With this view as a basis, the Buddha expounded the path of the
bodhisatva, which is usually called "the practise of the path of the
pāramitās". A pāramitā literally is "that which has gone to the other
shore". It refers to a practice which belongs to the side not merely
of the arhat's personal enlightenment taught in the first turning of
the wheel but to the side of truly complete enlightenment taught in
the second turning of the wheel. Generally, six pāramitās are taught
for the ordinary type of practitioner—generosity, discipline,
perseverance, meditative absorption, and correctly working mind or
prajñā—though there are ten in total. There are ten levels of
development of a bodhisatva with the level of truly complete buddhahood following the tenth level and each of the levels corresponds
to the practice and fulfilment of one of the ten pāramitās.

view = Theory
Meditation = Practice

Of the ten pāramitās, the sixth, called the pāramitā of prajñā, is crucial. Where the other nine pāramitās are assistive techniques for attaining truly complete enlightenment, prajñāpāramitā is the liberative development of insight that sees the view of reality, which is, as mentioned above, the emptiness of self of phenomena and persons.

"Prajñā" literally means the best (pra) kind of knowing (jñā). The definition given in Tibetan texts is "that mind which correctly distinguishes general and specific characterised phenomena". In plain English, it is a mind which correctly distinguishes any one thing from another, regardless of what that might be. Prajñā is one thing only—a mind which makes a correct distinction. However, tradition speaks of many prajñās because of categorizing what the prajñā is looking at. Thus, it is taught that the bodhisatva develops many kinds of prajñā as he treads the ten levels on his way to buddhahood, meaning that he develops a mind which is correctly distinguishing how it actually is in relation to many different things. However, the bodhisatva gives special importance to the prajñā that sees the actuality[29], as it is called, of persons and phenomena. By practising the prajñā pāramitā, he specifically develops the prajñā that determines the emptiness which is the lack of self in persons and the emptiness which is the lack of self in phenomena. Through the prajñā that sees these two emptinesses, he transcends cyclic existence. Therefore, when the Buddha first turned the second turning of the wheel, he taught the Prajñāpāramitā Sūtras that explain the development and application of prajñā as the basis for training in all of the other pāramitās of a bodhisatva.

One of the features of the Prajñāpāramitā teaching is that it constantly negates the mistaken phenomena fictitiously produced by samsaric mind. Specifically, it negates over and again all of those phenomena seen to exist by way of self-nature. *The Heart Sūtra,*

---

[29] For actuality, see the glossary.

which is the most condensed form of the Prajñāpāramitā sūtras, teaches this mode of negation very succinctly:

> ... noble Avalokiteśhvara, the bodhisatva mahāsattva, saw in this way: he saw the five skandhas to be empty of self-nature. Then through the power of the Buddha, venerable Śhariputra said to noble Avalokiteśhvara, the bodhisatva mahāsattva, "How should a son or daughter of the noble family train who wishes to practise the profound Prajñāpāramitā?" Addressed in this way, noble Avalokiteśhvara, the bodhisatva mahāsatva, said to venerable Śhariputra, "O Śhariputra, a son or daughter of the noble family who wishes to practise the profound Prajñāpāramitā should see in this way: seeing the five skandhas to be empty of nature. Form is emptiness, emptiness also is form, emptiness is no other than form, form is no other than emptiness. In the same way feeling, perception, formative[30], and consciousness are emptiness. Thus Śhāriputra all dharmas are emptiness. There is no form, no feeling, no perception, no formative, no consciousness, no eye, no ear, no nose, no tongue, no body, no mind, no visual, no sound, no smell, no taste, no touch, no dharmas, no eye dhātu up to no mind dhātu, no dhātu of dharmas, no mind consciousness dhātu, no ignorance, no end of ignorance up to no old age and death, no end of old age and death, no unsatisfactoriness, no origin of unsatisfactoriness, no cessation of unsatisfactoriness, no

---

[30] The name of the fourth skandha has been mistranslated for many years. All Abhidharma texts and commentaries on them explain that the meaning of "saṃskāra" in Sanskrit and " 'du byed" in Tibetan is that which "causes (skāra) the formation (saṃ)" of a future existence. In other words, the fourth skandha consists of the afflictions and other factors which are the creators of karma and obscuration; because of that, they are the factors amongst all the factors of the five skandhas which have the specific property of driving the formation of future states of a being's continuum within cyclic existence.

path, no wisdom, no attainment and no non-attainment. Therefore, Śhāriputra since the bodhisatvas have no attainment they proceed by means of Prajñāpāramitā ... "

There are a few things to note. Firstly, the long list of negation above is actually a catalogue of many of the phenomena that the Buddha had taught to be existent in the first turning of the wheel. Here, they are methodically being negated in a way that makes it clear that all of the phenomena that the Buddha provisionally claimed to be existent in the first turning are now being definitively stated to be non-existent by way of a self-nature. The lists goes through the main things taught in the first turning: the five skandhas, the twelve āyatanas, the eighteen dhātus, the twelve links of interdependent origination, the end of the twelve links, the four truths of the noble ones, and wisdom and attainment as well as non-attainment. This long list is usually abbreviated by Tibetans in philosophical discussions to the phrase "all dharmas from form up to all-knowing[31]" and you will find this phrase used in some of the texts translated in this book.

Note also the key point at the end of the sūtra which can be paraphrased, "Well, if all of these things are not there, how does the bodhisatva proceed with his life? He proceeds by remaining within the realization of the absence of the two types of self, which is the ultimate realization of the Prajñāpāramitā." That begs the question, "What is this ultimate Prajñāpāramitā, the means by which the bodhisatva proceeds on his way, according to the second turning of the wheel?" An answer is given in the *Praise to Prajñāpāramitā* that was composed by Rāhula, the son of the Buddha, who eventually found his father, joined the community, and became an arhat buddha:

Homage to Prajñāpāramitā inexpressible by speech or thought—
Unborn, unceasing, entity of space,
The domain of individual self-knowing wisdom,

---

[31] Where all-knowing refers to the total knowledge of a buddha.

Mother of the conquerors of the three times.

In other words, although one might repeatedly use a negation of false existents in order to arrive at Prajñāpāramitā, Prajñāpāramitā itself is neither the process of negation nor the dualistic analytical mind that goes with the process of negation. Rather, it is wisdom, meaning the non-dualistic type of mind which is totally beyond the dualistic mind of samsaric beings. That, in fact, is the message of the third turning of the wheel, the message that prajñā which sees reality is wisdom, which does exist. However, the Buddha did not teach that way at all in the second turning of the wheel and it is universally accepted that the second turning teachings focus on the absence of self-nature in all phenomena and persons. Because of that, the second turning is universally characterized as "the turning of non-essentiality".

THIRD OR FINAL TURNING OF THE WHEEL OF DHARMA

After the second turning was complete, the Buddha gave further teachings which he stated were a third turning of the wheel of dharma. The teachings of this turning were, unlike the first two turnings of the wheel of dharma, not given at a specific time or place but at varying times and places.

The third turning of the wheel can appear to be a mixture of teachings of various sorts. However, careful inspection shows that they have a common theme and style. Their common theme is that all of them present the understanding that there is a core of enlightened mind present within every mistaken and not-truly-existing samsaric mind. Their common style is that all of them teach not by negating something seen to be a mistake, as was done in the second turning where the mistaken phenomena of samsaric mind were negated, but by making positive statements about the non-mistaken actually-existing enlightenment mind[32] present in every being. These third turning teachings precisely and repeatedly distinguish that enlightenment mind in order to determine what it is. Thus, the third turning is characterized as "the turning in which precise distinctions are made".

Here, there is the common theme of a core to mistaken samsaric mind which is not mistaken and which is the cause of enlightenment for every being. That core is referred to with many names in the third turning teachings. For example, one of its key features can be understood through the Sanskrit name "gotra" which is commonly used to refer to it. In the context of third turning teachings, this term has often been translated into English as "family" or "lineage", both of which are indeed meanings of the word "gotra", nonetheless, commentaries clearly explain that, in this context, the meaning of "gotra" is "type" or "same kind of thing". The core of mind is of the same *type* as buddha mind and because of that, there is the possibility that anyone with it could become a buddha.

A major point taught by the Buddha in the third turning is that every sentient being has this core of mind. Because it is the same *type* of thing as a buddha's mind and because all sentient beings have it, there is the major point taught by the Buddha in the third turning that all sentient beings have the seed of buddhahood in them so can become a buddha. Therefore, in these teachings, this core of mind is further given the name "tathāgatagarbha", where "tathāgata" refers to a buddha and "garbha" literally means "a shell or husk containing something", like a seed. The tathāgatagarbha is that matrix which is the birthplace of a buddha or is the seed from which buddhahood can come.

Many of the sūtras of the third turning of the wheel teach tathā-gatagarbha in a general way—for example, the ones which teach the

---

[32] For enlightenment mind, see the glossary.

Mind Only approach. There also are sūtras which teach tathāgatagarbha directly and in a very profound way. Other Emptiness
advocates pick out the latter ones as the sūtras that show an even
more profound teaching on emptiness than the sūtras of the second
turning of the wheel. Those who do not accept Other Emptiness
either do not consider these to be teachings on emptiness and hence
consider that the teachings on emptiness are only to be found in the
second turning of the wheel or consider that the emptiness presented
in the second turning of the wheel is more profound.

The tathāgatagarbha is the seed of enlightenment contained in but
cloaked by the dross of an ordinary being's samsaric mind. A more
profound approach is that it is not merely a seed of enlightenment
within an ordinary being's mind but is actual enlightenment existing
within an ordinary being. This latter approach is the view held by
the Other Emptiness schools and is certainly the view of the tantras.
It is important not to mistake this latter approach for a proclamation
that ordinary beings are enlightened—they are not. However, they
do have something within them which needs no more than to have
the cloaking removed from it in order for them to manifest
enlightenment. The Kagyu and Nyingma schools will usually show
that this approach was taught by the Buddha by quoting the *Hevajra
Tantra*:

> Every sentient being is buddha itself,
> However, all are obscured by adventitious stains ...

In other words, when the Other Emptiness schools point out that
tathāgatagarbha does not merely mean a seed that has to be grown
but refers to an already-present enlightened kind of mind, they are
referring to the naturally pure buddha element that exists within a
sentient being's mindstream, not to the same thing when it has later
been freed from the adventitious stains by practise of the path. There
is a subtle but most important distinction there.

The Buddha himself states clearly in at least two of the major sūtras
of the third turning of the wheel that the sūtras of the third turning

constitute a major, further step in the sequence of the teaching. He teaches in the *Unravelling the Intent Sūtra* and *Dhāraṇeshvara Sūtra*[33] that there is a progression of profundity of his teaching through the three turnings of the wheel, with the teaching of the second turning being more profound than the first, and the third being more profound than the second, and gives clear examples to support his teaching. Broadly speaking, those in Tibet who accepted the Other Emptiness view accepted that teaching of the Buddha as definitive, while the others seemed to ignore the teaching in these sūtras with their proclamation that the second turning of the wheel was definitive, profound teaching while the third turning contains important but mostly provisional and non-profound teaching.

If we wanted to look into the discrepancy just mentioned, we would have to investigate two points. Is the third turning a further step in the overall presentation of the teaching? Which turnings of the wheel are regarded as definitive and which as provisional? As discussed in the introductory chapter, Jamgon Kongtrul makes a clear ascertainment of both points in his *Treasury of Knowledge* starting on page 214. It is recommended that the reader read through that now, or at least through the section that deals with the ascertainment of provisional and definitive within the three turnings.

CHARACTERIZING THE THREE TURNINGS OF THE WHEEL

Each of the three turnings of the wheel of dharma is given a name that sums up the main character of the wheel. These names are based on the way that the Buddha and the great Indian masters following

---

[33] The relevant teaching in each of these two sūtras can be viewed in the extract from *Treasury which is an Encyclopædia of Knowledge* starting on page 214.

him characterized the three turnings. For example, in the *Unravelling the Intent Sutra* the Buddha says:

> The first one, the four truths; the middle one, lack of characteristics; the final one, precise distinctions ...

The first one is characterized in various ways but they all come down to its being the wheel which gets beings entered onto the path through the teaching of the four truths. The second and third ones are referred to by Tibetans as the wheels of "lack of characteristics" and "precise distinctions" respectively, in accordance with how the Buddha himself described them, as mentioned earlier.

The first wheel taught a dose of reality to sentient beings, enough to get them on their way out of their highly unsatisfactory situation. It also taught profound reality partially, but not fully, enough so that they could at least escape from the burning house of saṃsāra. All Tibetan Buddhists will agree with that. In fact, even the practitioners of the Lesser Vehicles such as the modern-day Theravada would have to agree because their own teachings clearly show and they do themselves accept that the fruition of their journey is the fruition of the arhat buddha and not of a truly complete buddha.

The second turning of the wheel is called "lack of characteristics". A key point is that it starts out from the perspective of the person who is within cyclic existence. A second key point is that it does not look at the mind of that person except to note that it is deluded. Rather, it looks primarily at the phenomena which have been invented by the delusion. A third key point is that it does not show wisdom in the positive sense of "This is what you will attain to", but focusses on it from the perspective "You have a mistaken mind that invents a self-nature in all phenomena; you need to negate the wrong concepts in order to remove them and so go to wisdom". In other words, wisdom is focussed on as an absence of the twist that samsaric mind puts on it and the practice to go with it is to stop seeing everything in terms of conceptual characteristics. In short, the second turning takes the perspective of a person in saṃsāra who is wanting to escape and looks out at phenomena, investigating them to find the absence of solid characteristics in them. ✗ — ˙ViTAL

The third turning of the wheel is called "precise distinctions". Whereas the second turning looks out at phenomena, the third turning looks in at the mind that is perceiving the phenomena. It decides that there is an enlightened core to that mind, one whose entity is the entity of buddha mind. It then makes very precise distinctions about what is un-enlightened mind and what is enlightened mind. In doing so, it not only teaches that there is an enlightened mind but determines it through the use of precise distinctions that negate what it is not and which, in doing so, affirm what it is. — ViTAL

The style of the third turning can seem either to be in contradiction to or missing the teaching of the second wheel in which all types of conceptualized existence are to be negated. It is usually seen this way by people who are attached to the presentation of the second turning as the ultimate presentation. Nonetheless, the difference in teaching between the two wheels does not have to be seen as contradictory or faulty. Firstly, it has to be understood that the technique for presenting the teachings in the third wheel is different from that of the second wheel; each one uses a certain style of negation and the two styles are fundamentally different. The negation used in the second turning to arrive at an absolute absence of characteristics in persons and phenomena is an outright negation whereas the negation that the third turning uses to show what a buddha's wisdom is not also affirms what it is.

In short, the third turning as a whole has a positive presentation to it. It affirms the presence of enlightenment within mind that can be revealed rather than the presence of un-enlightenment that has to be negated. It meditates within that self-existing enlightenment rather than meditating in a struggle to exit ignorance because of using logic which is an aspect of that ignorance. It has the value that its positive approach of negation with affirmation of the enlightened side can act as an antidote to the habit of absolute negation which, practically speaking, is usually built up through the contemplations and meditations of the second turning of the wheel. All in all, it comes from the side of enlightenment by showing that there is a core to dualistic mind which is enlightened and which does not have to be cut off, negated, or otherwise given the treatment of the second turning of the wheel.

Thus, for the Other Emptiness advocates, the teaching of the third wheel has, in accord with what the Buddha himself said, the hallmark of being a further, more profound explanation than the teaching of the second turning.

The Fourth Turning of the Wheel

The three turnings of the wheel are public teachings that anyone can practise without particular danger. They show an approach to the journey to enlightenment in which you practise now in order to obtain a result later. They are also called the conventional teachings because they teach spirituality in a conventional way. They are also called the outer or exoteric teachings.

The Buddha also turned a fourth wheel of the teachings that were not public and which showed very special techniques for a relatively small group of people who could appreciate and practise them. They were called the tantras and showed an approach to the journey in which the result is practised now. They were also called the vajra teachings because they focussed on the vajra or indestructible, enlightened mind that is part of every sentient being's mind and which can be used as the means to enlightenment. The vajra teachings were exposed to the human world in the form of teachings given by the saṃbhogakāya aspect of the Buddha's enlightenment or of his appointee, Vajrapāṇi, which were later written down in texts called the tantras.

The vajra teachings embody the meaning of emptiness that the Buddha laid out in the second turning of the wheel. However, the language and style of the teachings in these two turnings of the wheel are very different. The vajra teachings also embody the meaning of tathāgatagarbha that the Buddha taught in the third turning of the wheel, though in this case the language and style of the two are very similar because both of them teach wisdom that exists within a person. It is true that there are certain special features of the vajra teachings that are not found in the conventional or exoteric teachings and these features make the vajra teachings special, unconventional, and esoteric. Nonetheless, the third turning tathāgatagarbha teachings and the fourth turning vajra teachings have a great deal in common.

Moreover, when the third turning teachings are presented in the Other Emptiness style, they become so close to the vajra teachings that there is very little difference between them. Therefore, the Other Emptiness advocates say that the sūtra Other Emptiness approach is a bridge to the vajra teachings which themselves are the ultimate kind of Other Emptiness teaching. Some readers might doubt this because it is not discussed in Other Emptiness writings. However, I heard the sixteenth Karmapa himself say this to the vidyādhara Chogyam Trungpa Rinpoche's student body when he was visiting in 1980 and I have heard it personally from my own teachers many times, including the vidyādhara Chogyam Trungpa and the others mentioned in the Important Background chapter. It might be worth mentioning that, when the sixteenth Karmapa was visiting at that time, he asked an assembly of the Western scholars of the community what their view was. They collectively gave answers that added up to the Gelugpa presentation, which was the only presentation of view available through books and academia to Western Tibetan Buddhists at the time. The Karmapa showed his considerable displeasure. He made a clear proclamation that theirs was not the view of the Kagyu—that Other Emptiness was. At the time, no-one knew what Other Emptiness was so there was some scurrying around after that to try to find out about it. That led to Chogyam

Trungpa Rinpoche informing those of us who were in his Nālandā Translation Committee that we needed to learn this view and he set us to work on one of Mipham's texts about it and asked Khenpo Palden Sherab to teach it to us. That in turn led, through the history mentioned in the Important Background chapter, to this and several other books on Other Emptiness.

All the Tibetan lineages that follow Other Emptiness are primarily vajra vehicle lineages, so it works very well for them to have a sūtra style Other Emptiness teaching that fits with and leads to the actual vajra teaching.

WISDOM IS THE KEY POINT

This whole Chapter is A "Must Read"!

When the Buddha's teachings given through the four turnings of the wheel have been understood, the realization dawns that the most important task in life is to gain direct access to one's own, innate wisdom. That might be a little jarring to theorists who are reading this book with the aim of understanding Buddhist views, but it is a fact. The Buddha taught his teachings not for the purpose of satisfying the intellect, but for the purpose of leading beings back to their original, enlightened condition, which can be summed up in the word "wisdom".

Most Tibetan Buddhists will be familiar with the Buddha's teachings taught through various vehicles, for example, the nine vehicles of the Nyingma and the three vehicles of the Kagyu, Sakya, and Gelug presentations of the teachings. The Buddha also spoke of "The Single Vehicle", which he called "The Buddha Vehicle". This is the one vehicle that all Buddhists tread regardless of which of the many other vehicles they follow. The point, as explained by the Buddha, is that all beings have the one goal of the unsurpassed enlightenment of a truly complete buddha. A truly complete buddha is a being of wisdom, no more and no less, and the point of the single vehicle teaching is that there is only one thing to be done and that is to become wisdom.

Someone might object at this point and say that a buddha consists of a mind body—the dharmakāya as it is called—and form bodies—the saṃbhogakāya and nirmāṇakāya as they are called. They might be thinking that a buddha is like we humans who appear to have a mind and a body in which the body is a basis for but different from mind. However, a buddha is wisdom and wisdom alone—the form bodies which are manifestations of the wisdom are that wisdom, despite how they might appear to a human observing them. Even at the sūtra level, there is talk of a buddha being wisdom no more and no less; for example this is mentioned in *The Sūtra of the Recollection of the Noble Three Jewels*[34]. The very highest teachings of the fourth turning of the wheel, found in the teachings called Great Completion or Dzogchen in Tibetan, explicitly say that everything of all possible types of existence both un-enlightened and enlightened—saṃsāra and nirvāṇa—are contained within a single unique sphere of wisdom. This kind of talk could easily lead off into a tome of highly interesting discussions of Buddhist philosophy regarding the status of mind and matter, but that cannot be pursued here. The point is that, in the final analysis in the Buddha's teachings on enlightenment, everything is either wisdom itself or a projection of it. According to that, the path to enlightenment is none other than learning to access that wisdom to the point where one is nothing but that wisdom. Thus, this chapter looks at how wisdom can be accessed and especially how the various teachings of the Buddha can be used for that purpose.

Sentient beings, meaning all beings who, in having mind to a greater or lesser degree, are less than fully enlightened, have a natural drive which is always leading them back to their innate, enlightened state.

---

[34] A particularly complete presentation of this sūtra, with extensive introductions, three commentaries, and Pali, Sanskrit, and Tibetan editions of the text, is available in the book *Unending Auspiciousness, The Sūtra of the Recollection of the Noble Three Jewels*, by Tony Duff, published by Padma Karpo Translation Committee, 2010, ISBN: 978-9937-8386-1-0.

That drive is their own, innate wisdom. Sometimes it is so obscured that it does not seem to be operative, for example in hardened criminals, but it is there. Sometimes it is operating, though with confusion—for example, there are many religions and movements such as new age movements in which, at least from the Buddhist perspective, sentient beings are obviously attempting to get to their wisdom, even if their efforts seem misguided. None of these sentient beings mentioned so far can be said not to be on the journey to enlightenment—they are. Understanding this, the Buddha taught an extra vehicle in addition to the three or nine and so on vehicles to enlightenment. This extra vehicle was called "The Brahmā Vehicle". It is the vehicle entered by all those who have not entered the vehicles taught by the Buddha as direct, unmistaken vehicles to enlightenment. Moreover, the Buddha used the term "tīrthika" to refer to all those followers of spiritual paths other than his own. This is usually translated as "non-buddhists" which misses the meaning completely and loses the important part of the Buddha's teaching which is being highlighted here. "Tīrthika" means those who have come down to the shore of a pond but who have not yet entered the pond on their journey to the other side. It is a very kind term. By using it, the Buddha was not simply brushing off followers of paths other than his—which is what comes with the words like "non-buddhists" usually used these days to translate it—but was including them as sentient beings who have undertaken the journey to enlightenment, even if they have not yet arrived at a path which is unmistaken and direct. They are beings who have arrived at the brink of the true journey to enlightenment.

The Buddha saw that all sentient beings are on a journey back to their innate wisdom, even if their confusion sometimes blocks it or leads it down confused paths. Some of them have confusion which is light enough that, if they are shown an un-mistaken, direct path to innate wisdom, they could follow it successfully. It is well-known that the Buddha taught his official teachings for such sentient beings, though there is a tendency to lose sight of the fact that he was a wisdom being who taught exactly what was needed for any given sentient being to return to innate wisdom, even if what he taught seemed to be contrary to that. For example, the great bodhisatva Mañjushrī had been assisting a man who had initially come before the Buddha for advice. The Buddha had advised the man to do something which Mañjushrī saw would put the man in hell. When Mañjushrī asked about it, the Buddha replied that it was true, but that what Mañjushrī could not see was that the man would then become fully enlightened in a certain number of aeons following his birth in hell; the Buddha told Mañjushrī that, if the man were sent on what the Buddha was teaching as the official path to enlightenment, the man would not be born in hell and also would not arrive at full enlightenment for twice as long as if he followed the Buddha's unusual advice that would land him in hell.

In short, the situation of all beings is wisdom, no more and no less, and, having fallen into un-enlightenment in regard to that wisdom, they are automatically on a journey back to it. There are many, many ways for them to return to their innate wisdom. The teachings of the Buddha contained in the four turnings of the wheel are a set of unmistaken and direct ways for sentient beings to do that.

THE MEANING OF "WISDOM"

The Buddha spoke of wisdom like this. All minds, whether en-lightened or un-enlightened, are an awareness or a knower, at root. The awareness that is an enlightenment mind is a very pure knower, one without all the rotten discharges that come along when it becomes infected with dualistic ignorance. For this reason it is called "without outflows" where outflows are the defilements that pour out of it when it becomes sick with dualism. It is also a very simple knower, one without all the complications that develop in when it becomes a dualistic mind. For this reason, it is called "free of elaborations" which also means "lacking the complexities of concept"³⁵.

Indian spiritual traditions, including Buddhism, referred to this pure knower as "jñāna", a term which conveys the sense of just awareness, pure and simple. The Tibetan translators did not translate "jñāna" literally. Instead, they translated it with "ye gnas kyi shes pa" meaning "that awareness which is originally or primordially present", then shortened that to "ye shes" for convenience. Not understanding this, English translators have translated "jñāna" simply on the basis of the Tibetan "ye shes", coming up with "primordial awareness", "primordial wisdom", and the like. These translations do not reflect the simplicity of the Sanskrit original and show a lack of knowledge of the meaning of "ye" within "ye shes". One usually very capable Western translator has translated "ye shes" with "timeless aware-ness". This is a major error which takes people very far in the wrong direction.

Given that the Tibetan term "ye shes" is an indirect translation of "jñāna", it would be best for Western translators to go back to the Sanskrit and translate into their own languages directly from that. Unfortunately, there is no one word in English which has the right connotations, so we are left with the problem of how to translate this key term. The vidyādhara Chogyam Trungpa said to his Nālandā Translation Committee that it would be best to use "wisdom" given that it is a single word, readily identified, and which could over time come to have the required meaning. After many years of oral translation in which I had the opportunity to try out "primordial awareness" and all the other ideas floated by Western translators as well as wisdom, I think he was right. Therefore, "wisdom" is consistently used in all my writings as the translation of "jñāna", the non-dualistic, enlightened type of knower of a buddha.

---

³⁵ For awareness, knower, outflows, and elaborations, see the glossary.

To be clear, the wisdom that we are talking about here is not conventional wisdom, not the wisdom of a wise sort of person who thinks using rational mind[36]. Rather, it is a non-dualistic, enlightened type of knowing which is utterly different from the dualistic, deluded knower called "mind" that sentient beings have.[37]

INCREASINGLY PROFOUND WAYS TO ACCESS WISDOM TAUGHT BY THE BUDDHA

Now we can focus on the paths officially taught by the Buddha as the unmistaken, direct paths back to wisdom. Combining the characterization of each of the four turnings of the wheel given in an earlier chapter with the wisdom theme of the Other Emptiness teaching, we see that the four turnings represent four specific methods of accessing wisdom:

- the first turning sutra wheel teaches entrance to wisdom in a provisional, meaning an indirect, way, requiring the use of conceptual, dualistic mind to overcome that mind, with the result that wisdom is entered very indirectly;

- the second turning sutra wheel teaches entrance to wisdom in a definitive, meaning direct, way, requiring the use of conceptual, dualistic mind to overcome that mind, with the result that wisdom is entered indirectly;

- the third turning sutra wheel teaches entrance to wisdom in a definitive way which does not require the use of

---

[36] For rational mind, see the glossary.

[37] Skt. citta, Tib. sems. The average Buddhist hears the word "mind" and gets the rough idea "all types of mind". However, the word "mind" is specifically used in Buddhism to mean samsaric mind and is in contradistinction to "wisdom" and many other terms which mean enlightened mind. It is of crucial importance when reading these texts to understand each of the terms for the various kinds of knower.

conceptual mind to enter wisdom and shows how to access it directly, but shows this in a slightly hidden way;

• the fourth turning tantra wheel teaches entrance to wisdom in a definitive way which does not require the use of conceptual mind to enter wisdom and shows how to access it directly and shows this openly, in the most uninhibited way possible.

The Buddha himself explained that he taught entrance to wisdom in this sequence of steps of increasing profundity in order to accommodate all levels of capacity amongst his followers. His explanation of the third turning being not only definitive but the ultimate definitive teaching of the sūtras is what is accepted by Kagyu, Nyingma, Jonang, and a segment of the Sakya traditions. The others, the Gelug tradition of Tsongkhapa and his followers and some Sakyas, accept the above characterization of the first wheel but claim that the second turning is where the ultimate teachings of sūtra are found. This difference of opinion over how the Buddha's teaching functions as an entrance to wisdom is at the root of the argument of whether the Other Emptiness teaching is valid or not and also the differences of approach of the major schools of Tibetan Buddhism mentioned above. It should be emphasized here yet again that, despite the prominence that the teachings of the Gelugpa school sometimes have, the majority of Tibetan Buddhists follow the other empty approach in which the four turnings of the wheel were taught as increasingly profound entrances to wisdom in the way just shown.

There are other ways to characterize the four turnings of the wheel according to the other empty approach. For example, Gyalwang Je in *A Juggernaut of the Non-Dual View, Teachings of the Second Drukchen, Gyalwang Je* characterizes them according to the non-dual teachings of the *Kālachakra Tantra*, a tantra intimately connected with the view of Other Emptiness. In his presentation there, first turning is non-ultimate provisional; second turning is ultimate provisional; third turning is non-ultimate definitive; and fourth turning is ultimate definitive. He does it that way because of wanting to emphasis that the approaches of resting in wisdom are direct where the approaches of using conceptual mind to eliminate itself in order to access wisdom are not, and then, within each of the two, there are less direct and more direct approaches.

WHICH WAY IS SUITABLE?

The teachings themselves say that a teaching on accessing wisdom which is beyond one's capabilities should not be followed, but that one should find an approach within one's capabilities and then work up to more profound methods from there.

For example, if an ordinary person is told "Simply rest in your own wisdom by leaving it to be itself", which is the basic message of the profound meditation instructions of the third and fourth turnings of the wheel, for example as given in the Other Emptiness, Mahāmudrā, and Mahā Ati teachings, he will not, except in the rarest of cases of someone who has trained extensively at that level in an earlier life, be able to do it. Even if he is able to rest his mind nicely, he still will not know what this wisdom thing is and will end up focussed intently in dualistic mind. Over time, that could create a serious problem. Precisely for this reason, the Buddha did not initially teach the profound instructions of directly resting in wisdom. Instead, he first explained how to use dualistic mind to defeat dualistic mind in a relatively easy, indirect way to access wisdom. That gave ordinary people a means by which they could gradually get to the point where they could successfully use the more profound instructions to directly access wisdom.

Thus, in terms of the paths to wisdom taught by the Buddha, the choices for those who want to access their wisdom boil down to two: it can be accessed by using dualistic, that is samsaric, mind to defeat itself so that wisdom is "slipped" into, or it can be accessed by directly resting in it, though each of those ways has variations which further allow for the varying capacities of beings to enter wisdom.

THE TWO PRINCIPAL WAYS TO ACCESS WISDOM

Samsaric mind sees every phenomena as having a solid or substantial entity, called "a nature" or "a self". In fact, these phenomena do not have or are empty of a nature. Does that mean that the phenomena do not exist as such? No. It means that the phenomena seen with a nature by confused samsaric mind do not exist as they appear. Is that true for wisdom, too? It is. Wisdom as known by samsaric mind is a fiction and as such does not exist as it appears. In Buddhist terminology, it is said to be empty. Well, if it is empty, meaning empty of itself, then how could it be accessed? Wisdom being empty of itself does not mean that wisdom simply does not exist; it means that wisdom as known by samsaric mind is a fiction and does not exist the way it is seen. How then can we get to actual wisdom, whatever that might be?

The Second Turning Approach

If we follow the teachings of the second turning of the wheel, we use a correctly reasoning mind, which in Indian language is called prajñā, to investigate the status of all things, both persons and phenomena. Specific types of logical reasoning are used to determine the status of persons and phenomena, one by one. The more we do this, the more it will be seen that persons and phenomena do not exist the way that our samsaric minds have been seeing them. The grip of the fundamental ignorance of samsaric mind will be weakened until finally, one day, samsaric mind will fall apart and wisdom will manifest automatically as prajñā seeing a space-like emptiness of persons and phenomena.

A question that often arises when thinking this process through is this: how could the prajñā of a dualistic samsaric mind cause wisdom, given that wisdom is not a dualistic mind? It is a very astute question.

Prajña as an operation of dualistic, conceptual mind can be used in an attempt to resolve the actual status of the persons and phenomena of our worlds. When that is done repeatedly, it will weaken the confusions of dualistic, conceptual mind. The prajna itself is conceptual but is correctly operating concept. Therefore, although it does not have the power to bring wisdom directly, it does have the power to undermine concepts. As the confused concepts are weakened and removed, the strength of dualistic mind weakens until, one day, a gap in it appears and the underlying, innate wisdom sees itself. The Buddha's reply to this question when it was asked by his close arhat disciple Kāshyapa was recorded in *The Sūtra Petitioned by Kāshyapa*:

> Rubbing two sticks together produces fire and
> Having been produced it incinerates the two;
> Similarly, the faculty of prajñā is produced and
> Having been produced it incinerates itself, too.

The same sūtra also says:

> Fire and Grass-Wood have started a fight. Some come up
> to Fire and, gathering Grass-Wood's group into a gang,
> say, 'We are gathered into a gang, aren't we!' Fire replies,
> "Your gang, however big it is, is my gang![38]

If you take the approach like that of using logic to get to the emptiness of all persons and phenomena, which is the path that the Buddha laid out indistinctly in the first turning and explicitly in the second turning, it will indeed lead to the wisdom of enlightenment, according to the Buddha himself. However, it is noteworthy that the journey is a very long one indeed. As the Buddha himself pointed

---

[38] I have translated the quote from the sūtra literally because otherwise the meaning is lost. The names Fire and Grass-Wood are the names of two people who have started a fight. In the end, Fire says, "Bring on as much Grass-Wood as you want; since all of it is fuel for my fire, all is actually on my side, not yours!"

out, to follow this journey to its end takes "three countless great aeons", which is the time for three universes like ours to come and go.

There are many reasons for the lengthiness of such a journey. A major one is that you, the practitioner, are continually taking the stance that you are on the side of ignorance, which means that you are not on the side of wisdom! Your use of the samsaric mind, even if it is the best type of awareness (the literal meaning of prajñā) possible in that mind, keeps you within the very mind you seek to remove! It is also said in these teachings that it is necessary to analyse every phenomenon down to its emptiness in order to get to wisdom, making it a very protracted method.

This method has the advantage for those who have not yet reached the capability of resting directly in wisdom that it uses the problem itself to get rid of the problem. It starts with the ignorant samsaric mind and uses that to defeat itself. Therefore, it is a very accessible method.

There is one difficulty with this method, which is that it requires a genuine prajñā, something which most people do not have to begin with. Prajñā does not merely mean the ability to run together strings of ideas and reasons into what seem to be logical statements. Westerners, who have been through years of compulsory schooling that has trained them to think, have not necessarily been trained to think correctly. I have seen, during years of oral translation of the Buddhist teachings in front of Western audiences, that Westerners often assume that they think correctly when in fact few of them have developed that capacity. Fortunately, the teachings on how to practise these investigations contain extensive information on the reasonings needed for the investigations and how to apply them. The Gelug tradition in particular is held in very high regard for its excellent explanations of how to develop the logical mind needed for these investigations.

The Third and Fourth Turnings' Approach

What if you took the stance that, because you are wisdom at root, you could go to that side of things directly? In that case, you would not have to analyse every single thing down to its emptiness in order to get to wisdom. Instead, you would acknowledge that wisdom exists within and follow a path which lets that wisdom manifest in any given moment. If you were actually able to discover your wisdom mind and knew how to let it manifest, it could be a much faster path to wisdom than the one just mentioned.

It is possible to bypass the step of analysis of phenomena as taught in the second turning of the wheel and go directly to resting in wisdom. However, there should be no mistaking that it is a much more difficult path to follow and is not something that everyone can do. For example, there are those who claim they are "resting directly in wisdom" but who have not obtained all of the instructions needed to do so or are mistakenly practising the instructions they have received. It is also a considerably more dangerous path. For example, it is easy for people like those just mentioned to mistake various dualistic spaces for wisdom spaces and then create a very powerful habit of remaining in those spaces. In that way, they create the seeds of animal or other rebirths within cyclic existence, just as Sakya Paṇḍita warned was possible in his infamous text, *Distinguishing the Three Vows*, in which he claimed that Kagyu practitioners of Mahāmudrā were doing that and nothing else:

> Stupid people's meditating on Mahāmudrā,
> Mostly turns into the cause of an animal ...

Are the approaches of the third and fourth turning teachings different? Both of them essentially teach directly resting in wisdom. However, the explanations of the view and practice in the third turning teachings are a little hidden. The actual way to do it in particular is usually not discussed and only shown by the guru to the disciple. The fourth turning shows the theory and practice directly and with nothing hidden. However, the fourth turning is even more demanding of the person who wants to use such methods than is the third turning, for example, the fourth turning also requires entrance into a deity maṇḍala which in turn requires the acceptance of particular hard-to-keep vows called "samayas", and so on.

Differentiating the Two Approaches

The Other Emptiness teachings make many distinctions between these two approaches to accessing wisdom. For example, the second turning of the wheel teaches that the phenomena of samsaric mind are fictitious and therefore empty. It uses logic to investigate the status of those phenomena to the point of eliminating them and so indirectly arrive at wisdom. The third and fourth turnings do not teach a process of investigating the false phenomena which are the products of a deluded mind but a process of looking directly at the mind which is projecting them in order to see the wisdom innate to that mind. In other words, they teach looking directly at the mind making the fiction so as to see its core of wisdom. They do not look out at the persons and phenomena projected by samsaric mind; instead, they look inwards at the mind which knows the phenomena. They do not use dualistic mind and its false phenomena to find emptiness; instead they directly access the core of dualistic mind, which is the wisdom of a buddha.

Many more distinctions between the two approaches are shown, as follows. When the two approaches are distinguished according to their style of teaching, the former is typified as the "lack of characteristics" teaching of the second turning and the latter as the "precise definitions" teaching of the third turning. When distinguished according to their style of meditation, the former is typified as "analytical meditation" and the latter as "resting meditation". When distinguished according to the way that their meditation works, the former is typified as "cutting elaboration" and the latter as "equipoise", "actuality", and "direct perception". When distinguished according to the type of person who does them, the former is typified as the "paṇḍit's approach to meditation" and the latter as the "kusalī's approach to meditation". When distinguished according to the type of analysis used, the former is typified as "attribute analysis" and the latter as "overall analysis"—both are a type of analysis that results in a comprehension of the view but the former uses rational mind in a conceptual way that takes the attributes of the thing one at a time whereas the latter uses wisdom in direct perception to see the whole situation as it is. A substantial listing of them with extensive explanation for each is given in *A Juggernaut of the Non-Dual View, Teachings of the Second Drukchen, Gyalwang Je.*[39]

Can the First Approach be Omitted?

Is it possible to jump directly to the style of the third and fourth turnings and not bother with the approach of the first and second turnings? Some people say that it is not all right to do such a thing because it has to be known that all things are empty in order to access wisdom, but this is a little tricky. Wisdom—meaning the actual wisdom of a buddha and not a concept of it—does not have any dualistic mind in it and does see the emptiness of all persons and phenomena directly. Therefore, if one could genuinely enter it, that would be enough and there would be no need for the emptiness known through the logical approach of the first two turnings. However, that is a very, very difficult thing to do without any error at all. Therefore, it is more usually taught that anyone who is going to follow the third and fourth turning approach should have at minimum an intellectual understanding of how persons and phenomena are empty according to the teachings of the first and second turnings. For that reason, the Other Emptiness teachers of Tibet have taught a two-fold other empty approach in which one first goes through the self-empty investigations and then goes to the other-empty approach in which one enters wisdom directly, as explained in an earlier chapter.

---

[39] See the glossary for more on these terms.

Two Principal Emptinesses

One of the earliest statements made by the Buddha following his attainment of enlightenment was made to two brahmans who approached him. He pointed out to them that, from his point of view, emptiness is the most basic fact of existence so that was to be the basis of all his teaching. This exchange, recorded in the sutras, is often used to highlight that the teaching of emptiness in general is the most important teaching of Buddhism. It also means that emptiness is a major door to accessing wisdom.

Many different types of emptiness have been taught. For example, within the Prajñāpāramitā teachings of the second turning of the wheel, there are the two emptinesses of self of persons and phenomena, the sixteen emptinesses, and so on. All of them were taught for the sake of showing the emptiness of self-nature, which is one door to accessing wisdom. Then there is the other emptiness of the other-empty system, which does not stand opposed to the emptiness of self-nature but was taught for the sake of showing another, more direct door to accessing wisdom.

Does directly accessing wisdom involve the sight of emptiness? When wisdom has been directly accessed, that wisdom will be seeing emptiness. It has to be so because wisdom sees both the emptiness of all phenomena as well as the phenomena. Is that emptiness any different from the self emptiness seen through the less profound analytical approach? Well, that which is the actual emptiness referred to by the word "emptiness" is only seen by wisdom. If you apply analysis to find emptiness, in the end you will have to make a leap from the concept-based prajñā looking at a concept of emptiness to wisdom-based prajñā which sees emptiness directly[40]. There really

---

[40] This point of two types of prajñā, one being conceptual and one being

(continued...)

is no other possibility. That is confirmed for example by Rāhula's *Praise to the Mother* quoted previously. So in the end, the emptiness seen has to be the same.

The person who accesses wisdom through analysis has the view that all the phenomena known by dualistic mind are aberrations produced by that type of mind and that, to eliminate them, they must be analysed down to their non-existence, their emptiness.

The person who accesses wisdom directly has the view that emptiness does not need to be discovered through analysis because wisdom, which constantly sees emptiness, is innately present. He might have direct experience of the emptiness of self of persons and phenomena through logical analysis or not. Either way, he has the view that wisdom itself does not have dualistic mind or any of its apparatus in it, therefore, he takes the approach that there is no need to analyse anything down to its emptiness in order to get rid of the samsaric mind which prevents the sight of wisdom. He understands that, if he can let go of the contaminating dualistic mind that prevents his innate wisdom from becoming directly manifest, that will be enough—wisdom will be uncloaked and he will have achieved his goal. When that wisdom is uncloaked, it will see the emptiness of a self of all persons and phenomena simply because the ignorance that produced the aberrations of a self-nature is gone. Nothing has to be done for that to happen except to remove from the wisdom everything which is other than the wisdom. In other words, with a view that his wisdom is "empty" of what is "other" than it, he can manifest wisdom directly through meditation which is consistent with that view, and when he does, the emptiness of a self in all persons and phenomena will be known at that time.

*① All of This is Refering to The Process of mipams "Lamp to Text Dispel of Darkness"

---

[40](...continued)
analytical, is not usually clearly made.

The last paragraph is written according to the ultimate approach to wisdom in which phenomena do not have to be emptied out by logical analysis beforehand. It corresponds to the other emptiness of the tantric approach, which is also taught in the sūtras, though it is not commonly shown. The commonly shown approach of the sūtras is the two step approach of self emptiness followed by other emptiness: emptiness of self is reached through the conceptual type of prajñā which individually discriminates phenomena, then emptiness of other is achieved through directly accessing personal self-arising, self-knowing wisdom. *Lamp to Dispel Darkness by Mipam.*

Self-arising, self-knowing wisdom does see the emptiness which is the emptiness of self, but is different from prajñā which is equipoised only on absence of a self. That is because it never wavers from seeing the space-like emptiness of self of all phenomena yet at the same time views the entirety of phenomena. Emptiness of other points to this ultimate wisdom which, when known in direct perception, is constantly viewing itself. Free of all contaminating influences of dualistic mind, it is on the one hand empty yet at the same time is free of all contamination that would otherwise hamper its view of all the phenomena both of the enlightened and the un-enlightened side. In this case, fictional truth is the entirety of samsaric phenomena and superfactual truth is the entirety of nirvanic phenomena. These two truths are not the same as the ones defined in the case of emptiness of a self, with fictional truth being appearance and superfactual truth being emptiness. The two different sets of two truths that correspond to the two types of emptiness of self and other are discussed at length in the later chapter on the two types of emptiness.

Emptiness of other is a very profound teaching which is very hard to grasp intellectually. In my own experience, you cannot really begin to understand the theory of it until actual glimpses of naked wisdom begin to be recognized in direct experience.

Read Mipam's Text – "Lamp to Dispel Darkness" for Direct Exp.

DIFFERING OPINIONS OVER
THE TWO WAYS TO ACCESS WISDOM

The question of whether it is necessary to use an analytical type of approach to get to wisdom or whether it is possible to discover wisdom on its own terms, without the analysis, can lead to strong opinions and polarization. Some people feel very strongly that analysis is required in order to access the true wisdom of a buddha. Others feel otherwise. Here are some stories ancient and modern which reveal how strong the issue can become.

Sakya Paṇḍita, an extraordinarily learned head of the Sakya school, was vituperous in his opinion that it was only possible to progress on the path if an analytical approach preceded all other efforts. Gampopa and the others in the lineage of the Kagyu were of the opinion that such an idea was completely wrong. They felt that, if you had the necessary inner instructions from a qualified guru, wisdom could be accessed directly and without any of the analysis. Sakya Pandita wrote a text called *Distinguishing the Three Vows* in which he insisted that analysis was required ahead of all else. In it, he made a very strong assertion to the effect that Mahāmudrā meditators—and he was talking about Kagyu practitioners of the time—did not know what they were doing and were only creating the cause of animal births by attempting to rest directly in wisdom. For him, it was necessary to engage in analysis to find the emptiness of a self in persons and phenomena first, as shown in the second turning of the wheel. His view was that, if the Kagyu practitioners were doing it that way, they would not be making a gross error in their Mahāmudrā meditation. Padma Karpo of the Drukpa Kagyu, a lineage which follows the other empty approach and which was famous for producing many highly realized beings through their Mahāmudrā practice of directly resting in wisdom, wrote cutting refutations of Sakya Paṇḍita's position[41]. He clearly set forth how a practitioner could arrive at wisdom without any of the analytical approach of the second turning of the wheel, using the other empty approach of Mahāmudrā. This interaction between the two poles of thought became very famous in Tibetan Buddhist history and is often used to highlight this issue very clearly.

Then there are the Jonangs, the ones who first termed the Tibetan term "other empty". Their tradition was very much practice oriented, with Kālachakra being their specialty, and were renowned for producing a fine crop of realized practitioners on the basis of their profound oral instructions having the view of Other Emptiness and the blessings of the practice of the *Kālachakra Tantra*. The Gelug hierarchs in Central Tibet, who strongly preferred the analytical approach of the second turning, tried to squash the Jonangs, insisting that the approach of settling into wisdom expressed by them was heretical—despite the very obvious fact of the time that large numbers of realized practitioners were appearing because of the teachings on settling directly into wisdom. This again is an interaction between the two poles of thought which became very famous in Tibetan history.

For a present-day example, here is a personal story from 1999. I was translating Tsoknyi Rinpoche's Dzogchen teachings at a retreat in Nepal. One of the people present was a surgeon by training, a man of exceptional academic qualification and standing. He had taken

---

[41] See the text "An Explanation of the Four Yogas Points out Superfact" in *Drukchen Padma Karpo's Collected Works on Mahamudra* by Tony Duff, published by Padma Karpo Translation Committee, 2011, ISBN: 978-9973-572-01-9.

a liking to the presentations of the Gelug tradition, famous for their insistence on the need for analysis according to the second turning. In their approach, you must search out the wrong concept of a self, then analyse what you find in order to arrive at its absence, and that will eventually lead to wisdom, as described earlier. In the Dzogchen approach being taught to him at the time of this story, one goes directly to wisdom based on the special oral instructions provided by the teacher. At one point, the good doctor asked a question in which he stated that, because the Dalai Lama said so, the only possible way to get to emptiness was through the analytical search just mentioned. An exchange ensued in which the good doctor was clearly shown that the other way was also possible. During the exchange, the doctor became increasingly strident in his assertions that the only approach was through analysis, because that is what the Dalai Lama had taught. In the end, he sat there, lecturing to Tsoknyi Rinpoche and the other students, effectively preaching to them that his understanding was the correct one. Tsoknyi Rinpoche was completely taken aback and muttered some unpleasantries under his breath about Gelug arrogance. I met this man a couple of years later in Dharamsala, the Gelug stronghold in India. He proudly told me how he was now a monk in the Gelug tradition and had been designated as a teacher authorized to teach this analytical meditation in various institutions around Dharamsala. It was a text-book perfect case of the attitudes described in an earlier chapter that followers of the Gelug tradition have become infamous for, this time being acted out by a Westerner who could not see past his own, very strongly developed intellect.

The last story illustrates two problems. The first is that Westerners, whose intellects have usually been very well trained during years of compulsory schooling, often find the logical approach to wisdom of the second turning to be very fitting and can easily be seduced into thinking that it is the only approach. The second lies in the perfect re-enactment of the other emptiness versus self-emptiness drama that happened so often in Tibet. In this case, the surgeon's powerful intellect just refused to acknowledge even the possibility of a non-intellectual approach to wisdom. Unfortunately, it did not stop there; his mind became increasingly powerful in its attempts to turn back this apparent threat to its cherished way so much so that he attempted to over-ride the teachings being given in a formal setting. In the end, he simply shut out the teachings being given from personal experience, about how wisdom could be accessed directly. Later on, he found a way to preach to everyone he could that intellect's way is the only way.

My own dharma journey is very relevant here. As a young man in the very early 1970's, I joined many others of my age and found my way to Kathmandu. There, I discovered Lama Yeshe and Lama Zopa, who were, with unutterable kindness, trying to impart the Buddhist teaching to the crazy hippies who were turning up in droves. Due to the force of karmic habit, I quickly became a monk and studied and practised Middle Way philosophy as taught by their Gelug tradition. It was very helpful. After some years, and realizing that I was still missing something, I went to study with the incomparable Chogyam Trungpa Rinpoche and the Kagyu and Nyingma traditions that he represented. It took me four years of intense study and practise in that community to shed sufficient of the baggage I had developed as a Gelug monk that I could get past the idea that logical analysis was required in order to access wisdom and to see the brilliance of the teaching of the third and fourth turnings.

There were several lessons for me in that. One was that I had—by accident or karmic force—lived the progression towards wisdom exactly as the Buddha taught it in the three turnings—first a monk practising the renunciation of the first turning, then a Gelug practitioner meditating on the emptiness of the second turning, and finally a Kagyu practitioner meditating on the other-empty emptiness of the third and fourth turnings. All Tibetan teachers that I've met get a good laugh when they hear my story—all of them know the theory but it is rare to meet someone who has actually done it in his own life and who can tell you about the progression of the three turnings from firsthand experience. Through this journey I had personally come to the renunciation taught in the first turning, meditation on emptiness using logical analysis taught in the second turning, and was very clear about the need to access wisdom directly, without the use of dualistic mind, as taught in the third and fourth turnings.

Another lesson learned on my unusual journey came from meeting practitioners in Chogyam Trungpa Rinpoche's student body who really did not have any analytical knowledge of emptiness but who were directly accessing wisdom because of the other empty-style tantric practice correctly shown to them by their teacher. I came face to face with people who embodied the fact that the analytical step can be skipped if you have the right teacher, teachings, and karmic good fortune to be able to go directly to wisdom.

Yet another set of lessons came from having lived on both sides of the Other Emptiness argument. I have seen that both sides have paths that are valid paths to enlightenment. There is no doubt in my mind that the other empty approach is more profound and more satisfying for those who can encompass it, but then I am equally sure that this is not something that everyone can do—it requires a great measure of karmic good fortune to be able to step into wisdom directly. In that regard, one should contemplate the fact that while the constitution of the United States might guarantee equality to the people of the country, it can never guarantee equality of karmic good fortune.

Therefore, there are two valid ways to access wisdom, one using an analytical approach and the other not. The former is less profound than the latter, which is the way it has to be done in the end. However, the issue practically speaking is not whether one is more profound or not but whether a person has the karmic accumulation needed to follow that particular path. Many more people will be able to follow the path in which analysis is used than the one in which wisdom is accessed directly simply because the karmic good fortune needed for the latter is much steeper than for the former.

It is far too simplistic to say that the Other Emptiness approach of going directly into wisdom is right and the Self Emptiness approach of logical analysis is wrong or vice versa. Rather, a very careful consideration of what it means to access wisdom, which in this case has come because of looking into the meaning of the Buddha's teaching and why he taught it the way he did, should lead to a much more encompassing view of our own existence and what is involved with it. In my own experience, having that larger view is essential to being able to properly appreciate the fullness of the Buddha's teachings throughout his turnings of the wheel.

One thing is certain in all of this: it would be an absolute crime to insist that, of the two, your school is correct and the others are wrong and then to use your logic and political power to try to harm and then to destroy the other school. This happened in Tibet, is still happening today amongst Tibetans, and now you can find it amongst Westerners who have studied with the intellectual types and been seduced by that so that they have not yet realized a further possibility. We do not have to repeat a bad mistake made formerly in Tibetan spiritual circles in the West. Hopefully this book might help to prevent it.

CLARIFYING THE TERMINOLOGY

PROVISIONAL AND DEFINITIVE

The terms "provisional" and "definitive" are contractions of "provisional meaning"[42] and "definitive meaning"[43].

Provisional meaning refers to a style of explanation in which the meaning is not shown directly in order to gradually guide someone towards a full, direct understanding of the meaning. Definitive meaning refers to the case where the meaning is shown directly. The classic example given in Indian and Tibetan Buddhism is that the first is an explanation which is like a finger pointing at the moon and the second is an explanation revealing the moon itself.

---

[42] Skt. neyartha, Tib. drangs don. One teacher calls this "indicative meaning" instead of provisional. This is not quite correct—indicative says that the meaning shown indicates something—but all meanings shown indicate something, including definitive meanings. The point is that the provisional teaching, while it does not show the whole meaning in a direct way, does show something that will serve to guide the student along to the whole meaning, presented directly, later on. As such, the English word "provisional" fits well.

[43] Skt. nītartha, Tib. nges don.

In Buddhism, it is important when attempting to ascertain the intent of the Buddha to know which teachings are provisional and which are definitive. Therefore, the issue of provisional and definitive teaching has become a major point in Buddhist scholarship.

Tibetan Buddhist schools universally agree that the first turning of the wheel is a provisional meaning presentation. The Buddha himself said that he taught it that way as part of his skilful means of presenting the teaching in stages. In it, he taught that phenomena substantially exist. It is not true. However, it allowed for those who were not ready to hear that the phenomena of samsaric mind simply do not exist in the way that they appear to stay with their journey and progress to the point when they could be told that kind of truth directly. Tibetan schools generally agree that the second turning of the wheel is definitive teaching; in it, the emptiness of phenomena is fully and directly taught.

Tibetan Buddhist scholars have found it necessary to make further distinctions within provisional and definitive when ascertaining the intent of the Buddha and this is seen in the discussions of the status of the various turnings of the wheel. For example, an Other Emptiness follower would conclude that both the second and third turnings of the wheel are definitive with one being more subtle in its presentation. In that case, he might call the less subtle one "provisional of definitive" and the more subtle one "definitive of definitive" or the less subtle one "non-ultimate definitive" and the more subtle one "ultimate definitive". A number of these types of distinction are made.

EMPTINESS

The Sanskrit terms "śhūnyatā" and "śhūnya", which have the Tibetan equivalents "stong pa nyid" and "stong pa" respectively, are translated into English with "emptiness" and "empty" in philosophical contexts. To say in Sanskrit that a vessel of any sort is empty, or to say that something is devoid of something else, you say that the thing concerned is "śhūnya". Thus, when we say that a phenomenon is empty of self-nature, the word "empty' conveys exactly the meaning conveyed by the original Sanskrit term "śhūnya". Note that the Sanskrit terms have other meanings which are related to the meanings "emptiness" and "empty", for example, śhūnya is the word in Sanskrit for "nought", "void", and "devoid of", all of which are applicable to its philosophical use when discussing emptiness of a self-nature.

THE HEART MEANING SUTRAS

There are those who see the emptiness described in the second turning of the wheel as the ultimate, definitive description of emptiness. Based largely on that, they assess the second turning of the wheel as the ultimate definite one. Other Emptiness advocates also see that understanding of emptiness to be crucial, which is why they usually assess the second turning of the wheel as definitive. However, they see a further type of emptiness within certain sūtras of the third turning whose teaching of tathāgatagarbha has a very profound aspect to it, one which is very similar to the tantric teachings. For the Other Emptiness advocates, these particular sūtras contain the very heart of all meanings that the Buddha was presenting within the sūtra context. Therefore, the Other Emptiness advocates call them the "Heart Meaning Sūtras". For them, this is the group of sūtras which contains the most profound teaching of all the Buddha's sūtra teachings so they refer to them collectively as the "Profound Sūtra Section".

These sūtras are usually listed as a set of ten or twenty sūtras. The listings are generally consistent though sometimes there are slight differences between them. One listing of the ten sūtras can be viewed in Khenpo Tsultrim's History of Other Emptiness in the next section of this book and a partial listing of the twenty sūtras can be seen in

Jamgon Kongtrul's introduction to his *Complete Commentary to the Highest Continuum*.

✳ TWO TYPES OF EMPTINESS AND TWO TYPES OF NEGATION ✳

All Tibetan schools agree that the second turning of the wheel eliminates the idea of a self in persons and phenomena. The emptiness arrived at is an outright negation of something which, because it is an invention only of ignorance, does not actually exist. The thing being negated is a self-ness that ignorance sees in persons and phenomena. The emptiness is an emptiness of such a self. The Other Emptiness advocates called that self-empty emptiness for convenience. The outright negation involved with the determination of the emptiness of a self is termed in Tibetan "med dgag" which is often translated as "non-affirming negative" though there are also other translations such as "non-implicative negative". The style of negation is one in which the thing to be negated is negated and with that negation there is no further implication or affirmation of something else being present.   ✳ *Negated OutRight.*

[handwritten left margin: 2nd Turning Negation]

The Buddha continued his teachings with the third turning in which he primarily taught that there is a core to mind, the tathāgatagarbha, which, as explained before, is the same type of thing as enlightened mind. The Other Emptiness advocates see that, based on the words of the heart meaning sūtras and the oral instructions for the view and meditation which have come down through Maitreya, this core cannot be negated outright, because it is the wisdom of a buddha which remains even after samsaric mind and its fictional projections have been removed by the self-emptiness meditations of the second turning. However, it is empty in the sense that it does not have within its entity the things of samsaric mind. Therefore, this emptiness of other is not arrived at using the non-affirming negation used to arrive at the self emptiness taught in the second turning. The means by which emptiness of other is arrived at is called an "affirming negation" or "implicative negation". It is used to deny one thing

[handwritten bottom: ✳ This whole Section is not only Vital but Essential to Understand, espiecially the Highlighted Asterick ✳ pART!]

within a larger context while either affirming or implying the affirmation of other parts of the context. For example, "That tree is empty of fruit", negates the presence of fruit on a particular tree while implying that the tree exists. The third turning makes many statements about sugatagarbha which are not intended to eliminate self-entity from it using non-affirming negation but which are intended to precisely distinguish it as being this way or that way using affirming negations. Thus, for example, sugatagarbha is stated "to be empty of all the things other than its own entity", a statement which eliminates the entirety of samsaric mind from sugatagarbha and which at the same time indicates that there is something there which is empty of those things.

Some people who have become used to the non-affirming negation style of the second wheel feel, when they first start reading the teachings of the third wheel, that something is missing, because the negating of everything back to emptiness is gone and worse, that perhaps something is wrong because there is a tone of affirmation. Some become a little nervous and think, "Where has the real teaching on emptiness gone?" That is exactly the problem that the detractors of Other Emptiness had, the ones who could not make the transition to the very profound style of emptiness that was being presented in the third turning. The solution is to realize that the emptiness of self is an emptiness assessed through non-affirming negation and cannot be directly compared with the emptiness of other assessed through affirming negation.

The third turning presentation with its precise distinctions has a more descriptive style than that of the second turning presentation, but this is part of the affirming style of negation used to teach other emptiness in the third turning of the wheel. This does not mean that the presentation of other emptiness in the third turning is like the "yakkity yak, this is this and this is that" gossip of normal conversation. This presentation is done using dharma language to make precise distinctions about the profound truth of wisdom.

It was pointed out in the Important Background chapter that you might notice that the explanations in this first section of the book have the same quality of being descriptive distinctions rather than logical negations. That itself is a sign of the third turning teaching being presented, a sign that the other empty approach is being exposed!

The heart meaning sūtras of the third turning use the naming conventions of the world—words, letters, and so on—to talk about something which has none of these things in it. They are using conventions to present something which, ultimately speaking, is beyond the reach of these conventions. On the one hand, it is understood that the skilful use of conventions to make precise distinctions using non-affirming negations brings us as close as possible conceptually to this wisdom which exists as something empty of everything other than it. On the other hand, it is understood, in the words of the self empty approach of the Other Emptiness system, that the thing itself is empty of the conventions being used to explain it. That is one way to understand the union of other emptiness and self emptiness which is the ultimate understanding of the Other Emptiness system.

"TRULY ESTABLISHED" BRINGS THE TWO DIFFERENT WAYS OF ASSESSING EMPTINESS TO THE FORE

In Tibetan, there is the word "bden grub" with two entirely different meanings. It is often used in discussions of emptiness where it opens the door to confusion. When it is used in presentations of self emptiness, it always means "truly existent". It conveys the understanding that the samsaric mind sees phenomena as though they truly—that is, really—exist. In this context, it is always a synonym for "that which exists by way of a self-nature" and is something to be removed by the practice of meditation.

When this same term is used in presentations of other emptiness, it has an entirely different meaning. In that case, it is used to make a simple distinction about something. It is used to the distinction "yes, it is true" as opposed to "no, it is not true" or "yes, that is true, we find that it is so" as opposed to the opposite of that.

Thus, when the Other Emptiness proponents speak about sugatagarbha and say that it truly exists, they mean that it is existent as opposed to non-existent. That must not be taken to mean that they are positing that wisdom is "truly existent" in the sense of having a self-nature. They explain this clearly to their detractors, pointing out that they are talking in an affirming negation context and that the meaning here is "Yes, it does exist as opposed to being non-existent." They say, "Look, we have already investigated the status of wisdom using the second turning of the wheel logic and understand that wisdom and everything else that you could name is in fact empty of being a truly existent thing. Having done so, and with that as a basis, we have moved over to another, more subtle way of accessing wisdom. In this approach, we precisely distinguish wisdom using conventions, then we access it directly in a mode beyond all conventions and elaborations. For us, samsaric mind is an aberration which can come and go, but wisdom never ceases to exist, conventionally speaking. In that sense, we are saying that it does really and truly exist. You cannot deny this type of really and truly existing: sentient beings did become sentient at some point and they do leave that and become buddhas at some point—the enlightened mind nature of their minds was there before they became sentient beings, is there while they are sentient beings, and will continue to be there when they again return to their original enlightened condition!"

Their opponents come back with the reply, "But you have just posited the actual existence of something, which is totally wrong view according to the Buddha's teaching." The Other Emptiness advocates patiently reply, "No, we have already determined that wisdom does not truly exist using the teachings of the second turning. We are not losing that but building on it and going a step further."

Strangely, their detractors do not hear what is being explained to them. They continue, like a broken recording, to insist that "truly existent" can only mean having a self-nature and now proclaim loudly that the Other Emptiness advocates are heretics who do not understand the teaching. This becomes a major theme in the arguments against Other Emptiness though this mistake is quickly and easily dismissed through knowing the difference in the use of the term "bden grub" as just explained and knowing the way that the two types of emptiness are assessed as explained in the preceding section.

All the Other Emptiness teachings warn that this step up to other emptiness is a step towards something that is very subtle and which really does not fit easily into the conceptual mind.

TATHAGATAGARBHA AND SUGATAGARBHA

Tathāgatagarbha and sugatagarbha are two terms which are, generally speaking, synonymous. Both of them refer to wisdom as a seed of enlightenment existing within the saṃsāric mind of sentient beings. However, tathāgatagarbha has a more theoretical sense whereas sugatagarbha has a more practical sense. "Sugata"[44] gives the sense of actually going on the journey to and arriving at enlightenment. Thus, when "sugatagarbha" is used in the heart essence sūtras of the third turning to talk about the seed of enlightenment, it is emphasising the idea that this is not merely a seed of enlightenment but a core enlightenment actually present in a sentient being.

Therefore, Other Emptiness presentations, which ultimately are intended to be the basis for meditation done to actualize one's own innate wisdom, tend to use the term sugatagarbha rather than tathāgatagarbha. They are speaking, using sūtra language, of what

---

[44] A complete explanation of both tathāgata and sugata and all that they entail can be found in *Unending Auspiciousness, The Sūtra of the Recollection of the Noble Three Jewels*.

the tantras explicitly show, which is the real, actually present, enlightenment within oneself as something which can be manifested by directly accessing it.

Thus, when Other Emptiness teachings speak of "mind's actuality, the sugatagarbha", they are using sugatagarbha to mean the core of mind, what mind actually is at root. They are using it to emphasize the idea of the wisdom of a buddha in the form of a seed that can be immediately actualized.

LUMINOSITY

Luminosity is one of the special terms of the heart essence sūtras and one of a few, crucial terms of the tantric teaching. It is also a term which has been singularly badly translated into English.

The word "luminosity" comes from the Sanskrit word "prabhāsvara". That word breaks down into three parts. "Pra" means to a great degree and modifies "bhāsvara". In practice, it adds no meaning and prabhāsvara was, therefore, frequently abbreviated to "bhāsvara" in Sanskrit texts. "Bhāsvara" is made of two roots: "bhāsa" is "light" as in radiant light. "Vara" means "something making clear or evident". The two roots joined together make a noun which means "illuminating light" or "that light which, in doing the work of illuminating, makes something evident". All in all, it means "luminosity".

When used in relation to mind, it is a metaphor for mind, given that mind has the quality of illuminating what it knows. In other words, this word is a metaphor for the knowing quality of mind, the raw illuminative property of mind. One well-known translator these days translates it with "cognizance" as an alternative to the meaning "knowing quality". However that also is a gross error since it loses the metaphor of the original.

The Tibetan translation of the Sanskrit term " 'od gsal ba" is very exact. Unfortunately, the word has been badly understood amongst a large group of translators who consistently translate it as "clear light". Interestingly, translators connected with practice-oriented lineages, such as the Kagyu, who have direct contact with their mind through meditation seem to understand it correctly whereas those connected more with study make this mistake. The Sanskrit "bhāsa" is translated correctly by the Tibetan " 'od" meaning light. The "vara" is translated correctly by the Tibetan "gsal ba" which is a verb meaning "to make evident", "to make visible", not an adjective meaning "clear", and so on.

Note that the original Sanskrit term has two roots joined together to make one word, with "vara" being a verb root and that the Tibetan matches that. Thus, it is wrong to think that the abbreviated form of the Tibetan " 'od gsal" should be taken separately and wrong to think that the "gsal" is an adjective. Any Sanskrit expert will immediately say that the Sanskrit word refers to a luminous source which is causing illumination. Thus, although the primary translation is "luminosity", there are also cases where the term is best translated into English with "illumination" and the like.

"Clear light" is a wrong translation in every way. It simply fails to take account of the Sanskrit original and its meaning and then shows a complete misunderstanding of the Tibetan grammar involved in the Tibetan translation of the Sanskrit. Above all, it shows a total lack of experience of one's own mind, of which it is a description. Worse still, it produces a wrong meaning in the mind of the listeners. It has lead to the idea in many dharma students that mind is some kind of light. I have met, in my role as a teacher of meditation, people who have been meditating incorrectly for years because this usage of words leads to that meaning.

It is important to get this right. The term does not mean that there is a clear kind of light, it means that there is a luminosity that causes illumination. The original term is a metaphor for the knowing quality of mind. It is very similar to the several metaphors of the English language in which understanding is referred to via light, for instance, "the light went on", "he had a moment of illumination", "that was an illuminating comment", and so on.

STAINS THAT OBSCURE

Mind's innate nature, described as "sugatagarbha", "luminosity", and so on, is the fact of enlightenment present within every sentient being's mind. Although it is present, it is not seen or not seen clearly by them because it has become obscured, as is said, from their view.

The most famous quotation from sūtra used to explain being empty of other is from the *Highest Continuum*:

> The element, sugatagarbha, is empty of that which has the characteristic of being separable, the adventitious stains …

The view of Other Emptiness is that mind's actuality sugatagarbha is empty of that which is other than it. That, re-stated, means that the very entity of sugatagarbha does not contain anything which is foreign to it. Nevertheless, for sentient beings in saṃsāra, the contents of samsaric mind pop up on its surface and obscure it. These things are foreign to it and not part of its entity so can be totally removed from it. Thus they are referred to as "the obscuration-causing adventitious stains".

Here, the term "stain"[45] means something that arrives on the surface of something else and dirties it. In other words, it has the meaning of foreign matter that has appeared on the surface of something and is obscuring it but which, because it is foreign matter, can be cleaned off.

---

[45] Tib. dri ma.

[handwritten note: '✗ of being Divisable i.e. Impermanent]

OBSCURATION BUT NO TAINTING

If the stains on a piece of clothing actually affect the clothing so that they are now part of it—like wine stains on cotton—the stains will not be removable. However, the stains on the surface of wisdom are not like that. They are surface stains that come and go. Thus it is said:

> Mind's actuality, sugatagarbha, is empty of adventitious stains because it is not tainted[46] by them.

"Taint" here means that some particular thing is changed by some other thing and is tainted and permanently spoiled in the process. For example, when vinegar is added to milk, the milk is not merely diluted by the vinegar but is curdled by it and fundamentally altered in the process, or when cotton is stained by wine, the cotton is permanently altered by the arrival of the stain. Mind's actuality, also called sugatagarbha and luminosity, has samsaric mind appear on its surface but the appearance of it does not involve any change being made to the luminosity. Thus, it does not cause any taint or spoilage of the wisdom mind.

THE GOOD QUALITIES

The most famous quotation from sūtra used to explain being empty of other continues on from above with:

> It is not empty of that which has the characteristic of not being separable, the unsurpassable dharmas.

Mind's actuality, sugatagarbha, is empty of all the samsaric mind's stuff given that those things are separable from it. Moreover, the sugatagarbha is not merely empty of those things, but has with it all the things that are part of its own entity. Those things are referred

---

[46] Tib. slad pa.

* of noT being IndivisAble, ie PermAnenT

*Indivisable, hence, Permanent

to here as "the unsurpassable dharmas" and in other places are called "the buddha dharmas" or "the attributes of enlightenment". Note that, in this context, "dharmas" does not mean "phenomena" but "qualities". Thus the unsurpassable dharmas, the buddha dharmas, are the good qualities of enlightenment.

The good qualities of enlightment are taught in all three turnings of the wheel to be "inconceivable" in extent. An example frequently seen in Other Emptiness writings is the Buddha's statement that they are "more in amount than the sands of the Ganges". There are extensive teachings in the third turning sūtras on the inconceivable good qualities of a buddha. Maitreya's treatises also have such teachings; for example, one of the seven vajra topics of the *Highest Continuum* is the topic of these good qualities and the *Ornament of Manifest Realization* details the thirty-two major marks and eighty minor marks as an explanation of the good qualities.

These inconceivable good qualities of enlightenment are most commonly summed up into the "kāyas and wisdoms", meaning the two form kāyas of sambhogakāya and nirmāṇakāya manifested for the sake of others and the various wisdoms which comprise the dharmakāya which a buddha manifests to fulfil his own needs.

Other Emptiness says that the good qualities of enlightenment are already present in the sugatagarbha and do not need to be developed but simply need to be uncovered. Tāranātha, a throne-holder and great scholar of the Jonangs, gave an example of this as being as though "one had a golden buddha sitting in one's heart". Those who do not follow Other Emptiness usually do not agree with this position, regarding the sugatagarbha to be purely a seed which has to have its good qualities produced and developed.

STYLES OF EXPLANATION OF OTHER EMPTINESS AND DIFFERING USES OF TERMINOLOGY

The various teachers who upheld Other Emptiness within Tibet each had their own way of explaining it. This led to what can seem to be a bewildering array of Other Emptiness presentations. However, when the key points of Other Emptiness are known, all of the ways of explaining it come down to the points that I have been developing in this first part of the book and which will be seen repeated in the Tibetan presentations contained in the later parts.

Khenpo Tsultrim made some observations about these different styles of explanation and differing uses of terminology:

> What are the differences in the styles of explanation given by the great masters who upheld the Other Emptiness view? Jamgon Kongtrul lists Dolpopa Sherab Gyaltsen, Karmapa Rangjung Dorje, and Drimey Ozer as the three greats of the Other Emptiness view, so we will look at what they say.

> Dolpopa made "luminosity" and "wisdom freed of elaboration" the principal terms for conducting the discussion then connected those terms with scriptural quotations from both the sūtras and tantras. He also quotes the *Great Vehicle Highest Continuum*:

>> That which is mind's nature, luminosity,
>> Like space is without change;
>> The adventitious stains come from not realizing
>>   the authentic, passion, and so on,
>> Do not change it to affliction ...

> to show that the entity is without stains and without change, then produces many, many scriptural references from the sūtras and also from tantras such as *Kālachakra*, *Reciting the Names of Mañjushrī*, and so on to explain the

words "without change", and so on. He does not say much about emptiness, but talks mainly about the factor of luminosity. That does not mean that he one-sidedly mentions luminosity and does not mention emptiness. Rather, when he wants to emphasize the empty aspect, he speaks of it in terms of luminosity-emptiness, which is a way of talking that belongs to the tantras.

Then, Longchen Rabjam and Rangjung Dorje, representing the tantras in general, also explain it as luminosity-emptiness inseparable. Rangjung Dorje mainly explains it as rigpa-emptiness which accords with the earlier tradition of the Kagyu Mahāmudrā. Longchen Rabjam talks about it mainly in terms of the rigpa that is a special feature of Mahā Ati and also explains it using other special terms of that system that are mentioned for instance in his *Treasury of Dharmadhātu*.

On another occasion, the Khenpo quoted from a song of Milarepa and then pointed out that it was a very high level explanation—meaning that it came from Mahāmudrā—but that it fitted exactly with the sūtra *Great Vehicle Highest Continuum*'s way of talking. The Khenpo said:

Milarepa, in the verse of *The Three Nails of Meditation* describing the fruition says:

> To explain Fruition's Three Nails:
> Nirvāṇa has nothing to be produced from
>   another,
> Saṃsāra has nothing to be abandoned to another
> I am decided that my own mind is buddha.

This is a very high way of talking but it does agree with the view of the *Great Vehicle Highest Continuum*, doesn't it? The second line shows that mind's actuality is natural nirvāṇa—natural nirvāṇa does not need to be produced from anything else since there is nothing to produce.

Anything that has to be produced from something else is
not a final attainment. Then the next line says that
saṃsāra is dream-like confused appearances, not the
actuality of mind and since those confused appearances
have no essence, there is nothing whatsoever to abandon.
What Milarepa is saying there is that the real actuality of
mind, which is the superfactual according to the Other
Emptiness way of explanation, is buddha. One's own
mind's actuality, luminosity-emptiness inseparable or
dhātu-rigpa inseparable is the absolute buddha, the
absolute dharmakāya.

TWO EMPTINESSES AND TWO TRUTHS

All followers of the Middle Way speak of "emptiness". Those who do not follow Other Emptiness accept that there is just one type of emptiness, the emptiness of self-nature of persons and phenomena taught in the second turning of the wheel, an emptiness which is arrived at through the use of non-affirming negation. Those who do follow Other Emptiness accept not one but two types of emptiness, which they call self emptiness and other emptiness.

These observations raise a number of questions. Are the two emptinesses accepted by the followers of Other Emptiness similar or different from each other? Then, given that the two truths are usually considered to be defined in relation to emptiness, are the two truths for self and other emptinesses defined the same way or not? The answers to these questions explain crucial points in the Other Emptiness philosophy.

The two types of emptiness proclaimed by the followers of Other Emptiness are not the same emptiness with differing names or slightly different presentations but are two types of emptiness having two entirely different definitions, uses, and modes of realization. Following on from that, the two truths defined in conjunction with each of those emptinesses are also very different from each other.

There is also the question: are the self emptinesses of the Other Emptiness school and non-Other Emptiness schools the same? The answer is that they are of the same type given that they are arrived at using non-affirming negation, but can be very different in terms of how they are defined. For example, the self emptiness described by the Other Emptiness schools is described as phenomena and persons being empty of themselves, whereas the self emptiness of the Gelug tradition is described as a phenomenon or persons not being empty of themselves but being empty of self-nature. A complete explanation of this one point would take another book in itself but would further highlight the particulars of the other empty view, this time showing clearly the self empty aspect of their view. These differences are partially covered in Khenpo Tsultrim Gyatso's presentations of the Other Emptiness system in the second part of the book.

Other Emptiness Explained Using Ju Mipham's Text

The great Nyingma scholar Ju Mipham Namgyal wrote many texts that showed the Other Emptiness view within the Nyingma teaching in general. He also wrote two that specifically addressed the view as mentioned in the introduction. One of them, *The Lion's Roar that Proclaims Other Emptiness*, focusses on the issue of emptiness and how it should be understood within Other Emptiness as a whole. It clearly defines the two types of emptiness and the two truths that belong to each type. Following that, it highlights the differences between the self empty aspect of the Other Emptiness view and the self empty views of other schools, mainly of the Gelug, in a long, mock debate between the schools.

Here, I will use the beginning of Mipham's text to look into the definitions of the two types of emptiness and the two truths that go with each. However, a proper examination of the differences between the self emptinesses of Other Emptiness and its opponents as given in the mock debates following that is outside the scope of this book[47].

The Basic Approach of Other Emptiness

Mipham starts by saying:

> In order to arrive at a certain[48] determination of the tenets of Other Emptiness, it is first necessary to determine, in accordance with the system of Guardian Nāgārjuna, that all dharmas lack self-nature. If that is not understood, then a determination of the way in which the fictional is empty of itself and the way in which the superfactual is empty of other cannot happen. So, to begin with, a determination has to be made of freedom from elaboration as the fact[49] that comes through the use of individual, personal knowledge[50] and, after that, the superfactual sort of fact, of being freed from elaboration, is realized by a subject which is no-thought wisdom.

These few words contain four major points. Firstly, he is saying that, in order to fully determine the other empty view, you first have to determine the emptiness of self taught in the second turning of the

---

[47] I plan to publish a complete book of Khenpo Palden Sherab's teachings on the text, with extensive explanations of all parts of the text in future.

[48] "In order to arrive at a certain determination ..." has the meaning, "If you are wanting definitely to arrive at a correct ascertainment ..."

[49] Tib. don. Fact here is an object as it presents itself to the face of mind. Note that first the practitioner is concerned with the object or fact known by mind and then second with the mind doing the knowing, which in that case is wisdom.

[50] The text says Tib. so sor rang gi rig pa. This is explained in the tradition to mean "so sor rang rig pa'i shes rab", where shes rab is prajñā. Thus, this is talking about wisdom, not prajñā.

wheel. Only when that has been done can you determine the emptiness of other taught in the third turning of the wheel. This point nullifies one major complaint made by the opponents of Other Emptiness, which is their claim that the other empty system does not include an understanding of the emptiness of self.

Secondly, he is pointing out that, for emptiness of self, the key point is that the fictional truth is investigated until it is found to be empty of itself[51], whereas, for emptiness of other, the key point is that the superfactual truth is empty of other. In the first step, fictional truth is investigated and, under the onslaught of proper reasoning, falls apart. The superfactual truth belonging to that is the emptiness in which all of the elaborations of ignorant mind have been removed. In the step following that, the superfactual truth that has been determined is realized not to be merely empty but to be only empty of those things which do not belong to what it actually is.

Thirdly, he points out that this progression corresponds to first looking out at the objects of mind and determining their emptiness, then looking inward at the mind itself and determining its emptiness. Here, when he talks first about the object of mind, he uses terminology found in Yogāchāra-style explanations—for example, he says "fact" rather than object but it means the same because all objects are "facts of mind" in the Mind Only system. Note though that he merely says "fact" for the first step but says "superfactual fact" for the second step. This contains the important point that Other Emptiness followers generally do not see the emptiness understood by analysis as superfact but see it as a conceptual understanding of emptiness. Only wisdom sees true superfact. However, with Other Emptiness explanations, there have been different ways of presenting whether

---

[51] Note the words "the fictional is empty of itself". This is the approach of schools who are other empty in view. It differs markedly from Tsongkhapa's approach that phenomena are empty of self-nature.

the first point is merely a conceptual understanding of emptiness or not.

Fourthly, he states what kind of mind is needed for these two steps of realization. The first must be done with prajñā, the second with wisdom. In the phase of determining the emptiness of the second turning of the wheel, the practitioner uses his own, personal prajñā to determine in personal experience that each person and phenomenon, one at a time, is empty of itself. After that, in the phase of determining the emptiness of the third turning of the wheel, the practitioner settles into wisdom. That wisdom, when discussed conventionally, will not be empty of itself because what it is will be present in the direct knowledge of the practitioner while being empty of anything which is other than itself. This does not mean that sugatagarbha is not empty of self in the way that one would talk about it in the second turning of the wheel. The reason for this is that the mode of emptiness being talked about in the case of wisdom is quite different from the mode of emptiness being talked about as arrived at through logic.

Alternatively, you could say that the first step that must be undertaken on the path is to undermine the fundamental mistake of co-emergent ignorance in which all phenomena are seen to arise with a self-entity. That leaves a space-like experience in which those self-entities are no longer present because the elaborations producing them have been eliminated. However, that is not sufficient. The realization must eliminate the dharmas of un-enlightenment, which it has just done, but it must also include all the dharmas of enlightenment, which might not have happened. Therefore, the second step emphasizes the need for the no-thought wisdom not merely to be empty, which was the approach of the first step, but to be full. The superfactual truth in this case cannot be no-thought wisdom focussed on an absence of mistaken dharmas but has to be no-thought wisdom that knows that emptiness and simultaneously knows all of the enlightened qualities that belong to it. When there is authentic wisdom, which is the wisdom that the teaching of Other Emptiness is emphasizing, that wisdom will be empty of the fictional and at the same time, at the superfactual level, will be empty of what does not belong to it and full of everything that does belong to it. That really is what this is about. However, do not think that because the first step emphasizes direct experience of emptiness with prajñā whereas the second emphasizes a conventional statement about how that superfactual truth should be, that the second one is somehow easier or less profound than the first. First, you have to achieve the profundity of the experience of emptiness, then you have to achieve the even more profound level of fullness within that emptiness. This is the one way that all of the sūtras and tantras have ever taught the development of buddhahood, including even the highest teachings of Mahāmudrā and Great Completion. This is talking about wisdom which is the utter unification of appearance and emptiness, and so on—there are many ways like that of characterizing it.

Although we have not exactly defined the two types of emptiness yet, the difference in how they are approached and what they are actually about should be clear from the last paragraph. One result of the difference in the two types of emptiness is that, when it comes to the emptiness of the third turning of the wheel, the advocates of Other Emptiness make the statement that "the superfactual is not empty of itself but empty of other", as Mipham partially mentioned in the quote above. To understand this sort of statement, you have to understand firstly that the superfactual truth that the other empty system is talking about is the entity sugatagarbha or actuality sugatagarbha or luminosity sugatagarbha as it is called. It is not merely a concept or fictional truth that is being referred to but sugatagarbha in actuality. Then you have to understand that that superfact is not being defined in terms of being empty of a false self, though that is true, of course. Rather it is being defined as not empty of itself, meaning that conventionally you have to say that it is there, as opposed to not being there. And not only that, but it is empty of other, meaning that it does not have in it anything which is different in entity from it. That actuality sugatagarbha does not have affliction in it because what sugatagarbha is and what affliction is are completely different entities. Therefore, the superfactual here is the sugatagarbha which is empty of that which is other than it, all the afflicted dharmas of saṃsāra. However, that kind of negation is not a non-affirming negation but one that simply removes one thing while affirming another. Therefore, it also implies that the suga-tagarbha is full of everything that is the same entity as it. In other words, it not only exists in the sense that there is wisdom as opposed to not being wisdom but it also is everything that wisdom is, which is that it has with it every single one of all the inconceivable qualities of enlightenment.

The Other Emptiness Way of Defining the Two Truths

Ju Mipham continues on from the earlier quote by saying:

> At that point, both object and subject having become the way things are and the way they appear synchronized are called "the superfactual" and objects[52] and subjects[53] when the way things are and the way they appear[54] are not synchronized[55] are called "the fictional". When analysis is done with a valid cognizer that analyses conventionally,

---

[52] That is, the object, emptiness.

[53] That is, the appearances realized by non-conceptual wisdom.

[54] Here appearance means that which is seen by wisdom, the appearances realized by wisdom. When the way things are is seen by non-conceptual wisdom, that is the way they are and the way they appear synchronized.

[55] "Synchronization" and "non-synchronization" are translations of "mthun" and "mi thun", which could also be translated as "in accord" and "not in accord". "Synchronization" seems to work better when a noun is required, and using two terms helps give a wider range of the feeling of the word. It also emphasizes the practitioner's approach, which is what I have wanted to convey in this book rather than the merely philosophical approach. In fact, I cannot take credit for this; it was the suggestion of Chogyam Trungpa Rinpoche to us in the Nālandā Translation Committee when we were looking into this material.

there are the distinctions deceptive and not deceptive, confused and not confused, so whatever is not deceptive and not confused is classified as superfactual and the reverse of that is classified as fictional. ✓

✓ With this, Ju Mipham defines the two truths according to the other empty emptiness. The two truths according to self emptiness are universally known amongst Great Vehicle Buddhists so he does not even bother to mention it. In that set of two truths, fictional truth is the appearances that occur to an ignorant mind and superfactual truth is the emptiness that is determined when those appearances are subject to logic that analyses for their truth or not. That set of two truths is posited in relation to ultimate analysis and whether, ultimately, dharmas are found to exist or not. However, in other emptiness, the two truths are posited, as Mipham says, in relation simply to a conventional analysis. In this type of analysis, one makes the simple but precise distinction (which is the hallmark of the style of teaching contained in the third turning) that you can have a situation which either is confused about things as they are or is not confused about that. The situation which is not confused will be one in which the subject, which is the knower, and what comes to that knower, which is its object, are synchronized. That is defined as the superfactual truth for the other-empty type of emptiness. And the situation which is confused will be the reverse of that and that is defined as the fictional truth for the other-empty type of emptiness.

Validating the Other Emptiness Definition of the Two Truths

The definition of the two truths which belongs to the other emptiness approach should be sufficient to nullify other, major objections of the Other Emptiness opponents. However, they will reply that they have never heard of such a thing. Therefore, Ju Mipham continues on by stating that the Other Emptiness advocates have not simply made this up to suit their needs but are using what appears in the sūtras and the treatises on them. He says:

> It is not that the advocates of other emptiness have made up a new classification of the two truths. The two ways of

positing the two truths—the definition as emptiness and appearance which is universally known and the definition as the synchronization or not of the way things are and appear just explained above—have been taught from the outset in the sūtras and great treatises on them. The latter one is taught in *Distinguishing Dharma and Dharmatā* and is also found in the *Highest Continuum* when it states:

> The dhātu is empty of the adventitious ones,
> Those with the characteristic of separability;
> It is not empty of the unsurpassable dharmas
> Those with the characteristic of non-
> separability.

And in the commentary to that which says:

> Tathāgatagarba is empty of that which is separable, that which could be removed[56], all the sheaths of the afflictions; it is not empty of that which is inseparable, that which could not be removed, the inconceivable buddha dharmas which surpass in number even the sands of the river Ganges.

And the great charioteer Noble Nāgārjuna said:

> Just as clothing which is cleansed by fire[57]
> That has been sullied with various stains
> Will, if placed in fire, have
> The stains burned up but not the clothing,

---

[56] Tib. bral shes pa. This is equivalent to Tib. bral rgyu yod. Here, the Tibetan verb "shes pa", usually meaning "to know", means "can be" or "could be".

[57] This refers to a cloth which the Indians believed existed in the god realms and which could not be harmed by fire. In our world, it would be the substance asbestos.

So, the luminosity mind[58]
Having the stains of passion, and so on,
Has the stains consumed by the fire of wisdom,
And not the luminosity.

The sutras that show emptiness[59]—
As many as were taught by the conqueror—
All turn away the afflictions[60]
But do not damage the element[61].

And the Dharma King, Rigden Mañjuśhrīkīrti, said:[62]

The emptiness of the attribute-analysed
    skandhas[63]

---

[58] Meaning the sugatagarbha with samsaric mind on its surface.

[59] Beginning with this line, Mipham aims to show that sugatagarbha is not empty and that the reason for teaching emptiness is to settle that all things and appearances are emptiness. The Buddha does this in order to overcome afflictions, but that does not mean that sugatagarbha is non-existent.

[60] Tib. ldog. Some have translated this verse with the sense "were taught for the purpose of turning away the afflictions". However, Thrangu Rinpoche stated that translating it with the sense "for the purpose of" (Tib. phyir du) is a mistake; the literal meaning of the lines here, that they do remove the afflictions, is correct.

[61] Tib. khams. "The element" is one of many names for tathāgata-garbha.

[62] In his major commentary on the *Kālachakra Tantra*.

[63] "Attribute Analysis" pairs with the term "Overall Analysis". Attribute Analysis is what prajñā does, the other is what wisdom does. The meaning here is "the mere and useless emptiness of all the phenomena of samsara arrived at using logical analysis compared to the substantial and useful emptiness arrived at by direct perception of wisdom". Mention here of the skandhas means all the dharmas of samsāra, but the skandhas are mentioned because the practical instructions on doing this
(continued...)

Lacks substance[64], like a plantain tree;
The emptiness having the excellence of all
    superficies
Is not like that.

---

[63](...continued)
kind of Attribute Analysis teach doing the analysis in relation to the skandhas.

Attribute Analysis corresponds to the self-empty approach and Overall Analysis to the other-empty approach. The first is the use of logic alone which results in the emptiness alone of phenomena and the second is the use of direct perception with wisdom which brings an emptiness unified with wisdom and hence with all of the possibilities of appearance. The emptiness arrived at through attribute analysis is useless, like a plantain tree, which has the characteristic of bearing fruit once then dying. The emptiness arrived at through overall analysis is not like that; when you contact that sort of emptiness, you have arrived at wisdom, which is always useful as it is the one, final and universal solution.

[64] Tib. chu shing. Here, this refers to a plantain tree. Some translators have thought that the meaning is that the tree is hollow and that the emptiness is that sort of empty thing. However, that is not the meaning. A plantain tree grows, bears fruit once, and then dies. It is useless in the sense that it does not continue to bear fruit. Emptiness known through logical process is the same; it works for a little but then its strength is exhausted. Thus, the words of the verse which literally say "lack of substance" or "lacking a core" actually mean that it is useless. This is the understanding of the lineage, by the way; several important teachers in both Nyingma and Kagyu have explained this to me very clearly. This useless emptiness sits in comparison to emptiness known through overall analysis, meaning direct perception with wisdom, which is a fully functional emptiness. In *Kālachakra* tantra this wisdom emptiness is specifically known as "emptiness having the excellence of all superficies", because it is not a mere absence but also has all of appearance in it.

The first quotation in the series above is regarded as one of the most important scriptural quotations in support of Other Emptiness. The next one is the commentary to that verse by the author, Asaṅga, in his commentary to the *Highest Continuum*. The next one is from *In Praise of the Dharmadhātu* by Nāgārjuna; it shows that even he, who the opponents of Other Emptiness take as their champion, also understood this profound meaning and was not a supporter only of the second turning of the wheel type of emptiness. Those quotations were from sūtra. The last quotation is from tantra. Note how all of them have the theme that samsaric mind is a superficial event, so its emptiness of itself is one thing, but that no-thought wisdom, which is the very entity of sugatagarbha, is not empty in the same way. It might be empty of self-nature in the same way but it is not merely empty, rather, it is full of the qualities of enlightenment, even if neither the sugatagarbha itself nor any of the qualities of enlightenment exist by way of nature. Again, it is important to understand that, when empty of other is being discussed, the analysis has shifted from ultimate analysis of the non-affirming negation type to conventional analysis of the affirming negation type.

Defining the Emptiness in Relation to the Two Truths

Mipham continues by defining the emptiness that goes with each of the two sets of truths and showing how they are two, fundamentally different types. By doing so, he nullifies yet another objection made by opponents of Other Emptiness, an objection that occurs when the opponents concerned believe that the two types of emptiness mentioned by the followers of Other Emptiness are the same type of thing:

> Following on from that, this statement that "the superfactual is not empty of itself", has been made in total accord with the latter formulation of the two truths. And, in regard to this, it is imperative to understand that this second set of truths is being proclaimed using the

difference of one stopped[65] and definitely should not be understood as a formulation of the two truths of appearance-emptiness done using the difference of many facets[66] in one essence.

The two differences mentioned, "one stopped" and "one entity, many facets" are the names of two of what are called "four types of difference" in Buddhist philosophy. The key point here is that the emptiness of the second turning corresponds to the difference of "one entity (which is emptiness) and many facets (which are the appearances of that emptiness)" whereas the emptiness of the third turning corresponds to the difference of "(an entity for which) one (other entity can be denied as being part of that entity and hence) stopped".

So, when the Other Emptiness advocates say, "The superfactual is not empty of self, it is empty of other", their opponents, not understanding this crucial distinction, find the other empty assertion particularly upsetting because it seems to contradict the emptiness of self taught in the second turning of the wheel. It sounds to their opponents as though the Other Emptiness advocates are proclaiming self-existence for an ultimate truth, so they loudly protest that this is in direct contradiction to the Buddha's teaching. The root of this problem is not very hard to understand, though, for someone who has been inculcated to believe that emptiness taught in the second turning of the wheel—emptiness of self—is the only type of emptiness that could function to fulfil the requirements of Buddha's dharma, it can be hard to overcome habit patterns that prevent the person from understanding what has just been explained.

---

[65] Tib. gcig bkag pa'i tha dad.

[66] Tib. ldog in this case means a facet or particular way that something appears, like the Tibetan word "ngos". Most have translated it in this context as "reversal" or "isolate" which is a technical meaning that does not apply here. See ldog pa in *The Illuminator Tibetan-English Dictionary*.

For the Other Emptiness advocates, the superfactual is not mere emptiness but is that emptiness in conjunction with luminosity in the form taught in the third turning of the wheel, the tathāgatagarbha or sugatagarbha. To emphasize this point further, the Other Emptiness advocates do not merely say sugatagarbha but refer to "superfactual sugatagarbha". This superfactual itself is, of course, empty of self when determined using ultimate analysis and the Other Emptiness advocates proclaim that just as much as do their opponents. In other words, they both agree on the emptiness of tathāgatagarbha when looked at from the second turning approach but those who do not follow Other Emptiness leave it there whereas Other Emptiness followers feel that it is still possible to go further and arrive at a more profound level of understanding.

So far, both advocates and opponents have agreed that all persons and phenomena are devoid or empty of the ignorance-based idea of a self nature. What would we do if we wanted to go further and see what is there, if anything, when the ignorance—and the ignorant idea of a self nature with it—ceases? Certainly we would not continue to use the logic that we were using to remove the false appearances of persons and selves. Why? Because we have already eliminated what there was to be negated using that logic and there is nothing more could be gained by using that approach! At this point, we have simply to step into what is, the situation beyond dualistic mind called non-dual wisdom. Having done that we could accurately report the situation to others because of having seen, in direct perception, what non-dual wisdom is like. To report it, we would use the conventions—the names and words—of the world to say "It is like this. It is not like that". However, we would have to point out to our listeners that, although we were using the convention "is", "is not", "exists", "does not exist", and so on in order to distinguish as clearly as possible what it is like to be in non-dual wisdom, non-dual wisdom itself has none of those conventions in it.

Thus, the other-empty approach starts with the self-empty approach of eliminating the fictions of ignorance using non-affirming negations. It continues by leaping into non-dual wisdom without ignorance. It ends by describing that experience to others using conventions together with non-affirming negations because that is the type of logic suited to how non-dual wisdom sits. However, that reporting is done with the full understanding and also disclaimer made to the listeners that the use of words and other conventions to speak about non-dual wisdom does not in any way mean that the non-dual wisdom has the conventions of dualistic ignorance in it.

The Two Truths Restated According to Other Emptiness

Ju Mipham continues on with:

> Following on from that, the appearances of the confusion of non-synchronization of things as they are and appear are called "fictional" for the reason that, even though they have appeared to the confusion, they do not exist in that way in fact. The appearances of the other situation[67] are called "existing in the superfactual" and "truly existent" for the reason that they exist in the way they appear to non-confusion's sight and are not harmed by valid cognition.

> This does not require that appearances that have become separated from emptiness are truly existent. The reason is that, from the outset, the dharmadhātu has been taken to exist as the unity of appearance-emptiness—emptiness having the excellence of all superficies—and then that kind of actuality has been proclaimed as superfactual truth.

---

[67] Mipham is using shorthand here for a repeat of the words that open the last sentence and give the subject of the sentence but that cast in the other possibility. For the words "the other side", read "the appearances of the non-confusion of synchronization of things as they are and appear".

With that, Mipham is re-stating the two truths according to other emptiness. Then, when he gets to the superfactual truth, he builds on what he has said to make a new point, which is that you can quite correctly refer to the superfactual truth with words like "existing in the superfactual" and "truly existent" because in this case you are not speaking ultimately, as you would be doing if you were using the two truths of emptiness and appearance but are speaking conventionally about the situation of wisdom. The words "truly existent" here are the Tibetan term "bden grub" that was discussed in the chapter on terminology on page 106; you might like to review that earlier discussion in light of this.

Furthermore, he gives proof of that by pointing out that the noble beings, whose sight by definition is not confused, actually do see the buddha qualities and that, therefore, beings in saṃsāra—whose sight is confused—simply cannot argue with their reports about it. In the language of valid cognition, the noble ones' direct perception of it is the valid cognizer that proves that it is so and their valid cognition cannot be argued with by samsaric beings, the ones who do not have that kind of valid cognition.

He then counters an objection which might arise, which is that for some people the words "truly existent" necessitate something that has been separated from emptiness. He points out that here, when using those words, they are only being used conventionally to speak about something which is, ultimately speaking, beyond all conventions. That thing which is beyond all conventions is none other than the dharmadhātu which is utterly empty and at the same time utterly full of all phenomena (dharmas). Conventionally speaking, you can say that those dharmas "really do exist", which is the actual meaning here of "truly existent", because you are simply using conventions to assert something which, conventionally speaking, is true even if the superfactual truth being discussed is beyond the domain of conceptual mind.

At this point in his text, Mipham has finished with his general coverage of the Other Emptiness view and begins a long, philosophical argument with his opponents, all of which is quite difficult to understand and not needed for the purposes of this book, though experts who are studying Other Emptiness will want to read it.

Looking at it Again

Very profound, Subtle Teaching + understanding.

The Other Emptiness proponents are saying to their opponents, "Look, we don't disagree that everything is empty of a self. We accept the Buddha's teachings of the second wheel as a perfect statement of emptiness and we agree that one has to understand that all phenomena are empty of a self in just the way that the Buddha expressed that view in the second turning. However, we also see that, when you merely posit emptiness as a lack of everything, then you are so busy negating things that you lose the fact of wisdom. The Buddha himself said that the teachings of the third wheel are more profound than those of the second. In it, he teaches the reality of the wisdom which is what sees the emptiness of all dharmas that he so precisely determines in the second wheel. To teach that, he takes the fact that wisdom has already been determined to be thoroughly empty according to the approach taken in the second turning. With that as a basis, he proclaims that there is a part of mind that corresponds to that wisdom. That part is the seed of enlightenment, sugatagarbha. At the most profound level, he discusses sugatagarbha as reality using the most subtle approach possible, which is that, based on its being thoroughly empty of self-existence, it can be talked about using conventions with them being understood as mere conventions being used to discuss something which in itself is free of convention."

If you wanted to talk about this particular approach and tie it to what the Buddha did teach about sugatagarbha, you could point out that sugatagarbha as mind's actuality is empty of everything that does not have the same entity as it. In other words, you would be teaching it as something that, while having an emptiness of any self-existence that would be present due to ignorance, was also something that was also empty of everything other than it, which is all of the dharmas of samsaric existence. By doing so, you have presented mind's actuality, sugatagarbha, in the way that the Buddha did through the three turnings of the wheel and also the way that his Regent Maitreya did in his five explanations of dharma, and especially in the one called *The Great Vehicle Highest Continuum*, as something which is beyond conventions and concepts but which does have all of the qualities of enlightenment in it.

And how is it that sentient beings have wisdom? They have it in the form of sugatagarbha which is empty. How is it empty? Well of course, if you want to eliminate self-grasping regarding that, you approach it as being empty of a self as in the second turning. However, if you want to discuss the way in which it sits—which is really inexpressible—then there is an even more subtle approach that you can take: you can say that it is there but that it is empty of other things than itself.

The Two Types of Negation

Non-affirming negation is the type of negation used in the logic of the second turning approach and affirming negation is the one used in the third turning approach.

Non-affirming negation means that something is negated in such a way that no other thing can come to mind when the negation has been done. It is an absolute type of negation. The idea of self-existence that comes up with the perception of any given dharma is analysed using logic that attempts to see whether it really does exist or not. When the analysis is complete, that thing is found not to exist and, importantly, no other possibility comes to mind in its place. In other words, it is an outright negation that simply eliminates items that do not exist the way that they appear to exist and that is the end of it. This non-affirming or outright negation is the type of logic used when determining empty of self emptiness.

→ (NON (OR) NOT-OUTRIGHT Negation)

✗ (Affirming negation) means that one thing is negated and by doing so
another is affirmed. For example, "this is white" eliminates all other
possibilities at the same time as affirming a "this" with the quality of
whiteness in it. Or, put the other way around, "this is not white"
eliminates the possibility of whiteness but at the same time affirms
this as something which does not have the quality of whiteness
present in it. Affirming negation is the logic used when determining
empty of other emptiness.

The superfactual truth is known to be not self-existent from the
investigations of the second turning. Nonetheless, the superfactual
truth can be affirmed using mere words, by saying that "It is such and
such" or "It is not such and such". The Buddha himself said that
there is sugatagarbha; he did not say that there was not sugatagarbha.
If this sugatagarbha is the superfactual reality, then we could not say
"is not" we would have to say "is".

Again, the Other Emptiness opponents have failed to realize that this
is how the Other Emptiness advocates are talking. They believe that
statements like this are statements that, having applied the logic of
the second turning, if such a thing does exist, it would mean that it
is a self-existing thing. However, that is not what they are doing.
The Other Emptiness opponents only ever use the logic of non-
affirming negation to do their analyses in relation to the emptiness
of self and only use affirming negation to do their analyses when
empty of other is being determined.

Emptiness of self goes together with a definition of the two truths
that is based on emptiness and appearance. This is the way of
defining the two truths which is well-known and accepted in all Great
Vehicle schools. In it, fictional truth is the appearing aspect and
superfactual truth is the empty aspect.

Emptiness of other goes together with a definition of the two truths
that is based on the synchronization and non-synchronization of
appearances and actuality. This is the way of defining the two truths

that is the feature of the empty of other presentation. It is not commonly known and is regarded by the Other Emptiness followers as the very profound, heart-meaning teaching of the third turning of the wheel. The fictional truth in this approach is defined as the situation when the way things appear and how they actually are do not accord with each other. The superfactual truth is defined as the situation when the way things appear and how they actually are do accord with each other. Fictional truth in this case is the appearances of sentient beings in saṃsāra, because their appearances are not in accord with the actuality of their own minds. Superfactual truth in this case is not merely emptiness as with the other superfactual truth but is emptiness together with appearance that accords with that emptiness. This is a superfactual truth in which emptiness includes the buddha qualities because they are what appears when appearance accords with emptiness. You could say that fictional truth here is saṃsāra and superfactual truth here is nirvana—that is what it comes down to, though here nirvāṇa means ultimate wisdom in which all of saṃsāra and nirvāṇa is included—the thing is that the wisdom knows all of it but without delusion.

The second set of two truths, based in the synchronization and not synchronization of how things appear and how they actually are, can be very difficult to understand, philosophically speaking. Fortunately, it does not have to be understood deeply in order to understand the Other Emptiness teaching and a full treatment of it has been left aside for another book, one in which Mipham's text will be presented with a full explanation. Nonetheless, here is a quotation from Khenpo Palden Sherab that comes from his explanations of Mipham's text which sums it up: ✓

> ✓ There are two ways of positing the two truths. The
> commonly known one is the two truths posited as
> appearance and emptiness. The other one is the two
> truths posited as the synchronization or not of the way

things are and the way they appear[68]. In the second one, superfactual truth is set forth as object and perceiver when the way things are and the way things appear are synchronized and fictional truth is set forth as object and perceiver when they are not.

Mipham says: "These were taught from the very beginning in the sūtras and great treatises so this is not a case of the advocates of Other Emptiness making up new classification." With that, he is stating that these two differing explanations of the two truths have been taught from the beginning in the great sūtras and treatises of the tradition. Thus, there could be the question, "In what great sūtras and treatises has such been taught?" The first way of presenting the two truths is so common that Mipham does not need to provide references for it. The second one, which some people would question, is chiefly shown in the teachings of the regent, Guardian Maitreya. Of those teachings, the *Great Vehicle Highest Continuum Treatise* is the one that shows it extensively and the *Distinguishing Dharma and Dharmatā* shows it by making the distinction between dharmins and dharmatā and the respective minds that know each of those two possibilities.

In the *Distinguishing Dharma and Dharmatā*, Guardian Maitreya taught the nature on the one hand of dharmin and saṃsāra and the nature on the other hand of dharmatā and nirvāṇa. On the one hand, dharmins are the items of the impure way things are and appear; they constitute the appearances of the three realms of saṃsāra for the impure dualistic mind of impure beings. The impure mind of an impure being has an object and perceiver in which the way things are and the way they appear are not synchronized. The appearances that occur

---

[68] Tib. gnas lugs dang snang lugs mthun mi mthun.

in that impure situation are, in the other empty system, called fictional truth. On the other hand, dharmatā is the entity of no-thought wisdom. No-thought wisdom is the pure mind of the noble beings, the ones who have reached nirvāṇa. The pure mind of a pure being has an object and perceiver in which the way things are and the way things appear are synchronized. No-thought wisdom, the wisdom of the mind of the pure noble ones, is the conventional situation of the object and perceiver when the way things are and the way things appear are synchronized and that is superfactual truth. That is how the distinction is made in the other empty system.

THE PRACTICE OF OTHER EMPTINESS

We have been steadily building a clear understanding of the view called Other Emptiness. With that, the sense of its having been enveloped in argument by its detractors has appeared. Because of that situation, Westerners have developed the notion that Other Emptiness is some kind of philosophical theory. The understanding that it is a profound view with a practice for directly accessing wisdom seems to have been lost.

Like any other teaching of the Buddha, Other Emptiness is intended to be a means for the attainment of enlightenment. Discussions of Other Emptiness these days focus mainly on the view, but Other Emptiness is a complete teaching of the path to enlightenment with a view, meditation, and conduct at both sūtra and tantra levels. The sūtra form is said to derive from Maitreya and the lineage was handed on from Maitripa to his main disciple Sajanna from Kashmir and then came into the Tibetan tradition. The hearing lineage of its practice is clearly explained in the introduction to Jamgon Kongtrul's *Complete Commentary to the Highest Continuum* in part four of the book. The tantric system that originally went with the term "other empty" was the practise of the *Kālachakra Tantra* according to the Jonang tradition. However, the great masters of Kagyus and Nyingma have always stated that as far as they were concerned, the view and meditation of the tantras has always been that of other emptiness.

The indisputable proof of the existence of the meditation practice in connection with the sūtra Other Emptiness view is found in the very last item presented in this book, the practice section taken from *Instructions for Practising the View of the Other Emptiness Great Middle Way, "Light Rays of Stainless Vajra Moon"*. The text was composed by Jamgon Kongtrul the Great as a record of the oral instructions of the Other Emptiness tradition he obtained from the Jonang lineage. The text shows the view but focusses on the meditation of Other Emptiness, both sūtra and tantra.

Part 2

Explanations by

Dolpopa Sherab Gyaltsen

Figure 5. Dolpopa Sherab Gyaltsen
and Members of the Jonang Lineage

The First Chapter on Tathagatagarbha of

"Mountain Dharma: An Ocean of Definitive Meaning"

From the First Chapter on Tathagatagarbha

Initially then, there is this to understand. In the ground beneath a poor man's house, there is a great treasure of precious things. However, it is obscured by earth and stones seven men deep, so the poor man does not see it nor know of it, and so, not obtaining it, remains in his unsatisfactory state. In just the same way, the great treasure of the qualities of luminosity-dharmakāya is always present in oneself and everyone else but, because it is obscured by adventitious stains, all these beings do not see it, do not know of it, and so, not obtaining it, forever remain in their unsatisfactory state.

They, whoever they are, will, through a holy guru's special oral instructions of special scriptures and perfect reasonings, understand within themselves what is to be attained and what is to be abandoned. This is analogous to beings who possess the divine eye[69] explaining nicely about that treasure due to which the audience comes to know that the great treasure can be obtained, and that the earth and stones covering the treasure must be eliminated. If that knowledge is not

---

[69] The divine eye or god's eye is one of the five eyes, which are five different extraordinary abilities at seeing. The divine eye includes the ability to see under the **earth**.

clear, they will not obtain the treasure, and, simply by its being clear, they will know to obtain it, which is analogous to the dharma. Having understood the matter like that, they need to get the experience of it, so, in order to dispel adventitious stains in their entirety, they persevere at accumulating completely pure wisdom and what goes with it, which is analogous to the clearing away of the earth and stones seven men deep. What they gain through their experiences is the great treasure which is the final result, the dharmakāya not covered with outflows, and the qualities which are not separate from it, which is analogous to nicely obtaining that treasure of precious things.

At this point you might ask, "From whom do we know about these things?" We know from the buddhas and bodhisatvas who have spoken nicely of them. As was said in the *Tathāgatagarbha Sūtra*:[70]

> Sons of the family, moreover, it is as follows. To make an example, there is in the ground underneath a poor man's house, under a covering of earth seven men deep, a great treasure of a treasury filled with valuables and gold. That great treasure does not tell the poor man, "Hey! I am here, a great treasure covered with earth!", because the great treasure, being the very essence of mind, is not a being with a mind. The poor man who owns the house thinks like a poor man, and besides, there is no cause for him to think that he is on top of a treasure, so the great treasure in the earth underneath is not heard of, known of, or seen by him.
>
> Sons of the family, likewise there is, underneath the strong clinging within the dualistic mind of every sentient being which is like the house, the great treasure of the treasury of the tathāgatagarbha with the strengths, fear-lessnesses, un-mixed qualities, and every other one of the buddha dharmas. However, those sentient beings, due to

---

[70] ... by the Buddha himself ...

attachment to visual forms and sounds and smells and tastes and touches, are in an unsatisfactory position and circle around within cyclic existence. Not having heard of that great treasure of dharma, they have not acquired it and are not, in order to totally purify themselves, making an endeavour towards it.

Sons of the family! Then the tathāgatas appear in the world and, amongst the bodhisatvas, fully and authentically teach this kind of great treasure of dharma. They too orient themselves towards then dig for the great treasure of dharma and therefore, in the world, become the ones called "the tathāgata, arhat, truly complete buddhas". They, having become likenesses of the great treasure of dharma, have become treasuries of the strengths, fearlessnesses, and the many other dharmas of a buddha and are the sponsors of the treasury of the great treasure who, through their assurance without attachment, become the teachers to sentient beings of the previously unavailable reasonings, examples, reasoning for activities, and activities.

Sons of the family! Moreover, such tathāgata, arhat, truly complete buddhas, viewing every one of the sentient beings through the totally purified eye of a tathāgata in that way do, in order to thoroughly cleanse their treasuries of a tathāgata's wisdom, strengths, fearlessnesses, and un-mixed buddha dharmas, teach the dharma to the bodhisatvas.

Also, as was said in the *Highest Continuum Commentary*:[71]

---

[71] Now he presents something from the bodhisatvas. *The Highest Continuum* is a text of the master of the tenth bodhisatva level Maitreya's teachings. The teaching was given to the bodhisatva Asaṅga, who wrote a major commentary to it, which is now quoted.

Within the afflictions, which are like the earth's surface,
Sits the element of the tathāgata like a treasure of
        precious things,
Just as in the earth beneath a poor man's house
There was an inexhaustible treasure.
The man did not know it nor did the treasure
Tell him "I am here".
Like that, the internal essence of the mind is a precious
        treasure,
The stainless and not-to-be-clarified dharmatā[72],
Yet, through not realizing it, the unsatisfactoriness of
        poverty
Is continuously and always experienced by these nine
        beings[73].

Just as in a poor man's house there was an internal, precious treasure
which the poor man did not know of because it did not tell him, "I,
the precious treasure, am here!", likewise, sentient beings have the
dharma treasure in their house of mind and like the poor man do not
know of it. However, so that they could obtain it, the ṛiṣhi[74] took
authentic birth in this world.

Moreover, what does the Bhagavat say about this and related matters
in the *Mahāparinirvāṇa*? In the version translated by Devachandra
it says:[75]

---

[72] "Not to be clarified" means that the dharmatā or reality is pure in
itself and needs no cleaning; it only needs to have the adventitious
coverings removed.

[73] "Nine beings" is a way of referring to all sentient beings. It means
beings in three locations in each of the three realms—desire, form, and
formless realms.

[74] In this case "ṛiṣhi" means the Buddha.

[75] The *Mahāparinirvāṇa* sutra recounts the situation at the time just
                                        (continued...)

"Self" means tathāgatagarbha. The buddha element does exist in all sentient beings, yet is obscured by the surface appearances of the afflictions. Even as it exists within them, sentient beings are not able to see it. It is like this. To give an example, in a great city, in one poor man's house, there is a treasure of gold which remains unknown. There is a poor woman staying there; she also does not know that there is a treasure beneath the earth of the house. A man who has the method to assist says to the woman, "There is a treasure in your house, but since even you did not know that, how could anyone else know to look for it?" He suggests, "Please seek it yourself", following which she digs inside the house for the treasure and discovers it. Having seen it, she is amazed and takes refuge in the person. Likewise, son of the family, the tathāgatagarbha is present in all sentient beings, but they are just unable to see it, like the poor woman with the treasure.

Son of the family, I will now completely teach this point that "Every sentient being has the tathāgatagarbha": just as the poor woman did not know it but was taught that she had a great treasure, likewise all sentient beings have tathāgatagarbha, but, obscured by the superficies of the afflictions, do not know it, do not see it, so the tathāgatas teach that to them and they, happy in mind, take refuge in the tathāgatas, and so on.

---

[75](...continued)
before the Buddha's passing, called his parinirvāṇa, and includes his teachings at the time which included teaching on the tathāgatagarbha. The Tibetan scriptures contain translations of the sūtra made from both the Sanskrit and the Chinese sources, which Dolpopa gives next. He includes the translations from both languages as part of making his point that there is scriptural authority for all of his claims.

Similarly, in the *Mahāparinirvāṇa* translated from Chinese, too, there are extremely extensive statements:

> Son of the family, I also say this. Sentient beings having the nature of buddha and the examples of a treasure of precious things in the house of the poor woman, and the vajra jewel which is the forehead jewel of great strength, and the chakravartin king's springs of nectar which are analogies of it ...

Also in the *Dharani of Entering into No Functioning of Discursive Thought* it says:[76]

> Sons of the family, it is like this. For example, under a solid boulder are various, large, precious wish-fulfilling jewels, all luminous; it is a great treasure filled to the brim with precious silver, precious gold, and precious diamonds in separate layers. Then a few people wanting a great treasure arrive and a person who has clairvoyant knowledge of the great treasure says this to them, "Hey you people, under that solid boulder there is a great treasure of precious things completely filled with luminous precious things. There is a treasure of precious, wish-fulfilling jewels under it, nonetheless, what you excavate at first will be only the nature of stone, now dig! When you dig, stone that appears to be silver will appear; you should not take that to be the great treasure, instead just understand it and dig! When you dig, stone that appears

---

[76] Skt. Nirvikalpāvatāra Dharaṇi. Tib. rnam par mi rtog pa la 'jug pa'i gzungs. The words "no functioning of discursive thought" are a way of talking about the tathāgatagarbha. Discursive thought is the hallmark of the dualistic mind that covers over the tathāgatagarbha. The tathāgatagarbha itself does not have dualistic mind functioning in it but only as a covering over it. Therefore, in this discourse, the Buddha used the phrase "no functioning of discursive thought" as an equivalent to "tathāgatagarbha". You will see its use following this.

to be gold will appear; you should not take that to be the great treasure either, instead again just understand it and dig! When you dig, stone that appears to be various precious things will appear; you should not take that to be the great treasure either, instead again just understand this and dig! Oh people! When you have made an endeavour like that, you will then, without having to put in further effort, see the great treasure of the precious, wish-fulfilling jewels. If you find that great treasure of the precious, wish-fulfilling jewels, you will be wealthy with great riches and have a high level of things for use because of it; you will have the power to benefit yourself and others.

Sons of the family, in order for you to understand all of the meaning in what I have just said, here is how the example was constructed. The "solid boulder" is a fitting metaphor for the formatives appearing as total affliction[77]. "Underneath, a great treasure of precious wish-fulfilling gems" is a metaphor for the space of no functioning of discursive thought. "People wanting a great treasure of precious wish-fulfilling gems" is a metaphor for bodhisatva mahasatvas[78]. "A person who has clairvoyance of the great treasure" is a metaphor for the tathāgata, arhat, truly complete buddha. "The boulder" is a metaphor for concepts that conceive of the nature. "Dig!" is a metaphor saying to practise non-engagement with

---

[77] For formatives, see the glossary. "Total affliction" is a name for saṃsāra; it is paired with the term "complete purification" which is a name for nirvāṇa. In other words, the solid boulder is a metaphor for the afflictions which themselves are what cause the ongoing formation of new births in the total affliction of samsaric existence.

[78] "Bodhisatva mahasatva" here means "those great beings, the bodhisatvas" in general.

mentation[79]. "Stone that appears as silver" is a metaphor
for the concepts of discursive thought towards the antidote. "Stone that appears as gold" is a metaphor for
concepts of discursive thought towards emptiness and so
on. "Stone that appears to be various precious things" is a
metaphor for concepts of discursive thought towards
attainment. "Find that great treasure of the precious,
wish-fulfilling jewel" is a metaphor for contacting the
dhātu[80] of no functioning of discursive thought.

Sons of the family, by that fitting example, one develops
an understanding of the entrance into the dhātu of no
functioning of discursive thought ...

and so on, he speaks of it extensively. These precious extensive texts
of the sūtra section and the profound commentaries on their intent
both must definitely be looked at.[81]

❀   ❀   ❀

---

[79] Mentation is the ordinary, dualistic mind's mentality.

[80] "The dhātu" is a name for the tathāgatagarbha.

[81] Up to this point, Dolpopa Sherab Gyaltsen has been showing the basic
idea that the enlightened core is present in beings. From here he shifts
to the next level of presentation which is that the enlightened core has
two aspects to it. The first is that beings do have fundamental reality
at the core of their being. The nature of fundamental reality is referred
to as "dharmatā". The aspect of tathāgatagarbha that corresponds to
that is called the "natural" type. It is your nature, you do have it. With
that as the basis, you can develop spiritual qualities for the benefit of
others. Therefore, a second type of tathāgatagarbha, called the "developing" type is identified. It refers to the development through practice
of the spiritual qualities of a great being. These spiritual qualities are
not your nature; you have to do something to develop them.

That dharmatā of no-functioning-of-discursive-thought and lumi-
nosity-dhātu, is the natural lineage[82]. Dependent upon that there is
the developing lineage: the seed of emancipation is sown and
nurtured and from it special virtue is properly taken up[83]. That
produces the form kāyas of a tathāgata, which is like the production
of a resulting, good tree.[84]

---

[82] This means that the fundamental reality of your mind is what is left
when you do not have discursive thought, with all of the ignorance that
causes it, functioning. That fundamental reality is both luminous—
meaning not that it is some kind of light but that it knows—and is the
dharmadhātu, the zone which is the basis for and within which anything
and everything can and does appear.

[83] This means that a person properly takes up the special virtue of the
Great Vehicle as opposed to some other form of virtue.

[84] This leaves us with the very important question of whether you have
to develop these qualities as a separate task on the spiritual journey or
whether it is possible, just by uncovering the reality which is your
nature, to obtain all of the spiritual qualities. The message of conventional spirituality is that it is not sufficient just to uncover the reality of
your own nature. It says that you have to look into the emptiness which
is the hallmark of your own nature on the one hand and that you have
to engage in the production of vast amounts of good works on the other.
By doing so, you develop the state of complete buddhahood. Unconventional spirituality, the teaching of the tantras, states that there is a more
profound possibility, which is that doing the spiritual work of clearing
the dirt that covers and obscures the reality nature at the core of being
is, in itself, enough.

The rest of the first chapter is taken up with quotations, mostly from
the tantras, which prove the point that, according to unconventional
spirituality, the entirety of enlightenment is contained within the mind
and nothing more needs to be done than to uncover it.

Part 3

Explanations by

Khenpo Tsultrim Gyatso

A Brief Discussion of the Rise of The Other Emptiness Middle Way, Called "The Music of Talk on the Definitive Meaning"

The eye which has become a valid measure of all dharmas is
The wisdom replete with goodness, the treasure mastered by the
  Bhagavat,
The dharma spoken by him roots out the plague of becoming,
And the supreme assembly holds to that—to those together I pay
  homage.

Those words, a progression of phrases praising the Three Jewels who are the supreme refuge, serves to open up the good path. Regarding that path, what is to be discussed here is the rise of the Other Emptiness Middle Way. The headings for the discussion are as follows.

I. How the tenet system of the Other Emptiness Great
   Middle Way arose
   A. How it arose in India
      1. How it arose in the Teacher's words
      2. How it arose in the treatises
         a. How the great master, the guardian noble one
            Nāgārjuna, taught it in the *Collection of Praises*
         b. How noble one Asaṅga's "Intents of Maitreya's
            Dharma" spread
   B. How it spread in Tibet
      1. How it spread at the time of the earlier spreading
      2. How it spread at the time of the later spreading
II. An analysis of the term "other empty".

I. How the Tenet System of the Other Emptiness Great Middle Way Arose

A. How it arose in India

1. How it arose in the Teacher's words

In this fortunate aeon in a suitable country, etcetera[85], the founding teacher, the truly complete buddha Śhākyamuni, faced by a retinue of the regent, the tenth level satva guardian Lord Maitreya, and many others having the Great Vehicle lineage, enacted the teaching of a group of many sūtras of the profound. The sūtras of that group, which these days are principally cited as the places showing this definitive-meaning tenet system, are the "ten definitive-meaning profound sūtras" or the "twenty definitive-meaning non-regressing

---

[85] This refers to the ten examinations made by the Buddha prior to his birth as a wheel-turning buddha to assess where, when, how, and so on he would take birth on this planet in order to be most effective.

sūtras of unsurpassable intent". The ten definitive-meaning, profound sūtras just mentioned are:[86]

1. The Sūtra Petitioned by King Dharaṇeshvara[87]
2. The Sūtra Petitioned by the Girl, Jewel
3. The Sūtra Petitioned by the Householder Uncouth
4. The Sūtra of Neither Increase nor Decrease
5. The Sūtra for the Benefit of Aṅgulimālā
6. The Sūtra Encouraging the Extra Thought
7. Wisdom Appearance's Ornament Sūtra
8. Point of Passage Wisdom Sūtra
9. The Great Drum Sūtra
10. Meeting of Father and Son Sūtra

2. How it arose in the treatises

a. How the great acharya, the guardian noble one Nagarjuna, taught it in the "Collection of Praises"

The great āchārya, the glorious guardian noble one Nāgārjuna has three sets of commentaries on the meaning of the intent of the tathā-gata's word. The commentaries on the intent of the first wheel are the *Collection of Stories*; the commentaries on the intent of the middle wheel are the *Collection of Reasonings*; and the commentaries on the intent of the final wheel are the *Collection of Praises*. He clearly

---

[86] Tib. nges zab mo'i mdo bcu. "The ten profound definitive-meaning sūtras" are the sūtras that the Other Emptiness tradition uses for scriptural reference to support its system. Of the following, Padma Karpo Translation Committee has translated and published the *Point of Passage Wisdom Sūtra* and *Sūtra of the Householder Uncouth* specifically for those wanting to study Other Emptiness.

[87] *The Sūtra Definitively Teaching the Tathāgata's Great Compassion* contains many chapters, several of which were spoken because of the questions of King Dharaṇeshvara so is also known as The Sūtra Petitioned by King Dharaṇeshvara.

teaches this definitive-meaning tenet system's understanding in the last set: for the ground context, he teaches the lineage element sugatagarbha using the examples of fine gold, a butter-lamp in a vase, and so on[88] and explains it from the perspective of dharmin and dharmatā[89]; for the path context, he explains it from the perspective of upāya and prajñā; and for the fruition context, he explains it through the three kāyas individually; and for the view he explains it from the perspective of self-entity.

Further, his disciple the accomplished great Āchārya Nāgamitra's treatises *Engaging the Three Kāyas*, and so on, also show the subject-matter in that fashion. ✓

✓ And further still, in the majority of siddhas such as accomplished great āchārya glorious Saraha, Lord Śhavari, and so on's Secret Mantra vajra dohās connecting with the unsurpassable, any mention of the view is seen to concur with this definitive-secret's tenet system.

And later on, Jowo Maitrīpa himself at the glorious mountain in the south, in order to obtain the heart, non-mentation dharma teachings and while staying with an intent to request it from the accomplished great āchāryas themselves without regard for his life did, as the fruit of unimaginable trials, meet with Nāgārjuna, father and sons, because of which he also obtained the kindness of this view of the profound.

b. How noble one Asanga's "Intents of Maitreya's Dharma" spread

Bhikṣhuṇī Prakāśh Śhīlā's prayer of aspiration that the Great Vehicle Abhidharma Basket flourish came to fruit in accordance with her aspiration aspired as follows. The great āchārya noble one Asaṅga was born to her. When he had become expert in the baskets of teachings of the Lesser and Great vehicles, he ran into difficulty because of poorly understanding the intent of the Mother of the

---

[88] ... in *Highest Continuum* ...

[89] ... in *Distinguishing Dharma and Dharmatā* ...

Conquerors, Prajñāpāramitā, so he did the practice of the guardian Regent Maitreya at Birdsfoot's Peak for a length of twelve years and finally saw Maitreya in person. Then, in the divine abode Tuṣhita for a length of twenty-five human years, Asaṅga listened to the entire definitive-meaning sūtra section. Back in this world realm after that, he spread their essence in the form of a set of five commentaries on the sūtra section's intent, called *The Five Dharmas of Maitreya*.

In addition, the āchārya himself composed many treatises to comment on it and his younger brother, the supremely expert Vasubhandu, composed several treatises some supporting his the āchārya's works and some commenting on others' works. These two āchāryas were clearly predicted by the Teacher as the ones who would make distinctions between provisional and definitive and, in accordance with his prediction, they did that, teaching Mind Only for ordinary beings to be tamed and explicitly teaching this definitive-meaning, non-regressing tenet system as a hearing lineage for extra-ordinary beings to be tamed. Then, the followers of their lineage, Āchārya Dīgnāga, Dharmakīrti, and so on composed treatises such as *The Seven Sections* and its sutra[90] that contain a meaning which is this ultimate understanding, one that concurs with this definitive-meaning tenet system.

Then, the amazing Āchārya Chandragomi verbally accepted this sort of tenet system, too. Also, the fearless great āchārya glorious Dhar-mapāla, set out a *Middle Way Collection of Reasonings* whose intent concurs with this and which is well known. Also, the extremely expert Shāntirakṣhita composed the treatise, *Ornament of the Middle Way*. Moreover, there were other highly expert Indians who wrote commentaries and the like on this subject that concur with this tenet system, and who are well known.

---

[90] The sūtra is Dignaga's *Compendium of Valid Cognition*. His main disciple Dharmakīrti wrote a set of seven commentaries to it called the *Seven Sections, The Complete Commentary on Pramāṇa*.

Of the five Maitreya dharmas, the *Ornament of Manifest Realizations of the Prajñāpāramitā*, *Ornament of the Sūtra Section*, and *Distinguishing Middle and Extremes* spread across India completely. The two documents *Distinguishing Dharmas and Dharmatā* and *Highest Continuum* were not so widespread though, at a later time, the master, conqueror Maitrīpa, saw light coming from a fissure in an old stūpa and, when he looked to find out what was happening there, saw texts of the two documents there. He withdrew them and supplicated guardian Jetsun Maitreya one-pointedly, whereupon he saw him and obtained his instruction. Thus conqueror Maitrīpa gained exactly the same understanding as the two great charioteers[91] who commented on the definitive meaning intent. He passed that on to Paṇḍita Nandakīrti and others, who in turn gave it to the great Kashmiri expert, Paṇḍita Sajjana.

The subject matter of this tenet system is clearly present in both of the two charioteer's textual systems, yet there are still some who say, "There was no such naming convention in use." I consider this tiresome debate to be meaningless.

B. How it spread in Tibet

1. How it spread at the time of the earlier spreading

All-Knowing Mipham Rinpoche says that the translation of the *Five Dharmas of Maitreya* was completed during the time of the early translations. Therefore, there can be no doubt that their explanations, transmission lineages concerning meditation, and so on did exist at that time. In particular, the definitive Buddha Word of the secret level[92] and the treatises which show the view of the Ati vehicle—the mind oriented, foremost instruction, luminosity Great Completion—of the earlier spread are in complete concordance with

---

[91] This is Nāgārjuna and Asaṅga, whose role was explained above.

[92] ... meaning the Secret Mantra Vehicle level or, as referred to in part one of this book, the fourth turning of the wheel teachings ...

the view of this tenet system (which also means that, if threefold hearing, contemplation, and meditation is done in relation to the *Five Dharmas of Maitreya*, it will be possible to develop knowledge consistent with those teachings of the earlier spread).

Not only that but All-knowing Longchen Rabjam and the Minling brother Rigdzin Tshewang Norbu, and others definitely were great propagators of this special tenet system.

2. How it spread at the time of the later spreading

Ngog Lodan Sherab, the great translator predicted by the Conqueror, went down to Kashmir personally and listened to the later four of Maitreya's dharmas from the great expert Sajjana, then translated and explained them. The resulting lineage, which has stayed without waning down to the present, is well-known as "The Explanatory System of Maitreya's Dharma[93]" and there exist various ways of commenting on it: some experts comment on the *Five Dharmas of Maitreya* as Middle Way; some experts as Mind Only, some as the Mind Only which is a third, intermediate Middle Way between the lowest and highest Middle Ways; and so on. Those can be known from the various commentaries on them composed by the experts who were so precise about them.

Also, in regard to the special definitive-meaning tenet system, the pair—"gzus dga ba'i dorje" and "btsan khao che" who was a disciple of the monk Abhijñavat[94]—listened to the *Maitreya Dharmas* in their entirety from the great expert Sajjana then provided others with various explanations and instruction on it, especially bringing the

---

[93] A point here is that an explanatory lineage is less profound than a hearing lineage. The words imply what is historically true, that Ngog Lodan Sherab did not get the definitive meaning heart essence level of instruction that others, such as Marpa, and Zu and Tsan, obtained.

[94] These two are usually referred to as Zu and Tsan. Tsan was a Chinese practitioner whose master Abhijñāvat was also Chinese.

great treatise, the *Highest Continuum* to life. Because of that, the lineage coming from them has become well-known as the "Meditation System of the Maitreya Dharmas". Moreover, the holders of this lineage who were lords of realization—the Tāntrika from Tsang, Rigpa'i Sengge and the greatly accomplished Yumowa Mikyo Dorje—brought this tenet system to life and their disciples—many yogins who themselves were lords of realization—passed this hearing lineage on, one to the other. The great renunciant "thugs rje brtson gru" of their lineage founded a seat at Jonang and started a tradition which upheld this tenet system. After him, the All-Knowing Dolpopa composed many texts to bring this tenet system to life and located many supporting scriptural references for it within the Buddha Word of sūtra and mantra and the treatises on them. He was greater than any of the other Jonang throne-holders—"great paṇḍita phyogs rgyal ba", and the rest—at presenting the arguments, so he became known as the greatest of "the lions of the non-regressing"[95]. After him in importance were the two ocean-like[96] regents, Jonang Jetsun kun dga' grol mchog and Je Tāranātha, and then the other regents of the Jonang throne. Similarly, in other traditions, the great conqueror Rangjung Dorje, the all-knowing Chodrag Gyatso, the mahāpaṇḍita Shākya Chogdan, the southern Drukpa Kagyu mahāpaṇḍita Shākya Rinchen, the all-knowing Tenpay Nyinje, the pair Jamyang Khyentse and Jamgon Kongtrul, and others after them openly showed this secret definitive tenet system in their works. Their various disciples also definitely held the lineage of this tenet system.

II. An analysis of the term "other empty"

According to what the supremely expert Buton and others accepted, two naming conventions for the Middle Way were present in India

---

[95] A name used in general for anything connected with the Heart Meaning teachings of the third turning but which the Jonang followers also used specifically as a title for the holders of the Jonang throne.

[96] ... in the extent of their works for others and the Jonang lineage ...

in general: the Nisvabhava Madhyamaka or the Middle Way of the advocates of lack of entityness and the Yogāchāra Madhyamaka or the Middle Way of those who practised yoga. Tibetan experts distinguished the first as having two possibilities and named them Svatāntrika Madhyamaka or Autonomous Middle Way and Prasaṅgika Madhyamaka or Consequence Middle Way.

Similarly, this tenet system was well known in India as "The Great Yogāchāra Madhyamaka" and the holders of the lineage were well known as "Yogāchāra Madhyamikas". In Tibet, a variety of naming conventions for it existed: it was known as "Maitreya's Dharma Meditation System", "False Aspect Madhyamaka", "Profound Luminosity Madhyamaka", and so on. The name "Other Emptiness Madhyamaka" which was produced later, in accordance with the subject matter of the tenet system, was used by All-Knowing Dolpopa Sanggyay and, it seems to me, officially designated by him. Before All-Knowing Dolpopa arrived, the tenet system's subject matter existed and also, in both India and Tibet, there were many treatises which showed this secret definitive view even though the term "other empty" had not appeared. The term "other empty" came to prominence in the statements and writings of All-Knowing Dolpopa and since then most of the āchāryas holding the lineage have used this name.

Later on, the mahāpaṇḍita Shākya Chogden explicitly used the name "Yogāchāra Middle Way" for the subject matter of the first three *Maitreya Dharmas* and "Superfactual Complete Certainty Middle Way" for the subject matter of the *Highest Continuum*, the last of the *Maitreya Dharmas*. Moreover, for the Self Empty Middle Way he sometimes said "View's Distinction-Making Middle Way" and for the Other Emptiness Middle Way he sometimes said, "Meditation's Gained by Experience Middle Way". Similarly, there are the naming conventions "Special Middle Way" and others used by the Southern Drukpa great paṇḍita Shākya Rinchen and others. Then again, the all-knowing Jonang father-and-sons lineage and others asserted that the garbha's wisdom being empty of adventitious elaboration yet the wisdom itself not being empty, the luminosity nature is truly existing due to which the convention "Luminosity Other Emptiness" came about. And the great conqueror All-Knowing Mikyo Dorje, the Garwang Chokyi Wangchuk, and the others of their lineage maintained that "the garbha's wisdom itself is free of elaboration" with the result that the name "Dhātu Other Emptiness"[97] also became well-known. Based on this key point, the practice lineage's lord of reasoning, Karma Trinlaypa[98], also composed a text called "A Small Text Showing that Self Empty and Other Empty are not Contradictory".

Furthermore, Jamzang Chodrag and others have asserted that single instants of consciousness are truly established and that that situation is empty of the all-labelling and the dependent characters; that and other such things lead me to think that a name of Other Emptiness Middle Way has also appeared in relation to a Middle Way which has been made to conform with Mind Only.

This short discussion of how the tenets of the definitive-meaning Great Other Emptiness Middle Way arose was received from the embodiment of the three kindnesses, the great khenpo and guru, Tsultrim Gyatso Rinpoche. It takes as its basis the statements made in the "Treasury which is an Encyclopædia of Knowledge", and so on. I have written it down just as the Lord spoke it at Karma Shrī Nālandā Dharma Institute.

---

[97] Here, dhātu is short for dharmadhātu but this has to be understood as meaning the place which is arrived at through achieving the full realization of self-emptiness.

[98] Karma Trinlaypa is well-known in the Karma Kagyu practice lineage as a great master of reasoning. He showed that the "Dhātu Other Emptiness" of the self-empty presentation is not at variance with the fullness of wisdom presented in Other Emptiness itself.

THE VIEW OF OTHER EMPTINESS INTRODUCED

In Tibet, there was a large group of followers of the Middle Way who called themselves followers of the Other Emptiness Middle Way school of thought. They explained that their system includes not one but two types of Middle Way, one called Self Emptiness[99] and one called Other Emptiness[100]. Other Tibetan followers of the Middle Way did not make this distinction into two types of Middle Way and did not even use these terms "Self Emptiness" and "Other Emptiness". As far as they were concerned, they just followed the Middle Way and so referred to themselves simply as followers of the Middle Way. Thus, if you are talking with others who do not follow the Other Emptiness approach, you have to put aside those two terms.

To understand the Other Emptiness school, we have to understand the two types of emptiness that the school proclaims: self and other emptiness. Self emptiness is the type of emptiness in which something is understood to be empty of a self-entity. Other emptiness is the type of emptiness in which one thing, having a certain entity, is empty of anything that has an entity other than its own entity. Note that entity here does not mean "essence"; it means what something actually is.

---

[99] Tib. rang stong.

[100] Tib. gzhan stong.

The Self Emptiness system arrives at its view through the use of five main types of syllogistic reasonings presented in the Middle Way system, such as the one called "beyond having a nature of one or many", that all dharmas are "not truly existing", "not existing by way of a nature", and "not existing by way of an entity". In short, it comes to the view that, whatever else the phenomena of saṃsāra and nirvāṇa might be, they are without a self-entity. Due to this style of assertion, it is also called "Entitylessness Middle Way".

The Other Emptiness system has the view that "mind's actuality, luminosity sugatagarbha, is empty of adventitious stains." It proclaims that in several different ways; for example, it also states that "mind's actuality, luminosity sugatagarbha, is empty of the elaborations of conventions". This type of statement is made to point out that the sugatagarbha does not have in it those things which have an entity other than its own entity. In other words, what sugatagarbha is is not the same as what the adventitious stains and all elaborations of conventions are. It is other than them and thus is empty of them. In short, the sugatagarbha is empty of everything whose entity is other than its entity, and that is the meaning of the term "other emptiness".

In Other Emptiness presentations, the terms entity[101], actuality[102], and innate character[103] all point at the same thing but from slightly different angles—the very entity of mind, its actual situation, its innate character or disposition respectively. That actuality of mind is *empty* of stains which are *other* than it, meaning that it is empty of the paraphernalia of samsaric mind, all of which are other than what it actually is. Moreover, the paraphernalia of samsaric mind can stain, that is, can temporarily obscure that mind's underlying actuality, but

---

[101] Tib. ngo bo.

[102] Tib. gnas lugs.

[103] Tib. gshis.

they cannot cause a taint which is a permanent change to it precisely because the paraphernalia are *empty of*, that is, have no *self*-nature.

What does it mean that mind's actuality, luminosity sugatagarbha, is empty of stains? When were they emptied out? The Other Emptiness system states that mind's actuality, luminosity sugatagarbha, is empty from the outset of the adventitious stains that appear on its surface. From a practitioner's un-enlightened perspective, it might be tempting to say that mind's actuality at first has stains but later becomes emptied of those stains due to their being cleansed away by practise of the path. However, that is not what is meant here. Mind's actuality is empty of the stains of the afflictions from the outset because its entity has always been, is, and always will be empty of these stains.

Similarly, what does it mean that mind's actuality, luminosity sugatagarbha, is empty of naming conventions? It means that it is, from the outset, empty of elaborations in just the same way as it is empty, from the outset, of stains. It does not mean that mind's actuality sugatagarbha first has elaborations of conventions and in the interim, through the buddha and bodhisattvas blessings or alternatively through the force of your own meditation, that the stains gradually fall away. It is referring to the fact that mind's actuality sugatagarbha is from the outset empty of conventions which are of an entity other than it.

Let us take the idea of naming conventions. In a meditation session, you might enter the actuality of your own mind at which time conventions, because they are not part of the actuality of mind, would cease. In the original actuality, the conventions of both things and non-things do not exist—it is beyond all conventions. However, in post-meditation, you would not enter it because in post-meditation there is no method for not falling into conventions and because without conventions no comprehension is possible.

Now let us take the idea of elaborations. Mind's actuality being beyond all conventions and mind's actuality being free from elaborations is not quite the same but practically speaking comes down to the same thing. Why? Well, the term elaboration is used to indicate that a convention has surfaced in the mind; the term means that one or more concepts have actually been elaborated from the mind. Therefore, if mind's actuality luminosity sugatagarbha is empty of or beyond every convention—existence and non-existence, appearance and emptiness, things and non-things, and so on—then no elaborations of those conventions could surface there, could they? In sum, it has been said:

> It is that which is beyond every convention
> Because it is beyond elaborations of conventions.

Now let us take the idea of luminosity. Mind's actuality is also called "luminosity sugatagarbha". "Luminosity" is a convention. Mind's actuality is beyond conventions. Therefore, the concept that we might have of luminosity in relation to the sugatagarbha is not present in mind's actuality sugatagarbha. If mind's actuality had an extreme of luminosity in it, then the other extreme of non-luminosity would be possible in it and would have to happen. Therefore, neither luminosity nor non-luminosity are there in the actuality.

The words of the previous paragraph point strongly at the actuality of mind and can be hard to understand. It would be wonderful if we could somehow drop the conventions and get right to mind's actuality beyond conventions. Unfortunately, it is very hard to do and we are stuck with the fact that without using conventions, we will not easily be able to get to an understanding of this actuality of mind. Therefore, in Other Emptiness we designate the actuality of mind with conventions like "sugatagarbha" and "luminosity" but we also make the point that these are designations only and that the actuality of mind itself has no conventions of "sugatagarbha" or "luminosity" in it. It is beyond the convention of "empty" too—it is beyond all

conventions of empty, not empty, self empty, other empty, and so
on.

The Other Emptiness system does not proclaim that self emptiness
is one type of Middle Way understanding, other emptiness is another, and the two are separate things unrelated to each other. The
Other Emptiness Middle Way starts with the self-empty approach
in which it is understood that all things, including sugatagarbha, are
empty of a self, then continues to the more profound other-empty
approach in which it is understood that there is an awareness which—
conventionally speaking—does exist.

If you think this through and understand all the ramifications, you
might conclude, "Isn't that enough? With it we have emptiness and
an awareness of that emptiness." However, there is an important
point made in the tathāgatagarbha teaching, and this is where the
need for other emptiness comes in—if the awareness that sees
emptiness really is wisdom, it will not be a samsaric awareness that
now has emptiness for its object. Mind's actuality sugatagarbha has
the quality of being empty of other, meaning that it simply does not
possess any of the apparatus of samsaric mind. Because mind's actuality sugatagarbha is empty of those in the particular style of being
empty of entities that are other than it, it leaves room to understand
that it is also full of whatever its own entity happens to be. Its own
entity is the enlightened type of mind, so it contains all enlightened
types of qualities. Thus, the Other Emptiness system neatly points
at the wisdom of a buddha, which does not possess anything of or
seen by samsaric mind but does possess everything of enlightened
mind, that is, all the qualities of enlightenment or buddhahood.

Thus, there is a progression. First one works at the self emptiness
understanding which is connected with the middle wheel of the three
wheels of dharma. In the middle wheel, there is the idea that the
objects known by mind are in an obscured condition, therefore, using
logical process, one removes the obscuration from each object, one
by one. Then, in the final turning of the wheel, one comes to an

understanding that, although all samsaric things might be ultimately non-existent, there is a wisdom knower that exists and is free of all obscurations to the entire zone of dharmas[104]

How the Two Types of Emptiness are Validly Known

Most generally speaking, there are only two types of awareness or knower: un-enlightened samsaric mind and its events and the wisdom mind of a buddha. This fundamental division into two types of knower is well-known throughout Buddhism. Nevertheless, to see it stated in one of the sūtras used as a scriptural support by the Other Emptiness system, the Buddha taught in the *Descent Into Laṅkā Sūtra* that "awareness is of two types, the fictional mind of conceptualized phenomena (dharmins) and the luminosity mind of the nature of phenomena (dharmatā)". The first refers to samsaric mind which solidifies everything so that phenomena (dharmas) are not merely phenomena but are conceptually overloaded with an accounting of what they are (dharmins). The second is the actuality of that mind, which is the wisdom of a buddha.

The self-empty approach uses samsaric mind and its events to study itself; therefore, a study of how samsaric mind works and, in particular, how it can be made to have valid knowledge of what it is viewing is a very important part of the self emptiness approach.

For an ordinary person, the type of thought commonly used to understand something is the general discursive thought of samsaric mind. It usually does not come with the correct logical reasoning needed to have valid knowledge of how something is. However, it is possible to develop a better type of samsaric mind, one which has the quality of making a correct decision when it is used. This type of mind was called "prajñā" in ancient India, literally meaning "best type of knowing". In English, it is probably better to think of it as

---

[104] Skt. dharmadhātu.

"correctly discriminating mind", which is how it is defined in Indian and Tibetan texts on mind and its operation.

In order to develop a correctly discriminating mind, mind can be trained so that discursive thought arises based on correct logical reasoning, as happens for example when thought is trained to follow the valid forms of logic called syllogisms. When thought follows a line of reason and ends up with a correct conclusion, in which something has been validly known, the approach to the knowledge gained is called inference and the valid knowledge that results is called a valid cognition. In Sanskrit, it is called "pramāṇa", meaning "best type of mental operation". Thus, there is the valid cognition which comes through the use of inference, and that is called inferential valid cognition. Again, inferential valid cognition is logical thought process which arrives at correct knowledge of what it is analysing.

The Other Emptiness approach does not use samsaric mind and its events to study itself. It bypasses that in favour of directly accessing wisdom. Wisdom does not have the process of discursive thought in it and to emphasize that feature is also called "no-thought wisdom". Therefore, unlike samsaric mind which uses thought to know about things, wisdom mind simply knows what is, as it is, and without any thought involved. This process of knowing through direct perception is never mistaken, never confused, and never has any of the deluded and confused knowing of the samsaric type of mind. Therefore, it is referred to as a valid cognizer—anything known by it will be correct, without further question. It is a "direct perception valid cognizer".

Inferential valid cognition relies on reasonings such as syllogisms based on the mere conventions belonging to fictional truth. Nevertheless, the second turning of the wheel when setting out the self-empty approach says that it is capable of arriving at a determination of the actuality of mind. That is how it is said. However, the third turning of the wheel when setting out the other empty approach says that this method cannot be used to arrive at a determination of the ultimate actuality of mind because the ultimate actuality of mind is beyond every convention and cannot be engaged using the elaborations of conventions on which inferential valid cognition depends.

If this is discussed in terms of prajñā, which was defined above, a worldly person's prajñās of hearing, contemplating, and meditating are aroused in a process involving thought. Because of the thought involved, it is contradictory to no-thought wisdom and hence cannot give birth to realization that is directly perceiving mind's actuality, sugatagarbha. Therefore, the third turning sūtras which teach mind's actuality sugatagarbha deem it to be out of the reach of the worldly hearing, contemplation, and meditation prajñā. A sūtra records that this was taught by the Buddha when he said:

> The buddhahood that is the realm of all-seeing wisdom
> Is not the object of the three awarenesses[105].
> Therefore, bodied beings must understand that wisdom
> Is beyond the range of concept.

They teach that mind's actuality sugatagarbha has to see its own face in direct perception. This is done using prajñā which is beyond the world, prajñā which is the wisdom itself. It is very important to understand the difference between a thought-based prajñā of samsaric mind which is seeing emptiness of self and a no-thought-based prajñā of wisdom which is seeing what can be called emptiness of other, but which in fact is the entirety of wisdom. Wisdom simultaneously sees the space-like emptiness of all the phenomena it knows and all of those phenomena, which includes all of saṃsāra and nirvāṇa. Moreover, it has with it all of the good qualities of the wisdom entity, which is the same as saying that it has all of the good qualities of enlightenment, too.

---

[105] The three prajñās of hearing, contemplating, and meditating.

The Process of Perception in Relation to Seeing Mind's Actuality, Sugatagarbha

In the normal perceptual process of an ordinary person, there is first a direct sense perception. This is not a wisdom direct perception—it is a perception occurring within the framework of samsaric mind without the involvement of discursive thought. In the next moment, a structure of thought or a concept, specifically called a generality is created to represent the actual object of the initial moment of direct perception. The generality is then used to think about the actual object whenever the process of thought is being used to consider it. Then, various conventions of names, words, images, and so on are created amongst people to have a common basis for communication about that same thing.

When an ordinary person thinks about a specific thing, the generality is used to refer to it in the thinking process. However, the confusion of samsaric mind causes the generality to be confused with the actual thing, then a relatively unclear image of the actual thing appears to the thinking mind. Because of the confusion that comes with generalities, the use of conventions to discuss or present something, followed by the process of studying it with ordinary thought, will mean that the thing being studied will be neither directly nor clearly seen.

Thus, when trying to understand mind's actuality as presented by the Other Emptiness system, you first read the conventions on this page. From that, you understand the names that the Other Emptiness system gives to mind's actuality—"mind's actuality luminosity sugatagarbha", "the awareness belonging to mind's actuality", "luminosity awareness", and "sugatagarbha awareness". When your discursive thought tries to understand the basis to which these conventions of names and words apply, it uses the concepts called generalities[106]. When the discursive thought that consists of these generalities and the actual thing of mind's actuality are mixed in together through the general confusion of samsaric mind, it becomes impossible to realize the actuality of the mind that you wish to know, because it is being obscured by the process that uses the generalities.

The approach of the middle turning in which logic is used to remove mistakes from phenomena, relies on these generalities. Through a process of logical negation and affirmation, it arrives at correct decisions over what is. When the reasonings of the Middle Way are used to conduct the logical negation and affirmation, the wrong concepts of samsaric mind are negated one by one. The result is an emptiness of those wrong concepts, an emptiness of self-nature, seen by prajñā operating within samsaric mind. Therefore, the emptiness seen is not the no-thought wisdom which is mind's actuality sugatagarbha.

The Other Emptiness system uses that first step to develop the samsaric mind so that it works better. It uses that first step to empty out the mistake of ignorance. However, it does not arrive at no-thought wisdom. To do that, everything other than no-thought wisdom must be emptied out of no-thought wisdom and that is the meaning of the teaching called Other Emptiness. This second step requires no logical analysis, it requires stepping into the ultimate situation of mind directly, which I have been referring to here as "mind's actuality". Yogins who discover the mind's actuality via prajñā born of non-conceptual meditation go to the ultimate without any conventions. If their meditation apprehends something having conventions or elaborations, it is not realizing mind's nature luminosity sugatagarbha but is conceptually comprehending obscurations.

---

[106] Tib. spyi mtshan.

SUPPORTING SCRIPTURE FOR
THE VIEW OF OTHER EMPTINESS

One of the most important scriptural quotations used by the Other Emptiness school to support its view comes from the *Great Vehicle Highest Continuum Treatise*. It says:

> The element is empty of that with the characteristic of
> separability, the adventitious stains,
> It is not empty of that with the characteristic of non-sepa-
> rability, the unsurpassable dharmas ...

These two lines define the meaning of being empty of other. Restated, they mean that mind's actuality, luminosity sugatagarbha is empty of that which has the characteristic of being separable from it, the adventitious stains of samsaric mind, but is not empty of that which has the character of being inseparable from it, the unsurpassable dharmas, that is, the superfactual dharmakāya's qualities.

The unsurpassable dharmas come into being in a process called spontaneous existence. If they did not, they would arise from causes and that would mean that they were compounded. If they were compounded, they would be worldly compounded phenomena and would disintegrate. If that were so, the superfactual dharmakāya possessing them, or you could say nirvāṇa, would become a place that was not trustworthy, and these presentations of the Middle Way would not be trustworthy as a means to emancipation.

175

Jamgon Kongtrul presents the view of Other Emptiness in his *Treasury of Knowledge* with this and other verses. He says the same as the previous quotation and adds a further point:

> Empty of the adventitious to be cleaned,
> Not empty of the unsurpassable dharmas,
> The realization of self-arising rigpa means
> That it is constructed-luminosity luminosity-less.

The first line says that mind's actuality, which is luminosity sugatagarbha, is empty of the stains that arise adventitiously on its surface. What are those stains? They are the passing experiences of ignorance, the afflictions that come from it, the karma that comes from the afflictions, and the various sufferings that later arise due to those three. Those three, which sum up the occurrences which appear adventitiously on the surface of mind's actuality, temporarily defile or stain it. The sugatagarbha is empty of the adventitious stains to be cleaned because they do not introduce a taint to it—being empty of a self-nature they could affect it at all.

The second line says that mind's actuality, sugatagarbha, is not empty of the unsurpassable dharmas. There are fictional good qualities and superfactual good qualities. Buddha is not empty of the unsurpassable dharmas which are the good qualities of the superfactual dharmakāya because these good qualities are spontaneously present. They are not there as a cleanliness that would come from cleaning off adventitious stains but are there spontaneously in it.

The third line states how mind's actuality, sugatagarbha, is to be realized. There is no cleaning to do that would result in luminosity; if there were, the resulting luminosity would be a freshly created or a "constructed" luminosity. Because there is no new luminosity to be created, the actual realization, a realization which is obtained simply through accessing one's innate self-arising rigpa, is luminosity that is without a luminosity of the constructed type. In other words, mind's actuality does not have to be newly constructed.

This is Amazing

Milarepa says in the fruition verse of *The Three Nails of Meditation*:

> To explain fruition's Three Nails:
> Nirvāṇa has nothing to be produced from another,
> Saṃsāra has nothing to be abandoned to another
> I am decided that my own mind is buddha.

VITAL

This is a very high way of talking which agrees with the view of the *Great Vehicle Highest Continuum*. The second line shows that mind's actuality is natural nirvāṇa. Natural nirvāṇa does not need to be produced from anything else because there is nothing to produce—anything that has to be produced from some other thing is not a final attainment. The third line says that saṃsāra is dream-like confused appearances, not the actuality of mind, and since those confused appearances have no entity to them, there is nothing whatsoever to be abandoned. The fourth line is saying that one's own mind's actuality, inseparable luminosity-emptiness, is the superfactual buddha, the superfactual dharmakāya. "I am decided" on that, means that Milarepa has arrived at this without any doubt of it.

Then Dzogchen Paltrul said in his *Crying to the Guru from Afar*:

> Purity the dhātu[107] sugatagarbha is ground dharmakāya;
> Purifier the path gains the equipoise dharmakāya;
> Purified like that it becomes the two-purity possessing,
>   ultimate dharmakāya;
> Guru who is inseparable with these three mind-streams,
>   please think of me.

What is the ground dharmakāya mentioned there? It is the pure dhātu, the sugatagarbha pure of stains, the ground dharmakāya, the ground buddha. Because of saying, "This mind's actuality is the ground dharmakāya", the statement comes that "Every sentient being is buddha itself". There is a lot to explain about this assertion that

---

[107] Dhātu here is short for dharmadhātu. It has the sense here of a space which has no elaborations and so is empty but which at the same time provides the space within which all dharmas can and do appear.

sentient beings are buddha. Kagyu and Nyingma traditions commonly explain this point with a quote from the *Hevajra Tantra*'s two parts which says:

> Sentient beings are buddha itself
> But are obscured by adventitious stains.

In the second line, the equipoise that realizes mind's actuality luminosity sugatagarbha in direct perception is the path dharmakāya. In the third line, prajñā arising from the equipoise of meditation having cleansed the stains on the wisdom, the resulting fruition is the dharmakāya having the two purities. The verse ends by supplicating the guru who, through great kindness shows the ground, path, and fruition dharmakāya, which in this Other Emptiness teaching is usually referred to as the ground, path, and fruition sugatagarbha.

Mind's actuality sugatagarbha has the nature of indestructibility, permanence, and non-change. The supporting scripture for this is found in *The Great Vehicle Highest Continuum*. Explanations of it point out that permanence here means the great permanence "beyond permanence and impermanence", not permanence in the normal sense, and therefore this positing of permanence does not impose true existence on mind's actuality. Mind's actuality sugatagarbha is beyond both permanent and impermanent, but it needs a convention to describe it, which is why it is "permanent".

Then in the next line, the equipoise that realizes mind's actuality luminosity sugatagarbha in direct perception is the path dharmakāya. Equipoise having cleansed the stains on the wisdom, the fruition resulting from the stains being cleansed by prajñā arising from meditation, is that which has the two purities. When, through the meditation of the path adventitious confusion's stains and latencies have been dispelled, the result is called the dharmakāya having the two purities. The dharmakāya having the two purities is the fruition dharmakāya. The verse ends by supplicating the guru who shows what in Other Emptiness is referred to as the ground, path, and fruition sugatagarbha.

KEY POINTS IN THE EXPLANATION
OF OTHER EMPTINESS

Point: The Buddha taught in the third turning of the wheel that the nature of all sentient beings is buddha. This teaching is the general basis for the sūtra Other Emptiness teaching.

It is sometimes thought that the Other Emptiness teaching comes with the assertion that sentient beings are actually buddhas at the same time as being sentient beings. However, that is not the case. When it is said in the Buddha's teachings of the third turning and the Other Emptiness system's presentation of them that there is buddha in the mind-stream, the buddha being referred to is the naturally occurring complete-purity of mind, not the "freed from adventitious stains buddha" which happens at the time of fruition. As it says in the *Hevajra Tantra*'s two parts:

> Sentient beings are buddha itself,
> But are obscured by adventitious stains.

❃   ❃   ❃

Point: The Other Emptiness system teaches two approaches to emptiness, one called self empty and one called other empty. What is the difference between the two?

In the Self Emptiness system, the principal thing is the dhātu free from elaboration. For example, the Consequence Middle Way teaches emptiness in which all phenomena are free from having a nature of one or many. In that sort of emptiness, the assertion of freedom from every elaboration—existence and non-existence, duality and non-duality, appearance and emptiness, things and non-things, and so on—means that elaborations in the dhātu are negated and stopped. In regard to this, it is said that itemized phenomena (dharmins) is what is apprehended by rational mind; what they actually are in fact—or what their dharmatā is—is the "dharma dhātu free from elaborations".

Other Emptiness, Mahāmudrā, and Mahā Ati are different to that. The principal thing for them is wisdom free from elaboration. They negate elaborations not in the object but in the subject which is luminosity or wisdom. To summarize, in the Self Emptiness system, the point is dhātu free from elaborations and in the Other Emptiness system it is wisdom free from elaborations.

Because of the above, it is said that Self Emptiness is the approach in which the emptiness of the object of mind, dharmas, is determined, and that Other Emptiness—which includes Mahāmudrā and Mahā Ati—is the approach in which emptiness of the mind's nature is determined.

Furthermore, the Self Emptiness approach is shown in the *Heart Prajñāpāramitā Sūtra* when it says:

> ... no path, no wisdom, no attainment, and also no attainment ...

This is teaching freedom from the elaboration of a wisdom having an essence that is born; it is not teaching wisdom free from elaborations. The idea that commonly arises from that sort of wording which is found in the *Prajñāpāramitā Sūtras*—that wisdom is only emptiness, that it is empty and nothing else—is a mistaken understanding. The Other Emptiness proclamation that wisdom is free from the elaborations of existence and non-existence has the effect of negating that mistaken understanding.

Therefore, I think we can say that Self Emptiness Consequence Middle Way teaches dhātu free from elaborations, that Other Emptiness teaches wisdom free from elaborations, and that Mahāmudrā and Mahā Ati systems teach dhātu and wisdom inseparable.

❊   ❊   ❊

Point: The Self Emptiness emptiness is the "dhātu free from elaboration' and Other Emptiness emptiness is the "wisdom free from elaboration". Are they the same?

Technically speaking, "wisdom" in "wisdom free from elaboration" refers to the nature aspect of mind's actuality, which is called "luminosity", and the "dhātu" in "dhātu free from elaboration" refers to the entity aspect of mind's nature, which is called "emptiness". In mind's actuality sugatagarbha, the empty entity and the nature luminosity are inseparable, therefore, stating that self emptiness is the one thing of dhātu free from elaboration and that other emptiness is the other thing of wisdom free from elaboration leaves the impression of the two not being inseparable. Therefore, it has to be understood that, when the Other Emptiness system proclaims wisdom free from elaboration, "wisdom" refers to superfactual wisdom having the inseparable two facets of an empty entity which is a dhātu free of elaboration, and of a nature luminosity which is a knower free from elaboration.

Ultimately, this inseparability of empty dhātu and knowing luminosity has to be posited. The Self Emptiness approach takes care of the first but that is not sufficient by itself. Therefore, Other Emptiness presentations go further and include the knowing luminosity aspect and not as a separate item but as something unified with the empty dhātu. For example, this statement in the *Great Vehicle Highest Continuum* makes the factor of luminosity principal:

> That which is mind's nature, luminosity,
> Like space is without change;
> The adventitious stains of passion and so on
> Coming from incorrect knowledge do not change it to
>   being afflicted.

Note that sūtra Other Emptiness does not usually mention the knowing quality (rigpa in Tibetan); luminosity alone is spoken of but this is sufficient because "luminosity" is a metaphor for knowing. Tantra Other Emptiness on the other hand places great importance on the knowing quality and always mentions it.

Thus, according to the Other Emptiness system, the view of self emptiness has to be determined as a preliminary. By doing so, the empty dhātu aspect is determined. After that, the meaning of other emptiness has to be accessed in direct personal experience, which is done by accessing the nature, luminosity. Unlike the first step, the second step is not done as a logical exercise but as an exercise of meditation in which one directly accesses the luminosity. Because of that, the luminosity accessed is the superfactual luminosity, which is conventionally known as "wisdom with both aspects of empty entity and nature luminosity inseparable".

Therefore, it is said that, if you have not completed the self-empty view beforehand, hearing about luminosity will not be helpful because you will understand it conceptually as a luminosity divorced from the empty entity. That would hinder you from arriving at the superfactual luminosity, therefore an explanation of the factor of emptiness is required to being with, isn't it? On the other hand, it says in Other Emptiness, "If the self empty view has been set as a basis beforehand, mind's actuality luminosity, an entity free from afflictions, will be seen."

❀   ❀   ❀

Point: Therefore, when the empty factor of self emptiness and the luminosity factor of other emptiness are made inseparable, they become the entity of inseparability, which the Other Emptiness system sets as the ultimate actuality.

This unification is the intent of Jetsun Milarepa's words in his song, *An Authentic Expression of the Middle Way:*[108]

> Existence appearing as things[109] and
> Non-existence, their inner reality of emptiness,
> Both are inseparable in entity, of one taste, thus
> Self-knowing and other-knowing are non-existent and
> Everything is a unification vast and open.

These lines present the self-empty view of the middle turning which principally determines the factor of emptiness. Mind's actuality is dhātu-knowing (dhātu-rigpa) inseparable; the master might have finalized his accomplishment of it but most disciples will not be able to understand it at the start.

The middle turning's view is principally a determination of the dhātu being free from elaboration. The stopping of true existence—existence by way of a self-nature—in all outer and inner phenomena results in emptiness being determined, which is said to be the teaching of the dhātu's freedom from elaboration. It is determined principally in relation to the objects, appearances.

Following that, emptiness in the Other Emptiness system is determined principally in relation to the subject, in relation to the mind knowing those appearances. This approach to determining

---

[108] See *The Theory and Practice of Other Emptiness Taught Through Milarepa's Songs, Including Teachings of Khenpo Tsultrim Gyatso* for a full presentation of the song with thorough explanation by the khenpo.

[109] Things here means conceptually-constructed things.

mind's actuality is one in which the easier realization of appearing phenomena's emptiness is obtained first, followed by determining mind's actuality in relation to the mind knowing those phenomena. Mind Only, sūtra Other Emptiness, and Other Emptiness as expressed through Mahāmudrā and Mahā Ati all follow this approach.

❀   ❀   ❀

Point: The way of bringing Self Emptiness and Other Emptiness into agreement is to see that in the case of self emptiness, dhātu empty of elaborations is taught, and that in the case of other emptiness, wisdom empty of elaborations is taught.

The Other Emptiness system points out that the dhātu empty of elaborations derived through self-empty hearing and contemplation is an externalized dhātu, one based on the use of logic. However, the dhātu empty of elaboration within the other emptiness realization of wisdom empty of elaborations is an internal dhātu, the dhātu of emptiness seen in direct perception by the wisdom itself. Thus, it is not that the realization of the self emptiness approach is joined into the realization of the other emptiness approach. Rather, it creates a means by which the other emptiness of superfactual wisdom can be seen directly and, in doing so, that the empty entity of that superfactual wisdom will be directly seen by the superfactual wisdom as its own internal expanse empty of elaborations.

Therefore, Milarepa said:

> If there is emptiness of a sort other than mind
> You are making a mistake …

And also:

> When one's own mind is realized as empty,
> Most, having the emptiness of one and many, have a
>   nihilistic emptiness …

If your emptiness is merely the external type of empty dhātu arrived at through the contemplative use of logic, it is an emptiness of one and many in which phenomena have been stopped. It results from the non-affirming negation of negating that which is to be negated. It is a mere absence of duality. Milarepa thus calls it a nihilistic emptiness. What is actually needed? Seeing the internal type of emptiness in union with wisdom's luminosity is the profound approach that is needed.

Ju Mipham said in his *Lamp of Certainty*:

> The Gahdan view is non-affirming negative.
> Others have affirming negative.
> What does the Early Translation school say?
> Affirming negative's negative is there!
> If you use non-affirming negation
> Affirming negation will not help.

The Gahdan is the original name for what is now called the Gelug tradition. They use and only use non-affirming negation to determine emptiness, whereas others like the Kagyu and Jonang schools start with that then end up using affirming negation. Those were the New Translation schools; what does his own, Early Translation school, say about this? First, it says that the negation used in affirming negation, unlike the negation used in non-affirming negation, leads to the presence, not absence of something. This exactly fits with the Other Emptiness approach of the others who are not like the Gelug tradition. In their other emptiness approach there is wisdom and that cannot be denied. Second, it says that in the ultimate approach to wisdom, such as in its peak approach of Mahā Ati, the non-affirming negation gets in the way, and there is simply no need for it. In that approach, which is also the approach of Mahāmudrā and tantra, Other Emptiness as taught in Kagyu and Jonang traditions, the practitioner enters wisdom directly without needing to bother with any logical analysis. In those cases, the conventions of logic are not helpful at all, but are a barrier to accessing wisdom.

He says in the first line that the Gahdan view is non-affirming negative and that doing it that way is all right for the sūtra system approach; in one sūtra it says:

Emptiness meditation is space-meditation.
Prajñāpāramitā meditation is space-meditation.

Moreover, there are many other statements which, like that, exemplify the approach to meditation taught in the Prajñāpāramitā teachings, so it is not only alright to talk that way in that context, it is necessary. However, in the case of mantra system, which is another emptiness approach, affirming negation, not non-affirming negation must be used. Unfortunately, in the context of Secret Mantra, the Gelug tradition continues to insist that non-affirming negation is required; that is not alright because in the mantra system innate mind beyond concept is the thing whose emptiness is being determined.

Sūtra Other Emptiness and the tantras both use affirming negation. They speak of mind's actuality using various words and conventions together with various affirming negations, all of which make mind's actuality existent. It is alright to use conventions to speak of what is present and not present. Doing so does not harm the actuality pointed out by the affirming negatives, nor does it cause it to become existent or non-existent by way of a self-nature because, in itself, it is beyond every elaboration of existent and non-existent. In other words, the temporary presentation of superfactual mind's actuality does not cause some type of fictional existence to become present in it. The Other Emptiness system's other-empty style of emptiness is asserted in this way: "Mind's actuality sugatagarbha is an entity which from the outset is pure of adventitious stains, free of elaborations, and beyond conventions, therefore it is empty of those." However, the system continues by stating "Conventions like 'sugatagarbha', 'luminosity', and so on have to be created because, if there were no conventions, negation and assertion and also the normal process of study could not occur. Nevertheless, they are only conventions and the actuality of mind that they point at has to be posited as beyond every elaboration."

❀   ❀   ❀

Point: When the Buddha spoke after attaining enlightenment, his first words expressed the Other Emptiness understanding exactly. He said:

> Peaceful, luminous, free from elaboration, not-
> composite ...

Mind's actuality is ultimate reality because its entity is free from stains and beyond conventions. This ultimate reality beyond conventions is, of the two, dhātu free from elaborations and wisdom free from elaborations, principally explained as the latter. This wisdom free from the elaborations of conventions is, in its actual fact, beyond all conventions. Nonetheless, it is necessary for us who are on the path back to this wisdom to give it names such as "self-arising self-knowing wisdom" or we would not be able to hear about it, contemplate it, and study it so that we could arrive at it. Designating it with conventions is not a fault because, given that mind's actuality has no conventions in it, naming it with a convention does not cause it to change into something with conventions. Other Emptiness is a system of designating conventions to what is beyond convention in order to arrive at what is beyond convention.

❀   ❀   ❀

Point: This is how Dolpopa Sangyay explained Other Emptiness.

He is known for using the three characters of Mind Only in his presentations. His view is often referred to as Yogāchāra Middle Way Other Emptiness. According to him, the Self Emptiness view is principally emptiness of the imaginary. It shows, through the determination that all outer and inner phenomena are not existent by way of nature, the emptiness of imaginary and dependent phenomena. It does not show the emptiness of the Thoroughly Existent. The way that the Thoroughly Existent is empty is taught in the sūtras of the final turning of the wheel which teach sugatagarbha. Using that approach, he explained that mind's actuality emptiness is the ultimate emptiness. His way of teaching was about the style of emptiness.

❋   ❋   ❋

Point: The seventh Karmapa Chodrag Gyatso explains the Other Emptiness system in his *Ocean of Texts on Reasoning and Pramāṇa* as follows. Regarding the Self Emptiness system, the view of the middle turning, it is said that, if it is first realized that all appearing phenomena are lacking existence by way of self entity, which is a coarse approach using the coarse phenomena of sights, sounds, smells, tastes, and touches that is easy for a beginner, then from that coarse determination one can enter what is more subtle, mind's actuality. Then, in the Other Emptiness system, the root of all phenomena is mind, so if the actuality of mind is determined principally in relation to mind, then, having already understood the emptiness of coarse phenomena—that sights, sounds, smells, tastes, and touches are not truly existent—which is easy to realize, the actuality itself becomes dhātu and knowing inseparable in the entity of the actuality.

❖   ❖   ❖

Part 4

Explanations by

Jamgon Kongtrul the Great

Figure 6. Jamgon Kongtrul the Great

Introductory Section From:

"The Lion's Roar of the Non-Regressing", A Complete Commentary to the Great Vehicle Treatise *The Highest Continuum* which Connects to the Heart Meaning Using the Explanatory System of the Path of Direct Perception

The ultimate intent of the conqueror, the heart meaning,
Was well documented in the text by his regent
    Maitreya.[110]
The way of explaining these matters using inferential
    reasoning is very well known but
Direct experience made as the path, which is the way of
    the Buddha Vehicle,
Does not fit with the degree of fortune of inferior
    sophists—
It is the special feature of the lineage of the archer, father
    and sons.[111]
This analysis will be done according to the meaning
    truthfully stated

---

[110] ... to be examined in this commentary, the *Highest Continuum*.

[111] "Lineage of the archer, father and sons" refers to the lineage of the Indian mahāsiddha Saraha and his followers, which is the Kagyu tradition.

By the supreme charioteers of the heart definitive
    meaning.[112]

I will explain here the king of treatises which is a commentary on the
Buddha's intent, one that tells the story of the highest basket or
which is at the peak of the baskets of the Buddha's teaching, the
greatest one because of being the supreme amongst all the various
modes of dharma that were well-taught by the leader amongst the
Śhākyas, the omniscient one, a truly complete buddha. This is the
story of the non-regressing dharma, the lion's roar that is the heart
of the whole teaching.

There are two parts to the explanation, a summary that provides an
overview of what is actually in the text and an extensive explanation
that unravels the meaning of the actual words of the text.

I. The Overview

This has eight parts:[113]

    1. Identifying what it is that is to be explained;
    2. The sources on which it is based;
    3. The ācharyas who made it;
    4. The lineages through which it comes;
    5. What meaning is to be explained;
    6. The way in which it will be explained;
    7. A synopsis of the text, from beginning to end;
    8. All of that connected with the needs of that explanation

---

[112] They were the Buddha, Maitreya, Asaṅga and so on, as clearly
explained in Khenpo Tsultrim's history.

[113] The first five parts are presented here.

1. Identifying what it is that is to be explained

Generally speaking, the particular texts of the Buddha Word found within the good teaching of the complete buddha that show the three natures—the dharmadhātu, all-pervading non-dual wisdom, is the nature of the family; what possesses the two purities because the two adventitious obscurations have been abandoned is the nature of dharmakāya; and what obtains it, the view free of all elaborations and the meditation of not discursively thinking, is the nature of the path—will be the highest or holiest of texts. If such a text is carefully analysed, it will be found to be three fold.

The first one is as follows: within a buddha's own appearances, there are the intonations of speech that belong to non-dual wisdom shining forth as all superficies, and the particular sub-division of that which is the speech of the Great Vehicle sūtra section in its superfactual aspect is the first one. This is of the same entity as the nature complete purity and also as the disconnection fruition, the dharma-kāya[114]. The second one is the sūtra section of the Great Vehicle having the collection of letters and grammatical names and phrases[115] that appear as the generalities of terms in the minds of both noble ones and individualized beings[116]. The third one is the wordings of

---

[114] This first one is the same entity as the ground—the complete purity nature of mind, and also as the fruition of the path, dharmakāya. There are several types of fruition, one particular type is called "disconnection fruition". The reason for mentioning it here is that it is the result in which one is disconnected from something, in this case the impurities that prevent the complete purity of the ground from being manifest.

[115] In English, letters make words which make verbal expressions. In Tibetan letters make grammatical names and grammatical phrases, which are both used to make verbal expressions.

[116] Generalities of terms are the various terms of language that appear in the mind as a conceptual approximation of the actual thing.
(continued...)

terms that are then expressed in correspondence with that and which are called its "continuity" as the definitive meaning sūtras of the Great Vehicle. The latter two are very different in entity from the three of nature, fruition, and path. Nonetheless, because they arise from the buddha's prayers of aspiration, they are causes whose result will be dharmakāya and have the potential and power needed to carry out the abandonment of the two obscurations, and are to be understood to be included within the un-outflowed dharmas, within that which references complete purification, and within the Thoroughly Existent.[117]

No matter how many texts of that sort are assembled into a collection of Great Vehicle sūtras, all will be contained within both the Word and Treatises; The *Sūtra Petitioned by Devaputra* says:

> All dharmas are contained within both the Word and Treatises. It is due to these, which are his well-taught dharma and the commentaries on his intent in them, that this the Śhākya's teaching will remain for a long time in this world system.

You might ask where the text to be explained here, the *Highest Continuum*, is identified within that?" From one point of view, it could be identified as words that come with the authorization or blessing of the Buddha because the conqueror himself, having placed

---

[116](...continued)
Generalities were discussed in Khenpo Tsultrim's Introduction to Other Emptiness chapter.

[117] Un-outflowed dharmas are those belonging to wisdom. That which is referenced as complete purification means all those dharmas which are considered to be part of the process of attainment of complete purity (the nirvāṇa side) as opposed to total affliction (the saṃsāra side). The Thoroughly Existent is the third of the three natures of Mind Only and is regarded as the superfactual side in Mind Only and Other Emptiness presentations.

the crown on Maitreya's head, invested him with the rank of his regent for teaching dharma and also because of what it says in the *Condensed*:[118]

> As many rivers as flow and as many flowers, fruit trees,
>   medicinal plants, and forests
> As there are in this Jambu Continent,
> All depend on the governor over nāgas, the nāga ruler
>   who lives in Manasarovar and
> Are the glory of the power of that ruler of nāgas.
> And the dharma teaching, explanation, and expressions of
>   it through knowledge,
> Of the conqueror's śhrāvakas as many as they are,
> And all production of the bliss of the supreme noble ones
>   and attainment of the fruition by it
> All are the power of the being who is the tathāgata.

Even Maitreya himself said that text was made as a commentary to expose the intent of the one who taught this teaching, the Lord of Capable Ones[119]. He said:[120]

> The whole body of the treatise, in short …

And, following on from his own assertion that it is a treatise, it will be a treatise having the two qualities of "creating and protecting"[121].

---

[118] This is from a Prajñāpāramitā text; the point is that it was spoken by the Buddha himself.

[119] For capable ones, see the glossary.

[120] … At the beginning of the *Highest Continuum* …

[121] All valid Buddhist treatises have these two qualities. The author has shown here that all of the sūtras which are determined to be the highest kind of text that he has defined must be either spoken by the Buddha or be a commentary on the Buddha's intent. Maitreya himself says that it is the latter. It is customary when examining a treatise before
(continued...)

Now, from among the limitless numbers of authors of treatises that are commentaries on the intent, there is nobody in this world like the regent, lord of the ten bhumis, Maitreya and the three Guardians of the Three Families[122]. Given that and given that their speech is not distinguishable from the Buddha's excellent speech, all of the learned and accomplished ones of the Noble Land and of Tibet, pronouncing it to be "a commentary on enlightenment mind", joined their palms at the crown of their heads. A treatise as great as that is what will be explained here.

2. The Sources on Which it is Based

The eminent Conqueror Rangjung[123] and All-Knowing Dolpopa, fathers and sons, held that it was based principally on the definitive meaning heart sūtras of the final turning.

Moreover, the complete buddha saw with his omniscience that the buddha element exists in all sentient beings. He also saw that, because they are obscured by the four obscurations of hostility to the dharma, and so on, sentient beings do not know that they have the buddha element in them and because of the five faults[124] engendered by that of being disheartened with themselves, looking down on others, and so on, they swirl about in the ocean of saṃsāra. So he taught them that the buddha element exists in all sentient beings and

---

[121](...continued)
commenting on it to examine it for validity. So here, he has provided the validation by saying that Maitreya himself has said it is a treatise.

[122] This refers to Vajrapāṇi, Avalokiteshvara, and Mañjushrī who, together with Maitreya, are three more of the eight heart son bodhisatva mahasatvas of the Buddha.

[123] Conqueror Rangjung and the like throughout the text refers to Karmapa III, Rangjung Dorje.

[124] The four obscurations and five faults are listed in the first chapter of the *Highest Continuum*.

taught the methods for dispelling the stains a step at a time. With each step he showed only the methods suited to the faculties of those to be tamed with that step. He taught them in a sequence of non-explicit, explicit, and highly explicit modes of teaching.

Of the infinite doors of dharma shown in those levels of teaching, the supreme or ultimate ones are the definitive meaning sūtras taught on account of those bodhisatvas who, because of having properly entered the entirety of vehicles, had purified their mindstreams and developed sharp and fully-matured faculties. The definitive meaning sūtras *Unravelling the Intent*, *Descent into Laṅka*, *Densely Arrayed with Ornaments*, and *Avataṃsaka*, which are well-known as the four sūtras of the Mind Only presentation, use ordinary reasonings to show that the dharmatā is the truly existing superfactual case. The definitive meaning sutras *Tathāgatagarbha*, *Great Drum*, *For the Benefit of Aṅgulimāla*, *Petitioned by Shrīmala Devī*, *Petitioned by Dharaṇeshvara*, *Great Nirvāṇa*, *Cloud of Jewels*, *Utter Peace Fully Ascertained*, *Holy Golden Light*, *Great Cloud*, and so on give the secret story in fine detail using the extraordinary tenet of what is inherently present primordi-ally—the tathāgatagarbha, the expanse of the authentic, the unchanging dharmakāya, permanence and steadiness and svastika which are the qualities of the superfactual, and so on. Now those sūtras are within the reaches only of the single sphere of all-knowing wisdom, so why bother to mention sophists, shrāvakas, and so on in this context[125] when even those dwelling on the noble levels do not realize it as it is? None of them realize it as it is because, as was said:

> The buddhahood that is the realm of all-seeing wisdom
> Is not the object of the three awarenesses[126] therefore,

---

[125] Just above, it says that these teachings were give as the culmination of a series of steps of teaching, with the earlier steps meant for sophists, and so on. So they are included in this, even if they cannot immediately understand it.

[126] The three prajñās of hearing, contemplating, and meditating.

Bodied beings must understand that wisdom
Is beyond the range of concept.

Because it is subtle, it is not the object of hearing;
Because it is superfact, it is not of conception;
Because the dharmatā is profound, it is not the object
Of worldly one's meditations, and so on.

The reason is that, like form in the case of a man blind
    from birth,
It has never been seen before by the childish and
Like the form of the sun in the case of a baby in the house
    of his birth,
Not by the noble ones, either ...

It is our position then that those less fortunate ones of dull faculty
are taken on and not rejected. Having done so, in order to prevent
them from becoming obscured by lack of comprehension or a wrong
way of understanding, this treatise was made to show clearly the
entirety of what those sūtras of the profound sūtra section are
attempting to express by condensing it down into seven vajra topics.

In that regard, Seer of All Knowables Rongton[127] and others like him
hold that this text is not merely a commentary on the intent that
relates only to the final wheel, but is a general commentary to that
section of the sūtras which shows the definitive meaning, which are
made out to be approximately fifteen in number and include the
*Showing Great Compassion, Showing the Extra Thought, White Lotus of
the Holy Dharma*, and so on sūtras.

3. The Acharyas Who Made it

Experts speak of "the three types of authors of treatises—best,
middling, and least". With that in mind, the author of this treatise
is commented for his expertise in the field of knowables and for his

---

[127] Rongton Choje was a Sakya master who was important in Middle
Way philosophy of Tibet.

having seen the truth of the dharmatā. Moreover, he has in the definitive meaning sense been a manifest, complete buddha during past aeons as many as the atoms in the ground but had showed himself in the form of a bodhisatva at the tenth level, the Cloud of Dharma, with only one life hindering him[128] and had already received the empowerment of the level of great regent and was on his way to appearing as the fifth world-leading buddha of the good aeon.

Invincible Guardian Maitreya[129], a conqueror who wields a mastery over inconceivable manifestations equal to that of the current buddha and who is a close son of the current buddha, announced in the presence of the Lord of Capable Ones and with the great roar of a lion that he would uphold, spread, and protect the holy dharma. In accordance with that and using his eye that has no obstacles preventing it from seeing the meaning of the excellent speech of the Buddha and using his extra perceptions, he first composed the *Ornament of Manifest Realizations*. With that text, he showed the dharma talk of the definitive-meaning Great Middle Way, just bringing out the main points. Then, he explained it clearly and extensively in the *Ornament of the Sūtras, Distinguishing the Middle from Extremes*, and *Distinguishing the Dharmatā*. Finally, in the *Highest Continuum*, he pinpointed the most subtle tenet involved, the one that is the extraordinary meaning found in the heart sūtras.

Āchārya Haribhadra holds that the five dharmas of Maitreya were composed for Āchārya Asaṅga. Abhaya explains that they were composed at the time of the councils on the Buddha Word.

Then, in regard to who made the treatises visible in the Jambu Continent, Āchārya Śhāntipa says in his *Ornament of the Madhyamaka*

---

[128] This means that he had only one more life to be experienced before becoming a truly complete buddha.

[129] Invincible is one of Maitreya's names, given that there is nothing can stop him from becoming the next world-leading buddha.

that it was eminent Ārya Asaṅga who was said to dwell on the third level, Light Maker; it says in the *Root Tantra of Mañjuśrī* that:

> A bhikṣhu who will be called "Asaṅga"
> Expert in the meaning of the treatises
> Will thoroughly distinguish the sūtras of the definitive
>   meaning sūtra section
> And also many of provisional meaning type.
> He will be a teacher of knowledge to the world and
> Will stay composing treatises.
> This, the means by which he produces knowledge,
> The mantra called "Sāladūti",
> Will through its power
> Produce in him an excellent rational mind.
> In order that the teaching remain for a long time,
> He will compile the suchness meaning of the sūtras.
> He will live for one hundred and fifty years and
> When his body ends, will go to the god realms.
> He will experience happiness for a long time
> Roving in cyclic existence then
> Finally the great being
> Will attain enlightenment.

Prophesied in that scripture, he accomplished the practice of noble one Maitreya by doing it for twelve years, then, having been accepted by Maitreya, stayed in Tuṣhita for fifty human years, heard the entire basket of the Great Vehicle from Maitreya, and, especially, brought the *Five Dharmas of Maitreya* to this Jambu Continent. He composed many treatises such as the five "levels"[130], and so on. In particular, he made a commentary to the *Highest Continuum* in which he clearly and extensively explained its extraordinary tenet. These works

---

[130] According to the *Illuminator Tibetan-English Dictionary*: 1) Yogacāra-bhūmī; 2) Yogacāra-bhūmau vastu-saṃgraha; 3) Yogacāra-bhūmau paryāya-saṃgraha; 4) Yogacāra-bhūmī-niraṇaya-saṃgraha; 5) Yogacāra-bhūmau vivaraṇa-saṃgraha.

became famous as a "great chariot" among the various systems that lay out the path.

His younger brother, the eminent Vasubhandu, an expert among experts who had memorized all the nine million nine hundred thousand sections of the Prajñāpāramitā, also made many treatises. His commentary to the *Twenty Thousand* called *Defeating Harm*, and commentary to *Distinguishing the Dharmatā* skilfully exposed the tenets of the definitive meaning Middle Way, so were great clarifiers of the system, but these days the lineage for them no longer remains.

4. The Lineages Through Which it Comes

The general tenets of this definitive meaning Madhyamaka and the set of three Maitreya dharmas—the two ornaments and the *Distinguishing Middle and Extremes*—were spread widely by many who had excellent lineages of instruction coming from Dignaga, Sthiramati, and so on. However, the extraordinary teaching, because it does not fit easily into others' minds, was passed from ear to ear in a hearing lineage by the best disciples and the texts of the *Highest Continuum* and *Distinguishing Dharmatā* were hidden away.

The set of three texts and teaching with it was translated and explained at the time of the earlier spread by the Tibetan translators Kawa Paltsheg and Zhang Yeshe Dey. The *Highest Continuum* and *Distinguishing Dharmatā* root texts and commentaries re-appeared later on when Maitrīpa, who became their owner[131], saw light coming from a chink in a stūpa and, upon investigating to see what it was, discovered the texts of these treatises. He supplicated Jetsun Maitreya who came in person and whom he saw in the clouds. Maitreya very nicely bestowed on him the transmission for the scripture. He in turn gave it to Paṇḍita Anandakīrti who went to Kashmir in the guise of a poor man. There, in the city Glory, a line

---

[131] Here, "owner" means that he was the one officially designated (by Maitreya in this case) to protect and teach them.

of paṇḍitas of unparalleled expertise had been continuing on for many generations. One of them, the Brahmin Ratnavajra, because of having achieved expertise and accomplishment in the entirety of tenets, inner and outer, had become known as the first Great Central Pillar. His son was known as "Paṇḍita Sugata" and Paṇḍita Sugata's eldest son Paṇḍita Sajñyana[132] recognized Anandakīrti, who had become known as a holy being, as very expert, and heard the two treatises from him.

After that, the bodhisatva mahāsattva Ngog Loden Sherab heard them while he was in the land of Kashmir learning dharma, and translated them into Tibetan while he was there. After that, he explained them widely in the land of Tibet. Prior to that, the elder of Yerpa, Jangchub Jungney, made a request of the great expert bodhisatva of the good aeon, Jowo Je, which led to their being translated by Nagtsho Translator Tsultrim Gyalwa. The great Sharawa[133] chose to explain it using Nagtsho's translation, though later, because most students preferred Ngog's translation, he was known for explaining it twice each time, based first on one and then on the other translation. Later, Patshab Translator, Marpa Dopa, and many others translated the *Highest Continuum*, but it seems that the lines of explanation and hearing that went with those translations did not stay for long.

The great Ngog Translator wrote a small ṭīka[134] on the commentary to the *Highest Continuum* and, based on that, his own disciples Lodro Jungney of Drolung and Chokyi Lama the renunciant from Zhangtshe each wrote a ṭīka. Then, Zhang's disciple Nyang Dranpa Chokyi Sherab made a commentary based on both of them and later

---

[132] This is the person who is mostly referred to as Sajjana. This is probably the correct spelling of his name.

[133] Sharawa was disciple of Dromtonpa who was one of the three closest disciples of Atisha.

[134] Skt. ṭīka. This is the most general name for a commentary.

on again, Phyvapa Choseng and his disciples Tsang Nagpa Tsondru Senge, Dan Phagpa Mraway Senge, and so on also collectively made many commentaries. Their followers Lodro Tshungmey, Phagdru Gyaltsen Zangpo, Seer of All Knowables Rongton, and so on—altogether many experts—covered greater Tibet with volumes of their commentaries, but all of these commentators being followers of the great Ngog, all sorts of unusual and inconsistent ways of using dharma terminology appeared.

Besides that[135], there was the pupil of the monk Abhijña known as Tsan Khawoche who had travelled to Kashmir in the company of the great translator Ngog and then gone his own way. He met Sajjana and made this request:

> I wish to do a death dharma practice that comes from
> Bhagavat Maitreya's dharmas so please instruct me and
> keep me in mind.

With Zu Gawa'i Dorje acting as the translator, Sajjana taught him all five dharmas of Maitreya. He also gave very fine instruction on the *Highest Continuum* to Tsan, a person of stainless prajñā, who then went to Tibet and explained it in U and Tsang. Zu Gawa'i Dorje made an ornamental ṭīka to the *Highest Continuum* that fitted Sajjana's teaching on it and translated *Distinguishing Dharmatā*, both root and commentary. This stream of teaching coming from Zu and Tsan, which also became known as the Meditation System of Maitreya's dharma, is the particularly special, extraordinary explanation and extraordinary practice of the text.

The line of teaching being presented here, also came through Zu and Tsan's line of teaching like this. All-knowing Rangjung Dorje, someone who had, through seeing wisdom, realized the intent of the Invincible Maitreya, summarized the meaning of the *Highest*

---

[135] ... story of Ngog, now there is another branch of the story coming from Kashmir at that time ...

Continuum in an outline of its topics. Karma Konzhon[136] and others commented extensively on it and the great Karma Trinlaypa[137] made a commentary to it that expanded the existing wording to make it more comprehensible.

Then, there was the great translator Go Zhonnu Pal[138] who composed very extensive explanations that were commentaries to Asaṅga's commentary on it and which were consistent with this system that came through Zu and Tsan.

Later, there was the great All-knowing Dolpopa who began an extraordinary system of teaching and the lineages that came from the followers of his commentary—both in general and in particular the one that went through All-Knowing Tāranātha, and so on—planted a tradition of explanation and practice whose lineage transmitting his original commentary is still present today.

Later still, All-Seeing Chokyi Jungnay heard it from the great glory Chokyi Dondrup[139] and explained it many times, and through the line of his teaching, the expert of experts, Zurmang Lhalungpa Karma Tenphel made an annotational ṭīka whose line of explanation has also continued on, being well accepted. Thus from then to now,

---

[136] ... a disciple of Rangjung Dorje ...

[137] ... a contemporary of the seventh Karmapa, famous in the Karma Kagyu for his erudition ...

[138] Zhonu Pal [1392–1481] is well-known for his very extensive commentary to Asaṅga's commentary to the *Highest Continuum*, a system of commentary that was consistent with the profound system that came through Zu and Tsan.

[139] Chokyi Jungnay is the eighth Situ, Chokyi Dondrup the eighth Zhamar.

the people involved[140] principally follow the eminent Conqueror Rangjung.

5. What Meaning is to Be Explained

The Bhagavat's statement that, "All sentient beings always have the buddha garbha", is set as the basis for the explanation of the heart meaning. There have been infinite different systems in both India and Tibet for explaining it, each one following its own tradition of scriptural authority, reasoning, and meditation, but the ācāryas of the definitive meaning Middle Way held it to be as follows.

Every type of definitive meaning found within the three dharma wheels is contained within the two non-selves. When the ultimate meaning of that is reached, it is emptiness of the duality of grasped-grasping which come due to the person and his dharmas respectively. The mode of the emptiness is that they are not merely a non-affirming negative. The *Distinguishing Middle and Extremes* says:

> Here, the absence of things of
> Person and dharmas is emptiness.
> That existence of thing which is absence of thing
> Is itself emptiness.

This means that the mode of emptiness here is that of affirming negation and that the entity resulting from it, self-knowing self-illumination, is taught as the tathāgatagarbha, and that is the definitive meaning's vajra. When this vajra is categorized into its phases, it becomes threefold. The text itself says:[141]

> According to the sequence impure, impure-pure,
> And the extreme of completely pure,
> They are expressed as sentient beings, bodhisatvas,
> And tathāgatas respectively.

---

[140] ... in the Kagyu transmission to which he is heir ...

[141] In the *Highest Continuum*.

This means that, when, in the samsaric phase, it is impure due to the adventitious stains, it is called "sentient beings", and in this case the element is called "family or element tathāgatagarbha". In the phase where it has both purity and impurity, it is called "persons who have entered the path" and, in terms of the element, it becomes the dharma and the saṅgha. For example, from the aspect only of the wisdom of the path of seeing, it is the saṅgha, and from the aspect of its being the unhindered path, it is the truth of path, and from the aspect of having the feature of the path of liberation, it is the truth of cessation. In the phase of extreme complete purity, buddha, it is called "sugata" and so on, and the element is called "dharmakāya". When this is divided into aspects, there are three: enlightenment, qualities, and activity.

That way, it has seven subdivisions, and it is correspondingly taught in the text as seven vajra topics. It is easy to understand that the entirety of the definitive meaning of the two later wheels is included in those seven topics. Still, one might ask how the definitive meaning of the first one, the not-self of a person, is included. It is included because all three of the base to be purified, the purifier, and the result of purification of the lesser path are included within the stained tathātā or suchness.

Therefore, the principal thing taught by this treatise is the mode of the tathāgatagarbha and the entire definitive meaning of the three wheels is included in that. On understanding that, you might think, "And what is this garbha?" The answer is that it is described within the Excellent Speech of the Buddha's in general as:

1. emptiness that is freedom from elaboration;
2. mind's nature of luminosity;
3. the ālaya base consciousness;
4. bodhisatvas and sentient beings.

Following on from that, there is an explanation of four points consisting of three self-characterized items of:

1. dharmakāya;
2. tathātā; and
3. gotra;

and one generally characterized item:

4. no discursive thinking.

Those, moreover, are ways of expressing the intent concerning the three phases mentioned above and the provisional and definitive. If you think, "Where are they explained and who exposed them skilfully?" then the answer is as follows.

✓1. Freedom from Elaboration

This is the definitive meaning that appears beginning with the second wheel and which is clarified by noble one Nāgārjuna and his followers using many avenues of scripture and reasoning. There is a point here: the basis for the characterization of emptiness, self-nature, and so on that is the nothingness of a non-affirming negation discovered by the power of reasoning as explained in the Middle Way *Collected Reasonings* is what most Noble Land āchāryas of the Autonomy and Consequence schools accepted and what the Tibetan Self-Empty Middle Way followers insistently establish only as non-affirming negation.

Eminent Bhavaviveka in his *Blaze of Reasoning* explained that kind of emptiness as the tathāgatagarbha and Chandrakīrti accepted that too. Ārya Vimuktisena and Haribhadra explain the gotra and svabhāvikakāya and Jñānagarbha explains the dharmakāya to be emptiness that is a non-affirming negation. Thus they do accept the garbha via this meaning.

Nevertheless, it was taught that emptiness that is the non-affirming negation found through the valid cognition of inference brings great sickness for a bodhisatva because it becomes a great fetter, the fetter of thinking discursively. Therefore, because the final wheel contains the meaning of entering into no discursive thinking, it is special indeed.

2. Mind's Nature, Luminosity

This is taught explicitly in both the middle and last wheels and in the mantra tantras and there are extensive explanations that explicitly state that it is the garbha in the *Highest Continuum* and the *Ornament of the Sūtras of the Great Vehicle*, and in Nāgārjuna's *In Praise of the Dharmadhātu, In Praise of Mind's Vajra, Enlightenment Mind Commentary*, and so forth.

3. The Base Consciousness Explained as Tathagatagarbha

This appears in many places such as *Descent into Laṅka, Densely Arrayed With Ornaments, Petitioned by Shrī Mālā*, the vajra dohās, and so forth. And, the Mind Only āchāryas proclaimed it according to the literal meaning.

4. Sentient Beings Explained as Tathagatagarbha

The *Clear Lamp* says:

> All sentient beings are tathāgatagarbha.

and:

> The element is taught as three phases
> By using three names.

The meanings of those quotations are explained at length below but to state it concisely here:

> Because buddha wisdom resides in the mass of sentient
>   beings,
> Because that stainless nature is non-dual, and
> Because the buddha gotra is named for its likeness,
> All migrators are taught to have the buddha garbha.

First, because the buddha wisdom resides in the mass of sentient beings, that buddha wisdom that resides in sentient beings is called the "tathāgatagarbha". Second, because mind's nature, the "tathātā" or suchness without stain, exists without difference in all buddhas and sentient beings, it too is taught as the "garbha". Third, what sentient beings have such as the skandhas, and so on being the same sort of thing as buddha are the buddha gotra so, because gotra means "very much the same sort", this gotra is given the name "tathāgata" then explained as garbha. In sequence, they are taught as "dharmakāya", "tathātā", and "gotra" respectively. The translator Go Zhonnu Pal accepts that the first one is the actual tathāgata and is named sentient beings' garbha; that the middle one, because it possesses the aspect of both buddhas and sentient beings is actual tathāgata and garbha both; and that the final one is actual garbha and is named tathāgata. "No discursive thinking" is to be understood as applying generally to all four points.

"Gotra", "element", "seed", and so on are synonyms. "Element" does not mean cause[142]; it is a term that also contains a connotation of "garbha" so is called "element"[143]. The set of nine meanings that go with the nine examples of buddha within a bad lotus, and so on are to the point that there is an entity actually present which has become obscured by something else present that is causing obscuration from the outside; as such, they provide examples of the element. And with that, the dharmadhātu is also taught to be the element and gotra.

The term "garbha" is used to mean existing in the middle of a husk that is wrapped around it so the tathātā or suchness is at the time of

---

[142] Skt. hetu.

[143] "Garbha" has the basic sense of a place from which something else comes. "Dhātu", which is the Sanskrit word translated here as "element", has twenty-two meanings. One of them is a range or zone which becomes the source from which other things can come. It is that meaning which is consistent with the meaning of "garbha".

the ground obscured by adventitious stains and appears to exist at the centre of them. "Hṛidaya" is used to mean the essence or the best part, so this tathātā or suchness is the essence or best part of all the dharmas. "Sāra" is used to mean hard and unyielding so tathātā or suchness is taken to mean always changeless.

The Section from
The Treasury Which is An Encyclopædia of Knowledge on Thorough Ascertainments of Provisional and Definitive Within The Three Wheels, and of the Two Truths

This second major topic has three parts:[144]

1. Analysis of the provisional and definitive within the three wheels
2. Analysis of the two truths
3. Analysis of interdependent origination

I. Analysis of the Provisional and Definitive Within the Three Wheels

A. Synopsis
B. The Details Laid Out

---

[144] The seventh chapter of the *Treasury of Knowledge* explains the higher training in prajñā in four major topics: the evaluators to be used to evaluate the meaning of the holy dharma; ascertainments of items to be evaluated before anything else; the main thing to be evaluated, the view; and what must be evaluated before practising the view, the four mind reversers. The first two parts of the second topic are presented here.

A. Synopsis

> The principal thing to be evaluated is the three wheels of
> the holy dharma ...[145]

The principal thing to be evaluated by those evaluators[146] is the house
of treasures of the precious holy dharma which is what is generally
known in the Great Vehicles as "the three different wheels of the
Word"[147]. A classification of the three wheels that is quite clear can
be found within the words of the Buddha in the *Unravelling the Intent
Sutra* where it says:

> The first one, the four truths; the middle one, lack of
> characteristics; the final one, precise distinctions ...

and in *The Extensive Jewel* also, though in just a few words. In the
Sūtra Petitioned by King Dharaṇeśhvara it says:

> In the manner of four truths, the manner of emptiness,
> and the manner of tathāgatagarbha ...

Jetsun Maitreya in the *Highest Continuum* says:

> The wheels of entering the worldly into the path of peace,
> fully ripening them, and giving the prediction ...

---

[145] Lines of the root verses are quoted for a topic then explained. This
is the line for this topic.

[146] The evaluators that will correctly ascertain, because they are valid
cognizers, whatever it is that is being ascertained.

[147] Tib. bka'. "Word" refers here to the Buddha's teaching. The word
involved actually means "command". It is what the Buddha has spoken.
The Buddha Word is given as a directive to sentient beings that they
should follow for their own sakes.

And Ārya Nāgārjuna says:

> At first the wheel that shows self, in the middle that shows
> lack of self, and finally that turns away all bases of
> views ...

the meaning of which was commented on by Āchārya Āryadeva with:

> At first the wheel that turns away no-merit, in the middle
> that turns away self, and finally that turns away all
> views ...

Then there is also the way of dividing them into provisional and definitive and with that, generally, the characteristics of provisional and definitive sūtras are as follows. The characteristic of provisional meaning sūtra is that it is sūtra which, for the class of beings who can be tamed for all three vehicles, principally shows fictional truth in order to have a method that could make the path of definite goodness arise in their mindstreams. And the characteristic of definitive meaning sūtra is that it is sūtra which, in face of those fewer beings to be tamed who can bear the profound meaning, principally shows superfactual truth for the attainment of non-abiding nirvāṇa through meditation on the path of definite goodness[148].

1. How their[149] individual classifications within the three wheels appear in the Buddha Word and in the commentaries on the intent[150]

This has two parts:

---

[148] The "path of definite goodness" is one of many names for the path of dharma taught by the Buddha. It leads definitely to final goodness.

[149] ... the provisional and definitive sūtras just discussed ...

[150] A commentary on the intent is a commentary made by a later person which attempts to get to the actual intent behind a teaching given by someone else. In this case, it means a commentary that attempts to show the Buddha's intent.

1. In the Buddha Word
2. In the commentaries on the intent

a. In the Buddha Word

The following appears in *The Noble One, Unravelling the Intent*:

> The Bhagavat first, in the place of Varaṇāsi, at Ṛiṣhis Dropping in the deer park, for those to be truly placed into the Shrāvaka Vehicle, completely teaching the four truths of the noble ones[151], fully turned the amazing and wondrous dharma wheel which to that time had not been turned in the worlds either of gods or humans, the worlds conducive to dharma, for a first time. That turning of the dharma wheel by the Bhagavat moreover was surpassed, was temporary, and was provisional meaning that could be a ground for debate.
>
> Then the Bhagavat, beginning from no entityness of dharmas, beginning from no birth, no cessation, and primordial peace and naturally perfect nirvāṇa, for those to be truly placed into the Great Vehicle, with the aspect of stating emptiness, turned the even more amazing and wondrous second dharma wheel. That turning of the second dharma wheel by the Bhagavat moreover was surpassed, was temporary, and was provisional meaning that could be a ground for debate.
>
> But then the Bhagavat, beginning from no entityness of dharmas-ness, beginning from no-birth-ness and no-cessation-ness, primordial-peace-ness, and naturally-perfect-nirvāṇa-ness, for those to be truly placed into all vehicles, turned with its precise distinctions the extremely

---

[151] Although sometimes translated as "four noble truths", the Buddha himself clearly stated in a sūtra that it is the four truths fully seen only by noble ones, that is, the ones who have attained the path of seeing.

amazing and wondrous third dharma wheel. This turning
of the dharma wheel by the Bhagavat was not surpassed,
was not temporary, was definitive meaning, so could not
be a ground for debate.

The *Sūtra Petitioned by King Dharaṇeshvara* says:

> Son of the family, it is like this. For example, there is a
> skilled jeweller who knows the craft of jewellery well. Of
> the various types of precious jewel, he has taken a
> precious jewel which is completely dirty. He wets it with
> a penetrating, chemical salt solution then thoroughly
> cleans it with a hair cloth and in that way gives it a
> thorough cleaning. He does not stop his efforts at just
> that, either. Beyond that, to clean it he wets it with a
> penetrating decoction then thoroughly cleans it with a
> woollen flannel and in that way gives it a thorough
> cleaning. He does not stop his efforts at just that, either.
> Beyond that, to clean it he also wets it with a strong
> chemical liquid then thoroughly cleans it with a fine
> cotton cloth and in that way thoroughly cleans it.
> Thoroughly cleansed and free of encrustation, it is now
> called "an excellent type of Lapis Lazuli".
>
> Son of the family, in the same way, the tathāgata,
> knowing the element of totally impure sentient beings[152],
> uses the story of renunciation which is about
> impermanence, suffering, lack of self, and impurity to
> arouse disenchantment in those sentient beings who like
> cyclic existence and to get them into the taming that goes
> with the noble dharma. The tathāgata does not stop his
> efforts at just that much, either. Beyond that, he uses the
> story of emptiness, signlessness, and wishlessness to make
> them realize the mode of a tathāgata. The tathāgata does

---

[152] Element is a name for tathāgatagarbha as described in the previous
selection.

not stop his efforts at just that much, either. Beyond that,
he uses the story of the non-regressing wheel and the
story of the three spheres of total purity to make those
sentient beings who have the cause of varying natures to
enter the tathāgata's place.

b. In commentaries on the intent

The root master of commentary on the intent, Regent Maitreya,
commented on the meaning of the later sūtra scripture and said that
the reason for the three turnings is as follows. The first wheel enters
those to be tamed who are attached to cyclic existence into the path
of peace by urging them on with the story of renunciation. Then
they are thoroughly ripened in the Great Vehicle with the story of
emptiness. And the final one causes them to enter the tathāgata's
place and to obtain the great prediction with the story of the non-
regressing wheel.

Noble one Asaṅga, summarizing what was said, cites scripture from
Unravelling the Intent and makes the final wheel the ultimate definitive meaning, and Vasubhandu and others follow. Still, noble one
Asaṅga and his brother do not say that the middle one is provisional
in meaning; in the *Vyakhaya-yukti*[153], root and commentary, they say
that it has to be referred to as definitive, and the great charioteer,
glorious Dharmapāla, in the *Vijñaptisiddhi* explains both wheels even
to be definitive meaning.

Noble one Nāgārjuna makes the third approach in the *Dharaṇeśhvara
Sūtra*[154] definitive meaning and Āryadeva does likewise. Tibetan
teachers have no choice but to make assertions that concur top to
bottom with these commentaries on the intent, because that is really

---

[153] One of Vasubhandu's eight Prakaraṇa.

[154] See the earlier quote from this sūtra.

how it is! Later commentators who held the real lineage of Maitreya did not go outside the system mentioned above.[155]

Now in regard to this, note that Chandra in his commentary to Nāgārjuna's tradition[156] did not make this type of classification by going through everything from top to bottom but made his distinction merely on the meaning of provisional and definitive contained in the *Sūtra Taught by Inexhaustible Intellect*. Many blather-filled dissections of the middle and final wheels into provisional and definitive, higher and lower meanings have been seen to come from Tibetan teachers on the basis of an incomplete examination of the meaning of the intent contained in that sūtra. Moreover, others who speak about the eight sections that analyse provisional and definitive in this sūtra do place both middle and final wheels equally on the definitive meaning side. Even though Chandra, basing himself on the eighth section about lack of self, posits just emptiness of the two selves as definitive, Asaṅga and brother together with followers show

---

[155] This is a clever way of criticising the Tibetan Buddhist schools who made a point of defining provisional and definitive within the three wheels according to their own interpretations but whose definitions did not fit with the Buddha's own statements or those great Indian masters in the tradition. If Buddha and his most important followers all say it is a certain way, then how on earth could someone later, such as Tsongkhapa, claim some thing else and still be within the Buddhist tradition? This is a key part of the debate between the Other Emptiness followers of Tibet and their opponents. It is a particularly important point for readers to note.

[156] ... Chandrakīrti in his text *Entering the Middle Way* which is intended as a commentary that would perfectly elucidate the meaning of Nāgārjuna's approach ...

through precise distinctions[157] that the meaning there is a lack of self as determined by the childish. It says in the *Unravelling the Intent*:

> ... if realization is in regard to self, it is unsuitable; this I have not taught to the childish ...[158]

And, in the *Aṅgulimālā*:

> The bhagavats say to search all dharmas carefully but that self of worldly ones is a mere thumb ...[159]

down to:

> ... that self referred to with "it is like this" is something that none of the buddhas and none of the śhrāvakas have been able to find; manifest buddhas explain this to living beings.

and so on. And, the *Descent Into Laṅka* says:

---

[157] ... as done in the third turning of the wheel ...

[158] In other words, the Buddha did teach realization in relation to a self as a lesser approach that was suitable for less mature beings. That sort of realization, ultimately speaking, is not suitable, but he did not say such a thing to the less mature beings because it would not help them on their journey.

[159] There are two points here. Firstly, as with the preceding quote, the buddhas tell less mature beings to seek for a self in all dharmas so that it can be negated. However, that is a much lesser approach to dharmas that could be put, from a higher perspective, as still part of worldly dharma. From the higher perspective, such as that taught in the tathāgatagarbha teachings of the final wheel or in the tantras, such teaching on self and selflessness is a minor thing compared to the final teaching of reality.

Aṅgulimāla was a man who killed people and cut off their thumbs. He had been told by a false guru to make a rosary of one thousand such thumbs in order to attain liberation. The Buddha caught up with him on his 999th thumb and brought him into the order. Later he became an arhat. The reference to "thumb" is not accidental.

The tathāgatagarbha teaching is not the same as the
Tīrthikas propounding a self ...

and so on, and:

Overt clinging to a self is not to be done.

The meaning of those and other statements having been determined,
we accept that the middle and final wheels are equally definitive
meaning and that definitive meaning is specialized into non-ultimate,
which is the cutting of elaboration, and ultimate, which shows
actuality[160].

B. The Details Laid Out

This has five parts:
1. The system accepted in common
2. The system of advocates of lack of entityness
3. The system of Yogāchāra
4. Linking with the noble ones' acceptance
5. Turning away wrong conceptions of provisional meaning and
   establishing same intent

1. The System Accepted in Common

The first is provisional meaning, everyone concurs.

Every one of the Great Vehicle advocates concurs that the first wheel,
since it is defined principally in view of fictional truth, is a teaching
predominantly of provisional meaning.

2. The System of Advocates of Lack of Entityness

The advocates of lack of entityness accept that "The

---

[160] He is stating his final acceptance in the matter, that is, what he will
assert as his position.

middle one is definitive meaning and the final one principally provisional meaning".
There are no actual scriptural references; it is established
through agreement with reasoning.

The advocates of lack of entityness accept that, "The middle wheel
is the teaching of ultimate definitive meaning and the final one a
teaching principally of provisional meaning." They have no actual
scriptural references from the sūtra section that clearly define it that
way. For them, it is established as being in agreement with reasoning
that relies merely on scripture that generally distinguishes provisional
and definitive.

3. The System of Yogāchāra

The middle one cuts elaboration, it is non-ultimate
definitive meaning;
The final one determines the superfactual, it is ultimate
Definitive meaning", is the Yogāchāra system.
Scriptural references are those stated by the Conqueror
himself and
The system of the prophesied maker of distinctions, the
third-level noble one that
Connects with the examples and meanings in the
reasonings of cleaning a jewel, and so on.
"Rangjung", "Dolpo", "Drimed Ozer", and so on
Accepted principally this later one, others the earlier one.

The middle wheel, because it cuts elaborations of grasping at
extremes on the sides of the view, is the non-ultimate definitive
meaning. The final one, because it is what explicitly determines that
superfactual actuality, individual self-knowing wisdom itself, is the
ultimate definitive meaning", appears in the Yogāchāra followers
textual system. And, as mentioned in the scriptural sources cited
above, the conqueror himself sanctioned this, actually saying so in
the sūtra section and furthermore, in the *Great Drum Sūtra* with:

Whoever might teach emptiness, all are to know which
ones have the intent. They are to know that these ones
like this unsurpassable sūtra are not ones that have the
intent.

Thus, he over and again differentiates extremely clearly the modes
of provisional and definitive in the sūtras demonstrating the garbha.
But that is not all, there is the system of the prophesied maker of
distinctions into provisional and definitive, the noble one who had
gained the third level, Asaṅga, together with his brother, in which
connections are made with the examples and their meanings like with
the reasonings taught in the *Dharaṇeśhvara Sūtra* of cleaning a jewel
in stages, and so on.

From among Tibetan āchāryas, the All-Knowing Conqueror Rangjung, the great All-Knowing one, Dolpopa, All-Knowing Drimey
Ozer, and so on, together with their followers, appeared as the
principal acceptors of this later system and most other very well-
known Tibetan teachers accepted the earlier one.

4. Linking With the Noble One's Acceptance

In particular, he accepted that non-virtue, view of self,
and all bases of views,
Are reversed in the first, middle, and final wheels,
Though there is acceptance of connection
With three types of dharma wheel ...

In particular, noble one Nāgārjuna and lineage holders have said:

Someone who understands that
In the first non-merit is reversed,
In the middle one self is reversed,
And in the final one, all bases of views are reversed is an
expert.

In other words, he said that non-virtue, view of a self, and all bases
that turn into views are reversed in the first, middle, and final ones

respectively though Tibetan teachers accept a step-wise connection with the three types of dharma wheel, too. Moreover, the first was for the purpose of establishing beings un-mistakenly in adoption and rejection within fictional truth so that they could see superfactual truth; the second was done for the sake of reversing self-grasping through teaching the accountable superfactual truth which is a cessation of one side of elaboration; the third, done for the purpose of reversing every basis of view—existence and non-existence, and so on—was the actual showing of superfactual truth which is beyond all elaborations. Following on from that, the earlier explanation that "The middle wheel itself is posited as the final one" is what the self empty and the other empty groups accept. The Other Emptiness advocates as other emptiness advocates say that "turning away self" is connected to the meaning of "establishment of lack of self which is freedom from elaboration" and that "turning away all bases of view" is connected with the meaning of being "beyond the emptiness of attribute analysis" and this is explained as concurring with the intent of both the sūtra and scripture cited above and the sequence given in them.[161]

And also, in regard to that, All-knowing Rangjung's personally stated acceptance was:

> Noble one's "wheel that turns away all views" and Jetsun Maitreya's "prophesy wheel" both do, in general, come down to the same one point; the final wheel, if it is that, is the wheel that shows freedom from elaboration because that is the common key point. It is done from the perspective of several special particulars, not one: the earlier one was not spoken of due just to freedom from elaboration and the later one comes from specifying that the freedom-from-elaboration wisdom is what is experienced

---

[161] Attribute and overall analysis were explained previously in the author's explanations in the two truths and two emptinesses chapter. They are also explained in the glossary.

by individually self-knowing wisdom. "But", you query, "Nāgārjuna and his lineage-holders did not accept free-from-elaboration wisdom, did they?" That is not so, because it was explicitly taught in the *Collection of Praises*, the Yogāchāra *Four Hundred*, and other places[162].

5. Turning Away Wrong Conceptions of Provisional Meaning and Establishing Same Intent

> One person's concept that provisional meaning not being
> true is false
> Is a wrong concept; the Buddha Word does not have
> falsity in it.

One person who, not possessing the eye of stainless prajñā, has the concept that everything of provisional meaning that was spoken, because it is not true in superfact is false and not something that could be taken as a reliance. That is a wrong concept that comes from one's own rational mind's hundreds of confusions; the Buddha Word does not ever have falsity and deceptiveness in it. Provisional even is true as a provisional meaning because of which it truly does lead to the profound actuality.

Thus, saying, "We are Middle Wayists" is derided in other places in the Excellent Speech. And saying, "I am a Secret Mantra person" is tossed away like grass in the śrāvakas's baskets of teaching, and so on. And especially, as Lord Mikyo Dorje said:[163]

---

[162] ... all of which were written by Nāgārjuna.

[163] The ninth Karmapa was complaining that some Nyingma followers are so busy with Guru Rinpoche as the source of their teaching and so involved with only that teaching that they put Guru Rinpoche above the Buddha as the founding teacher and do not even make the effort to listen to the basic teachings of the Buddha, such as the thirty-seven factors conducive to enlightenment, and so on.

These present-day so-called Nyingma followers who do not accept Buddha Śhākyamuni as the founding teacher and have never even heard the dharmas conducive to enlightenment cannot be included in the line of the insiders.

Therefore one needs to examine and analyse the issue of dharmas that are to be abandoned, then pay attention to it.

> The way of appearances' elaboration cutting and actuality
>   are explicitly taught
> So it is accepted by the great charioteers, and so on, that
>   all dharmas have the same intent.

The modes of teaching which are the cutting of elaboration of the fictional that is the way that things appear and the explicit teaching of the superfactual actuality were taught because of the grades of faculty, coarse and subtle, that occur. Thus, it is accepted by the great charioteer eminent Nāgārjuna, and the others that all the dharma doors taught by the conqueror have the same intent.

Further to that, the *Root Prajñā* says:

> The bhagavat by knowing things and non-things
> Did, in oral instruction to Katyāyana,
> Negate both existence and non-existence ...

meaning that all of the teaching that the āyatanas exist that appears in the first wheel is known to be intended in regard to mere appearance because of the oral instruction of freedom from the extremes of existence and non-existence existing in the first wheel. And it says:

> That nirvāṇa is a single truth
> Is taught by the conquerors.
> At that time, the extra "wrong"
> Is something no expert attempts to realize ...

which means that, in the middle wheel, form up to omniscience is given as the fictional, compounded extra that is wrong and, with an entity of being empty of elaborations, uncompounded nirvāṇa is taught as a single truth. And, in the *Middle Way Stages of Meditation*:

> By pure prajñā like that
> This self-entity of superfact
> Is established in the extreme, therefore,
> By examination it does not become other, a thing.

This means that the explicit teachings of the meditational meaning concur with the final wheel. Especially, the contents of the *Collection of Praises* brings to life the meaning of the final wheel. Then, the *Enlightenment Mind Commentary* also, through linking that so that it is unified with the profound meaning of mantra, does not engage in the cessation of one thing by another. And, it is also illustrated by the clear statement of noble one Asaṅga:

> Advocates and opponents of the sūtra section are abandoning the holy dharma.

So it is that Jetsun Maitreya said:

> To this, the way that it has to be taken, defined by the Buddha himself and given by him as un-muddled, carefully arranged advice, not able to keep my palms separate, I join them indeed[164].

II. Classifications of the Two Truths

This has two parts:
  A. The limits of the explanation

---

[164] The Buddha, knowing how the three wheels should be presented, taught them as advice in a perfectly clear and unmixed way. This is amazing and worthy of prostration, so Maitreya puts his hands together at his heart in the standard Buddhist gesture of homage.

  B. The actual classification

A. The Limits of the Explanation

The holy dharma was spoken based on the two truths.

Every one of the doors of holy dharma taught by the tathāgata were spoken based on the two truths. The tathāgata said in the *Meeting of Father and Son:*[165]

> The Knower Of The World gave his teaching
> Through the two truths themselves, not from listening to others.
> They were the fictional and the superfactual;
> There was no third truth given at all.

following on from which eminent Nāgārjuna said:

> The dharma taught by the buddhas
> Really is taught as the two truths;
> They are the worldly fictional truth and
> The superior one's factual truth.

B. The Actual Classification

This has five parts:
  1. Entity
  2. Precise definition
  3. Characteristics together with enumerations
  4. Divisions
  5. The need for understanding

√ 1. Entity

> Their entities in overview are contrived and
>   uncontrived—

---

[165] This sūtra came from the meeting of the Buddha with his son Rāhula.

> Ordinary being's rational imputation and noble one's
> equipoise fact.

For those truths, the individual way of assertion for each of the various tenets results in many varying identifications of what they are. However, generally what those of the Great Vehicle accept is that fictional truth is contrivance and exaggeration and that superfactual truth is no contrivance and no exaggeration. Then specifically, according to the peak of tenets, the Consequence system, it says in the *Entrance*:[166]

> He said, "By seeing all things as correct and false,
> Those things are taken as two entities.
> That which is the object of correct seeing is superfactual
> And of false seeing is fictional truth."

This means that each of these dharmas from form up to omniscience is observed as having a twofold nature or entity. According to that, there is the entity which the childish get without examination or analysis of things which is obtained via rational mind engaging things simply as such and there is the entity which the noble ones get in their equipoise which is obtained via wisdom that has no conceptual thinking.

The former of the two is called "fictional truth". Ignorance is obscured in relation to seeing suchness, so it is called "fictional". When ignorance apprehends that fiction as true and does not realize its suchness, it makes a fact in accordance with the grasped aspect and, because for the childish ones that fact is not deceptive, it is called "truth"[167]. This is covered by what was said there:[168]

---

[166] ... *Entrance to the Middle Way* by Chandrakīrti.

[167] Ignorance does not see things as they are so it is given the name "a fiction". The ignorance itself becomes the perceiving side of mind that is holding or has grasped the things of the fiction to be true. As long as it is doing that and does not realize suchness—which would then stop

(continued...)

✓"Ignorance, because it obscures the nature, is fictional,
And what it contrives appearing as true
Is fictional truth". That is how the Sage said it.
Things[169], having been contrived, are fictional.

The latter one is called "superfactual truth". The noble ones'
equipoise wisdom that has no conceptual thinking engages actuality
just as it is, so is called "superior"[170], and its domain, because there
is no deceptiveness about any of its facts[171] or you can say superficies,
is "truth".

2. Etymological Definition

Etymological definition: compounded is true in fiction.
One is true as the superior fact.

---

[167](...continued)
the whole, fictional process—it creates what it thinks of as an external
object, which in fact is just the other aspect of mind from the grasping,
the aspect that appears as the grasped at object. This grasped at object
is a fact for this dualistic mind. Because it is taken as a fact for mind that
really is so, with nothing deceptive about it, it is called "truth". This
explanation of duality in the style of a grasper and grasped at duality
follows the Mind Only, Other Emptiness, and tantric presentations of
the working of dualistic mind, and is part of Jamgon Kongtrul's
presentation as a follower of Other Emptiness.

[168] ... in the previously referenced text, the *Entering the Middle Way* ...

[169] Tib. dngos po. The things of an ordinary person are actually concept
labels, so in these discussions "things" does not mean an external thing
but a conceptually created thing.

[170] Tib. dam pa. This term means "superior" or "high type of thing" or
"holy".

[171] Tib. don. "Fact" is the name for what appears on the surface of any
given mind. Another word for the same thing is "superfice".

The etymological definitions that go with the meanings of the terms for the two truths are as follows. In Sanskrit language, the application of "later augmentation" results in the term "saṃvṛti", which is in Tibetan, "kun dzob"[172] [and in English "fiction"]. It is explained that it is used with the meanings: "the true situation obscured", "assemblage" or "collection", "(the contrivance of) a sign made up to communicate meaning" or "convention", "individual distinction", and "falseness"[173].

---

[172] The Sanskrit word here is "samvṛtti". This word is constructed in Sanskrit by starting with the root "vṛtti" which gives the main meaning and then joining the modifier "sam" to it to give further meaning to the root. This results in "vṛittisam". However, the Sanskrit grammar rule called Later Augmentation states that modifiers like this have to be moved into the prefix position. This results in "samvṛtti". The parts of the term are translated into Tibetan with "kun" translating "sam" and "rdzob" translating "vṛtti". Although the etymology of the Tibetan and the Sanskrit is well-stated by Jamgon Kongtrul, it is necessary for us to go back to the Sanskrit in order to gain a correct translation into English. When that is done, we find that "samvṛtti" is a term that was in regular use in Sanskrit, not only for spiritual purposes but in normal language, too. It means something that is a deliberately created falsehood, designed to deceive another. In fact, it turns out to be the exact equivalent of the English "fiction" or "fictional".

[173] Jamgon Kongtrul gives these equivalents according to the meanings that have been given in Sanskrit by earlier Indian commentators. What is crucial for the reader to understand is that principal meanings for the original Sanskrit are "deliberate distortion" and "the actual situation deliberately obscured". The sense of "collection" and the like comes from the idea of several things being put together to create a fiction, more like in English, a "construction". The sense of "conventions" and other things made to communicate a meaning is the sense of something that has been deliberately invented to convey a certain meaning but which again means a fiction, not the actual situation.

For the first of those, we get that ignorance which is an afflicted thing functions as an obscurer of the nature of the authentic, that is, superfactual truth, so is called "fictional", and, for the mindstream of the person controlled by it, the composite dharmas that appear to the valid cognizers which it rules, because of being true within the fiction are designated as such[174]. The *Entrance* explains it with:

> Ignorance, because it obscures the nature, is fictional ...

For the second of those, we get that those assemblages exist in a mutual dependence of one upon the other, like a house and its rafters, not because of a single solidly-existing thing that could be pointed to. Thus, they are "fabrications".

For the third of those, we see in *Clear Words*:

> Alternatively, saṃvṛtti comes to mean in the end, "(the contrivance of) a sign used to communicate meaning[175]", that is, "convention used in the world". Alternatively, it is that which has the characteristics of expressor and that to be expressed, knower and that to be known, and so on.[176]

For the fourth of those, we see in *Blaze of Reasoning*:

---

[174] This is the main meaning of the Sanskrit etymology and the one that fits closely with "fiction".

[175] This is the word in Tibetan and Sanskrit for a word or other symbol which is used to convey meaning to others. In English we do call these conventions and likewise, in Tibetan and Sanskrit, they are called "conventions" as a synonym for "sign used to communicate meaning".

[176] The meaning here is "a contrivance" made up by the world for the purpose of conveying meaning. Again, this fits with "fictional" which is the main meaning in the Sanskrit word saṃvṛtti.

> Things of form, and so on, because all of them are
> individual distinguished items, are fictional ...[177]

For the fifth of those, we get that, because of meaning "unable to withstand analysis", it is "a fiction". Āchārya Haribhadra said it like this:

> Unable to withstand the onslaught of thorough analysis,
> therefore, "fiction".[178]

Then, the other one, the term "paramārtha satya" translated into Tibetan with "don dam bden pa" [and into English with "superfactual truth"] is parsed as follows: the "parama" or "dam pa" [or "super"] actually there in the term[179] is the wisdom of the mindstream of a noble one remaining in equipoise; the "artha" or "don" [or "fact"] refers to the emptiness which has become its domain; and "satya" or "bden pa" [or "truth"] refers to their being no deceptiveness in relation to all the superficies of that emptiness.

Then there is the assertion that it can be parsed as follows: there is what corresponds to that "parama" or "dam pa" [or "super"]— inferential reasoning consciousness—given which "artha" or "don"

---

[177] All the things of form and so on known to ordinary beings are items that are produced in a conceptual process of distinguishing each one individually, one from the other. This does not represent their actual nature but is purely an invention. This again accords with the sense of "fiction".

[178] The "falseness" given in the list of possible meanings at the top of this section specifically means something that is being shown as something which it actually is not. For example, putting on a smile when feeling very angry, and so on. This also fits closely with the primary meaning of saṃvrtti and again closely matches "fiction".

[179] The Tibetan is "dam pa'i don" which is often reduced to "don dam". Thus he is saying, the "dam pa" which really is present in "don dam".

[or "fact"] refers to the emptiness that has the characteristic of non-affirming negation and which has become its domain, and "satya" or "bden pa" [or "truth"] to its not being deceptive in the face of reasoning that examines and analyses. This latter one is spoken of as "corresponding" or "assessed" superfactual truth and every engagement in analysis of the two truths in the Middle Way treatises has been argued only from this, not the other, because in actual superfactual truth there is no activity of conceptual thought analysis involved. That conventionally there are two superfactuals and what their respective characteristics are is clearly stated in the *Blaze of Reasoning*.

3. Characteristics Together With Enumerations

> The characteristics: objects of non-analytical, confused
>   awarenesses and
> Objects of un-confused noble ones are deceptive and un-
>   deceptive.
> The apprehension styles of the subjects[180] are confused
>   and un-confused.
> Those are taught through many enumerations of names.

The individual characteristics of the two are as follows. The falsity which is the sight of an exaggerated or contrived entity, the obtained fact[181] obtained on the face of a non-analytical, childish awareness, has the character of fictional truth. The authentic which is the sight

---

[180] Tib. yul can. That is, the awareness or that which has objects.

[181] Tib. rnyed don. The obtained fact is what an awareness comes to know, what it discovers or obtains.

of not exaggerated or un-contrived entity, the obtained fact obtained on the face of a noble one's reasoning, has the character of super-factual. Pha Tshab's chief son Ma Bya Byang Tson[182] said:

> The object of non-analytical confused awareness is
>   fictional;
> The object of un-confused noble one's awareness is
>   superfactual.

In accord with his explanation, many awarenesses are posited as "confused awareness" due to their simply being confused in regard to the appearing object. In the same way, reasoning awarenesses, which are inferential, also are posited as such; they are analytical awarenesses, but, because of the foregoing definition, the term "non-analytical" will be put with them. Nonetheless, in this case here, the object's truth or falsity is being set based on its being deceptive versus not deceptive and the subject's truth or falsity is being set based on its style of apprehension of it being un-confused versus confused.

There are very many enumerations of their names because of the acceptances of the individual tenet systems. According to the Middle Way system, as the *Middle and Extremes* says:

> If emptiness is summarized,
> Suchness and authentic limit,
> Signlessness and superfactual,
> And dharmadhātu are its enumerations.
> Other[183] names are not mistaken.

And, when the sūtra by noble one Droldey[184] is followed, eleven enumerations are explained. And, Āchārya Chandra also explains many enumerations. Then, the other side of that will be the

---

[182] He was an important translator of early Tibet and his son also was a translator.

[183] These other ...

[184] Tib. grol sde. He was an Autonomous Middle Way master.

enumerations of the names of fictional truth: "mere sign that communicates meaning", "mere name", "mere designation", "mere convention", and so on are expressed for it.

4. Division

This has five parts:
 a. The things to be distinguished
 b. The reason for the distinctions
 c. Definite count of two
 d. Same or different?
 e. The ways of assertion of the individual tenets

a. The things to be distinguished

This has two parts:
 1. General distinction
 2. Particulars of the distinction

(1) General distinction

> On the basis of distinction, the mere un-analysed knowable,
> The way things appear and their actuality, fictional and superfactual, are distinguished.[185]

Generally, the Buddha said in sūtra that fictional is that there is not a knowable in face of rigpa and that superfactual is that there is not a knowable in face of confusion[186] but that, without having made the

---

[185] Root verse.

[186] Rigpa is the knower when superfact is seen and confusion is the knower when fictional is seen.

distinction, this mere knowable that comes in the face of no examination, no analysis is the basis of the distinction of the two truths. As he said:

> That which could be known is exhausted in just these two
> truths.

Regarding that, it says in the *Root Prajñā*:

> The world is fictional truth and
> Superfactual truth.

Like that, two truths are distinguished with the dharmas of deception being fictional truth and the non-deceptive ones being the super-factual truth, or two truths are distinguished from the perspective of the ways things appear and the way they actually are, their actuality.

(2) Particulars of the distinction

> The way they appear, confusion, the rational mind
>   appearances of migrators are
> Mostly accepted as un-confused path and fruition.
> Beings and noble ones, worldly ones and yogins, fictional
>   and
> Superfactual inseparable in entity, the three
>   characteristics.
> Through the door of itemized dharmas the sixteen,
>   etcetera, are distinguished.

In terms of the way that things appear, there are two ways of appearance: confused and unconfused. The confused way of appearance is as follows. As much as shines forth in the rational mind of migrators of confused appearance, confused grasping, confused knowing, it is deceptive and not true, so from hell-beings up to buddhas, the whole extent of appearance that can be conceived of and expressed is designation made with rational-mind-made imagery. Because of that it does not connect with fact, so is explained as confusion. Further to that, the ability to function as a fact that occurs with appearances of the four elements, and so on is posited as correct fictional and the inability to function as a fact that occurs with appearances like those of two moons is posited as wrong fictional[187].

Unconfused fictional is of two sorts. Coming from the fruition, non-confused path wisdom together with its good qualities increases whereby one journeys to the place of impermanence and the inner character; in relation to that, there is non-confusion. And, from having obtained the fruition, unconfused buddha wisdom together with the form kāyas resides in Akaniṣṭha. These are mainly accepted by the Svatāntrika. Further, this system's acceptance of authentic fictional, the direct perceptions of the faculties apprehending forms, sounds, and so on of a mindstream which is looking hither, is so because of the influence of their assertion that their own appearing object is not confused. The Prasaṅgikas, because of asserting that those awarenesses are also confused regarding their own appearing object, do not accept them as correct fictional and proclaim that, if they are fictional, they must be wrong. Additionally, assertion and non-assertion of establishment by self-character also comes into play with this, therefore the latter group who are involved with character-istics say "It is a very subtle topic".

Alternatively, it becomes the two types of fictional of ordinary beings and of noble ones. The first is distinguished because of the moons reflected in water, echoes, and so on, which even the childish resolve as being false and deceptive dharmas. The second is distinguished because of the forms, sounds, and so on which are strongly clung to by the childish but which the ones who see the noble one's dharmas

---

[187] These definitions are connected with the Sūtra Followers school in which appearances of things that can actually perform a function are not only fictional truth but are correct fictional truth. Things like the appearance of two moons that comes when you press your eyes while looking at the moon cannot perform a function and are defined as wrong fictional truth.

consider to be illusion-like constructions, dummy-like and essence-less things.

Alternatively, a distinction into two types: worldly one's fictional and yogin's fictional has been taught. Shāntideva said:

> For yogins there is no fault in being fictional ...

and Chandra said:

> The way that what the seven types make out as non-
>   existent[188]
> Is claimed "to exist" is an existence not found by yogins.

The basis of a name—the coarse itemized dharmas on the face of non-examining, non-analytic confusion—are the fictional of the worldly ones. The obtained fact of a rational mind that has conventions in the face of slight analysis such as subtle impermanence, and the post-attainment appearances of noble ones starting from the no-more-training shrāvakas and going up through the bodhisatva noble ones is the yogin's fictional.

For the enumerations of name also, for the former one there are "unexamined", "childish ones' reasoning awareness", and "un-related fictional" and for the latter one there are "analytical", "noble one's reasoning consciousnesses", "related", and "Middle Way followers fictional". The wrong and correct fictional of this context here are also posited as the two truths of the world's own level, too.

---

[188] Yogins, by using the seven reasonings of a chariot given in Chandrakīrti's text *Entering the Middle Way*, know that what ordinary people say exists is non-existent.

There is no distinguishing done from the perspective of the entity
in superfactual truth because it is a totality of one-taste like space and
because it is beyond the objects of conventions; the *Stack of Jewels*
says:

> Bhikṣhus! This superior truth is one. It is like this; it is a
> non-deceptive dharmin[189] of nirvāṇa.

If distinguished using mere verbal expressions, two were spoken of:
from the lesser truth there is the assessed superfactual truth and then
the un-assessed superfactual truth. The first is being separated just
partially free from elaboration; it is like absence of birth where birth
has merely been prevented. The latter is freedom from elaboration
in its entirety.

If distinguished from the perspective of what is to be negated in the
assessed superfactual truth, it is both the lack of persons and lack of
self of dharmas. If distinguished from the perspective of its characteristics, it is the three emancipations of emptiness, signlessness,
and wishlessness, or with four parts, no manifest gathering. If distinguished from the perspective of itemized phenomena (dharmins),
it will be distinguished as the sixteen emptinesses or, with others
included, the eighteen or twenty emptinesses.

b. The reason for the distinctions

> The difference in style of apprehension of noble and
>   childish ones and
> Based on a defined relationship ...

The reasoning behind distinguishing the two truths is this. It too
comes from the differing apprehension styles of rational mind of the
two persons, noble ones and childish ones. For that reason, it is a

---

[189] Usually dharmin means a phenomenon known by a samsaric mind.
However, here it means something known within the nirvanic context.

distinction into two truths from the perspective of the subject[190]. It is not that, with regard to the fact, it is present as two, because if it were present in the fictional fact, it would change to being the fictional, and if in the other, it would change to being two superfactual truths.

For that reason, it is also not the case, as seen in some presentations, that "In not being present in the fictional fact, it is superfactual"; because it is defined in mutual relation to the classification of apprehension of truth.

Thus, the statement "The meaning of free from extremes is the superfactual truth and the other is fictional truth" which comes in connection with the verbal statements of those having strong grasping resulting in the proposition that fictional is on superfactual's side is not defined anywhere in the system of the Middle Way itself. For as long as the meaning of "freed of expression" has not been realized, for that long it also is not the Middle Way, because the Middle Way's meaning in that case has not been realized.

c. Definite count

It says:

> Definite as two truths ...

meaning that the truths definitely have a count of two—the fictional and superfactual. *Descent Into Laṅka* says:

> Fictional and superfactual;
> There is no third arisen from cause.
> Fictional is concept's designation;
> That exhausted is the noble ones' domain.

---

[190] ... meaning the knower, not the object known.

and, the *Meeting of Father and Son* says:

> The tathāgata fully comprehended both fictional and
> superfactual so all that could be known is done with in
> this fiction and superfact.

For acceptance and rejection, which is principally done from the side
of reasoning or method, it would not be suitable to have no fictional.
For what is principally something to be taken up, complete purity
without references, it would not be suitable to have no superfactual.
If there were less, not everything would be included, and by just this
amount all the needs of a being are fulfilled, so for this reason more
are not necessary.

Alternatively, the subject, the rational mind is definite as two, confusion and non-confusion and, because it would not be acceptable
to have no classification of fictional in relation to the former and
superfactual in relation to the latter, the truths are definite as two.

d. Same or different?

> Conventionally, one nature with different facets;
> Superfactually, same or different cannot be expressed.[191]

Concerning the truths' mode of being the same or different, the tenet
systems do not concur, they have their individual ways of acceptance.
However, Glorious Rangjung verbally stated:

> These two truths that have been explained, dharmas and
> dharmatā, are within just exactly what is, within total
> liberation from one thing and something other, so their
> sameness or difference cannot be expressed.

Like that, we accept that the two truths taken in the face of non-
analysis, that is, just conventionally, are different facets of one nature,

---

[191] This is the root verse for this section.

whereas in superfact whether their entities are the same or different is altogether inexpressible.

Additionally, if they were the same, many faults would accrue: the childish would as they comprehend fictional truth also realize superfactual truth, so there would be the consequence that they would have effortless liberation; there are the consequences that, the fictional would, like superfact, be without distinctions and would be the cause of complete purification, and that superfact would, like the fictional, have a variety of distinctions and would be observed as something that increased total affliction, and so on. If they were different, many damaging arguments would accrue: there would be the consequences that yogins would realize the superfactual but would not be able to abandon strong grasping at the fictional, that the superfactual would not be the fictional's dharmatā, and so on. For these reasons, the *Unravelling the Intent* says:

> Formative's elements[192] and superfactual's characteristic,
> Have the characteristic "free of same and different".
> Any realization of it as same or different
> Is to have entered something which does not correspond
>   to their actual situation. ✕

e. The ways of assertion of the individual tenets

> If destroyed or eliminated, apprehension of it could be
>   rejected.
> Non-rejected coarse things and awareness's continuum
>   are fictional;

---

[192] Formatives are the contents of the fourth skandha, for the most part they are the afflictions. They drive the formation of future samsaric versions of any being. Beings produced in this process have a certain set of elements which are their constitution, karmically produced by the formatives.

The partless are superfactual truth. That is the
     Particularist system.[193]

Generally speaking, just classification into two truths is declared by all advocates of tenets. Additionally, the śhrāvakass advocate that:

When something is destroyed or by rational mind other-
     eliminated[194],
It is not engaged by rational mind.
For such as water-pots existing in fiction,
The superfactual existence is other.

If things are destroyed by destroyers such as hammers, and so on, or substantial dharmas are individually eliminated by rational mind, their rationalizations are not engaged. Thereby, pots which could be rejected and the water, etcetera, inside them, are fictional and where such rationalization of them is not rejected by destruction or mental dissection, the consciousness generated independently, the apprehenders of forms, sounds, etcetera are superfactual. Both of those, the thing and what exists as its essence, are posited as truths. In summary, the Vaibhaṣhikas assert that coarse things and the

---

[193] The tenets of the four philosophical schools of Buddhism will now be presented. This is the root verse for the lowest of the two Lesser Vehicle philosophical schools, the Vaibhaśhika or Particularist school.

[194] Tib. gzhan sel. From *A Partial Commentary to "The Miraculous Key Which Opens A Door to The Treasury Of Knowledge and Sums Up The Reasonings in The Ocean Of Texts on Reasoning"*: "Other elimination is a particular mode of something being removed from knowledge in rational mind. The definition of an other eliminator is a phenomenon that is realized through negating explicitly its object of elimination. It is eliminating with explicit words through conjoining the words. For example, if you say 'this is a man', then that eliminates that it could be a woman. If you say 'it is daytime', then that eliminates that it is night. So, through connecting those words you have eliminated an object to be eliminated. Thus it is an other eliminator. Other elimination is the mode of engagement of a conceptual consciousness."

continuum of awareness are fictional and that things' partless atoms and awarenesses' partless instants are superfactual truth[195].

❁   ❁   ❁

> The self- and generally-characterized of being able and
> not able
> To perform a function in superfactual is the Sutra
> Follower system.[196]

In the *Complete Commentary*[197] it says:

> What in superfactual is able to perform a function,
> That here is superfactual existence;
> Other is fictional existence.

---

[195] Khenpo Tsultrim Gyatso said, "What this amounts to is that both outer substantial things which are made up of indivisible atoms and inner mental things which are made of indivisible moments of consciousness are reducible either by external means such as physical destruction or internal means such as mental dissection. When such things are reduced and hence eliminated, their rationalization has been eliminated, that is, they no longer appear to the mind. Such things which can be reduced in that way are said to be fictional truths. When such a process is applied to something and it does not result in the removal of the appearance of the object to the rational mind, the consciousness apprehending that thing, whatever it is, is an independent consciousness. The partless atoms themselves which cannot be reduced and the partless moments of consciousness themselves which cannot be reduced and which give rise to independent consciousnesses are superfactual truths."

[196] This is the root verse for Sautrāntika or Followers of Sūtra school. This is the second of the four philosophical schools of Buddhism and the highest of the two Lesser Vehicle philosophical schools.

[197] *The Complete Commentary on Pramāṇa* of Dharmakīrti.

Those are asserted to be self- and generally-characterized[198].

Like that, that such as a pot or pillar which is able to perform a function in the superfactual is superfactual truth and that such as space, a pot generality, or a pillar generality which is not able to perform a function in superfactual is fictional truth. In short, what exists as self-characterized and what exists as generally-characterized are asserted to be those respectively and existence is asserted to be the meaning of truth. Here, some later experts have explained that, "Superfactual truth, impermanence, thing, compound, and self-characterized have the same meaning and fictional truth, permanence, non-thing dharma, non-compound, and generally-characterized have the same meaning."

❀   ❀   ❀

---

[198] Khenpo Tsultrim Gyatso said, "The Sautrāntika system, the higher of the two philosophical schools of the Lesser Vehicle, presents the two truths in terms of what is not able and able to perform a function in superfact. Additionally, what is not able to perform a function in superfact is said to be generally-characterized and what is able to perform a function in superfact is said to be self- or specifically-characterized. The distinction between generally and self-characterized phenomena can be seen through the example of a tent pole. The superfactual tent pole is the one that has its own, specific characteristic of being able to hold up a tent; without such a pole, the tent really would fall down. The fictional tent-pole is the one that has the characteristic of being the generic image of 'tent-pole' that appears in the mind and which refers to the general category of tent-poles. The generality in the mind cannot perform the function of actually supporting the tent, therefore it is a fictional truth, not a superfactual truth. In this system, things such as tent poles which are superfactual truths are impermanent, and things that are fictional are permanent."

> Positing of object and subject, the dualistic appearances of
>   grasped and grasper, and
> Non dual awareness is the Mind Only system[199].

Positing object and subject that are dualistic appearances of grasped and grasping as fictional truth and mere awareness without the duality of grasped and grasping as superfactual truth is the Mind Only system. In the *Compendium of Wisdom's Birthplace* it says:

> So-called "part-possessors" are non-existent.
> Atomic particles also do not exist.
> Individual appearances are not observed but
> Are experienced in a dreamlike way.
> Consciousness which is released from grasped
> And grasper exists as the superfactual truth.
> Those gone to the other shore of the ocean of
> Yogāchāra texts proclaim it in those words.[200]

---

[199] This is the root verse for Cittamātra or Mind Only school. This is the third of the four philosophical schools of Buddhism and the lowest of the two Great Vehicle philosophical schools.

[200] Khenpo Tsultrim Gyatso said, "Of the two, parts and part-possessors, part-possessors are being stated to be non-existent; this is like the limbs of a body which are parts and the body itself which possesses the parts where the body is being said to be non-existent. Not only that, but subtle atomic particles do not exist either. These two statements refer to the Vaibhashika way of presenting the two truths and are refuting that presentation. Furthermore, individual appearances (sights, sounds, smells, and so forth, again as mentioned above in the Vaibhashika presentation) also are not observed, yet these things are experienced and the way that they are experienced is like that of a dream. Consciousness which is released from that mode of experience, that is, which no longer has the mode of dualistic grasped-grasping's experience occurring in it, is the superfactual. That way of presenting the Mind Only system is renowned due to those who have gone to the other shore, that is, who have fully comprehended, the vast ocean of texts in the Yogāchāra

(continued...)

Additionally, when the three characteristics are applied to this[201]: the Imaginary[202] is fully-characterized fictional because it does not exist substantially and because it is established merely conventionally. The Dependent[203] is fully-characterized assessed superfactual and assessed fictional because when analysed by reasoning it is truly established and because it obscures seeing suchness. The Thoroughly Existent[204] is fully-characterized superfactual because it is that which is the domain of the noble one's wisdom.[205]

Appearances fictionally existing, similar to illusions;
Superfactual not existing, space-like, is the Svātantrika
     system.[206]

---

[200](...continued)
tradition."

[201] ... to the two truths ...

[202] Tib. kun brtags. The term literally means "nothing but the product of concept-based thinking.

[203] Tib. zhan dbang.

[204] Tib. yongs grub.

[205] An excellent explanation of the three characters as they apply both to Mind Only and Other Emptiness is contained in *The Three Characters of Mind Only*, teachings of Khenpo Tsultrim Gyatso on the matter compiled by the author and available free on the PKTC web site.

[206] This is the root verse for Svātantrika or Autonomy Middle Way school. The Middle Way school is highest of the four philosophical schools of Buddhism. It has a number of branches. The two main ones are: this school and the Prāsaṅgika Middle Way school. This school is the lower of the two.

That all appearance, however it comes, being fictionally existent similar to the horses, elephants, and so on of a magician's illusions is fictional truth and that the superfactual not existing whatsoever, being like space, is superfactual truth is the acceptance of the Autonomous system. *Defeating Confusion* says:

> Associated with reference, it is fictional; in superfactual
> There is total release from referenced and referencer.[207]

This system's divisions of fictional are as stated above.

❀   ❀   ❀

> Imputations by rational mind are fictional, expressed
>   following the world, and
> Freedom from elaboration, beyond thought and verbal
>   expression, is the Consequence system.[208]

The Consequence system is that "Imputations made by rational mind of speech, thought, and expression are fictional truth; they are expressed following the way that they are known within the world. The innate character that is free of elaboration, beyond all thought and verbal expression is superfactual truth". There is no positing of something to be realized because this system is beyond the superficial things of a position to be taken and a positer of it and beyond an entity to be realized and a realizer of it. Nonetheless, there is an imputation of such in those words for the production of a rational mind that is concordant with superfact. Regarding this last point, Chandrakīrti said:

---

[207] For referencing, see the glossary.

[208] This is the root verse for Prāsaṅgika or Consequence Middle Way school.

For the production of a rational mind concordant with
emptiness, there is the verbal expression, "emptiness is
realized", nonetheless, emptiness is not realized.

This for example is like realization that opens up an understanding
of space's nature being space itself become inseparable with rational
mind.

Now, at this point, consider what All-knowing Drimey Ozer[209] in his
Commentary to Resting up in Mindness said:

Here, if we distinguish clearly in accordance with foremost instruction: taking the object, dharmadhātu, as such
for the basis of making the distinction, these factors of
appearance which are similar to magician's illusions,
mirages, water moons, and so forth that come from it are
natures that do not exist in the appearances so they are
called "fictional truth". As it says in the *Sūtra Petitioned by
Living Tree*:

In the circle of a mirror, as though real,
An image of the moon appears, and like that
Living Tree should understand that
Dharmas are not established by nature ...

Following on from that, ordinary beings see appearances
as truly true but yogins, taking them as mere dreams do
not see them as definite. Thus for yogins these mere
hazy, indistinct happenings do appear when not examined, but because they are known to be only non-existent
when examined, that is called the "realization of fictional
truth" and at that time, the yogins are not harmed by the
circumstances of the appearances.[210]

---

[209] Longchen Rabjam.

[210] Appearances, for ordinary beings are circumstances from which
samsaric states of mind can come. Yogins who have examined them to
(continued...)

If they become trained in that, yogins accomplish the miraculous abilities of travelling through these appearances unhindered, and so on, and, the appearances—however they arise—not being proclaimable as anything one way or another, do lack nature, and the mind is trained in the absence of some truth different from that[211]. Thus, they obtain a noble one's wisdom and then it turns to appearances of the fields[212] and so on, but because there is no clinging to truth in that appearance, it is called "authentic fictional".[213]

We assert that, "All thoughts of mind and all appearances of rational mind with clinging to truth are 'wrong fictional', and that all that shines forth and all appearances without clinging to truth are 'authentic fictional'."

There is the superfactual, or mindness which is the natureless actuality, and there are all phenomena included within no clinging to truth, of water-moon nature. Thus,

---

[210](...continued)
the point of realizing them for what they are are not only not affected but are never harmed by these appearances that could be circumstances for harm.

[211] This cleverly expresses how a yogin trains in the dream-like fictional aspect of truth and combines it with the lack of nature of that fictional aspect so that there is a realization of the combined two truths, not a realization in which there is a difference between the truths.

[212] This refers to the many types of fields such as the sambhogakāya and nirmāṇakāya fields that exist in the purity of perception of those who have a noble one's wisdom.

[213] This is a very skilful presentation. By using this quotation, Jamgon Kongtrul is going past the usual presentation of Consequence Middle Way in which appearance is always seen as impure and is showing how, in fact, pure appearance has to come together with the wisdom that sees the lack of nature in the impure appearances.

confused appearance is mere baseless appearance so is
known to be a natureless entity. When the concepts of
rational mind—existent, non-existent, and so on—are
liberated into expanse it is called "realization of
superfactual's actuality". Realization of the superfact that
is present as that sort of innate character is called "The
rational mind that realizes superfact".

✓ Rāhula's *Praise of the Mother* says:

> Homage to Prajñāpāramitā inexpressible by
>   speech or thought—
> Unborn, unceasing, entity of space,
> The domain of individual self-knowing wisdom,
> Mother of the conquerors of the three times.

Like that, we accept that individual self-knowing wisdom
is superfact and what is realized by it is superfactual truth.

Additionally, the two truths are not different like the two
horns of an animal. Fictional's actuality when viewing
something such as a moon in water is like this: from the
factor of appearance of a moon's form there is the fictional; from the factor of no truth to the moon there is
the superfactual; those two not existing in the pool of
water yet appearing is inseparability of the truths as
though they were one entity, which is unified
superfactual; and the rational mind realizing it like that
refers to the realization of "the two truths" …

❀   ❀   ❀

That Imaginary and Dependent are fictional truth, and
    that superfactual

Is the Thoroughly Existent, self-knowing wisdom is the
Other Emptiness system.[214]

Making Imaginary and Dependent the fictional truth and superfactual the Thoroughly Existent, self-knowing wisdom is the system
of the Other Emptiness Middle Way advocates. To go further with
this, All-Knowing Dolpopa accepted that the Imaginary, not even
true as fictional, is equivalent to a dream, that the Dependent is true
just conventionally, and that the Thoroughly Existent exists as
permanent, stable, and true. Serdog Panchen[215] said that the former
two are equivalent to what is stated in the case of Mind Only and that
the latter is the same as for Dolpopa.

Eminent Leader of Conquerors Rangjung's way of accepting it will
be explained[216]. His acceptance is like the great Jetsun of the Jonang's
statement[217] which sides with Dolpopa's intent:

> We posit that all dharmas included within dualistic ap-
> pearance—things and non-things, grasped and grasping,
> etcetera—are fictional and that wisdom which is
> superfactual's expanse, empty of duality, the self-knower,
> is superfactual. Thus, rather than positing the
> superfactual as mere freedom from elaboration, we are
> positing it as the rigpa which is isolated from the elabora-
> tions of duality's grasped and grasper. Following on from
> that, of the three characteristics, this is that the Depend-
> ent is an awareness of the sort that has confused appear-
> ances, the Imaginary is the confusion that appears to it,
> and the Thoroughly Existing is that awareness empty of

---

[214] This is the root verse for Other Emptiness Middle Way school.

[215] A Sakya scholar who was a great proponent of Other Emptiness.

[216] Below, in the section on mantra and the two truths, Rangjung Dorje's
way of acceptance is explicitly stated in the root verse and shown in full
in the commentary on that.

[217] Tāranātha.

the confusion of the duality of grasped and grasping and not empty of self-knowing essence. That being so, the Imaginary, except for just being posited by signs and conventions absolutely is not existent; the Dependent exists fictionally and not superfactually; and the Thoroughly Existent exists superfactually.

❀   ❀   ❀

In mantra, they are adorned with extra features.
Especially, the fictional is appearances of grasped and
    grasping,
Expressed as truthless appearances like a moon in water;
Superfact's entity is the eighteen emptinesses,
Its truth is non-dual wisdom.[218]

In mantra, the way of accepting the two truths is adorned with extra features over and above the individual views of Middle Way explained as object and subject being the sphere of the maṇḍala and great bliss respectively. Eminent Ācharya Jñāna said that it is called "profound luminosity's non-dual view".

Moreover, the following is accepted. Fictional saṃsāra is adventitious appearance that is non-existent like the appearance of a snake where there is a multicoloured rope. Superfactual is mind's non-dual profound luminosity that is like the actual rope. Saṃsāra for a confused being is like adventitious awareness apprehending a snake in a multicoloured rope; to have made nirvāṇa manifest is to have cleared off the adventitious awareness so that, the apprehension of a snake having been turned away, the rope's nature is seen. The meaning of saṃsāric mind being naturally nirvāṇa is like the rope naturally not being a snake and instead remaining as its own phenomenon. The meaning of natureless cyclic existence naturally

---

[218] This is the root verse for Secret Mantra.

being nirvāṇa is that saṃsāra's profound nature, which is a nature of unstopped luminosity that merely appears as saṃsāra, also is the support and supported of the maṇḍala and that the awareness that makes the appearances in the luminosity also has the nature of an uninterrupted stream of great bliss. The luminosity nature is nirmāṇakāya, the bliss nature is saṃbhogakāya and, given that those are luminosity, the two also, like a mirror and what appears in the mirror, are present in unification.

In particular, eminent All-Knowing Rangjung accepted that:

> The fictional is grasped-grasping's appearances and due to conceiving of a fact which is not there, it is the Imaginary, the appearances of vessel and contents, etcetera, and truth is that, because they are said "to appear but are without nature, like a moon in water" they are merely true in the face of confused rational mind. Superfactual is the emptiness nature which is thoroughly explained as the eighteen emptinesses of internal emptiness, and so on, and truth, expressed as "self-arising wisdom which is without the duality of grasped-grasping", also exists superfactually.

Further to which, it is the meaning stated in the *Jñānavajrasamucchaya Tantra*:

> The intent of the two types of truth is like this. It is fictional truth and superfactual truth. Son of the family, fictional is unstable and fluctuating. Its truth is like a water moon. Superfactual truth is the eighteen great emptinesses. Its limit is presence.

5. The Need for the Explanation

> Knowing this, one is not ignorant regarding the Sage's
>   word and
> Practises what is method, accepting and rejecting, and

Seeing the meaning which is the result of the method
    goes to saṃsāra's other shore.

When the actuality of such two truths is not understood, the suchness
of the profound is not understood. So, by knowing these, one is not
ignorant regarding that subject which is unmistaken, the meaning
pointed to by the word spoken by the teacher, the leading Sage. And,
those skilled in fictional truth, having understood the entire subject
of the method, abandoning and accepting, practise it and, by realizing
superfactual truth, entirely know the result of the method, which is
the three vehicles' nirvāṇa, the nature which is complete purity, free
of adventitious stains, and go to the other shore of cyclic existence,
the level of non-dwelling nirvāṇa. This is seen in *The Two Truths*
with:

Those who understand the divisions of the two truths
Are not ignorant regarding the Sage's word;
Every one of them having accumulated the
    accumulations,
The accumulations are perfected, which is the other
    shore.

The Practice Section From:

Instructions for Practising the View of the Other Emptiness Great Middle Way, "Light Rays of Stainless Vajra Moon"

by Jamgon Kongtrul Yontan Gyatso

1. To make this the path of extraordinary Great Vehicle, first take refuge:

> As for mind, its nature is luminosity,
> The virtuous sugatagarbha[219].
> As for sentient beings' appropriation[220],
> The extremes of existence and non-existence are
>   completely abandoned.
> Just as by burnishing gold colour
> And Sa-le-dram[221] and five-metal alloy
> Are seen, likewise

---

[219] "Virtuous sugatagarbha" is the original dharma term which Chogyam Trungpa Rinpoche famously translated as "basic goodness". It means the actual sugatagarbha which in itself never falls into samsaric afflictions and therefore could always be said to be virtuous. Of course, at the superfactual level, sugatagarbha is beyond being virtuous and non-virtuous.

[220] For appropriation, see the glossary.

[221] "Sa-le-dram" is a name from Ancient India for particularly pure gold.

> In the aggregates, sentient beings and persons
> Do not exist and aggregates do not exist
> But buddha wisdom without outflow,
> Permanent peace, is fully meditated on—
> In that I take refuge.[222]

Arouse enlightenment mind:

> The supreme advocate fully taught
> That mind's nature which is luminosity
> Falls into association with the afflictions of
> Mentation, and so on, and a self.
> In order to dispel them, I will meditate on the supreme
>   path.

Repeat those whilst remembering their meanings.

2. Setting yourself in equipoise on no-thought freedom from elaboration corresponding to the middle wheel, then crossing over to the profound dharmata

On a comfortable seat, set your posture according to the usual points of the body[223]. Cultivate yearning devotion. If you have previously determined the view by hearing and contemplating, put yourself into equipoise on that view remembered. If you do not have the needed hearing and contemplation, determine that this mind of yours has no entity at all—which is lack of self of a person—then decide that every appearing object does not exist other than as an appearing

---

[222] Mind's nature is luminosity and the karmas and afflictions that drive the process of sentient beings taking on samsaric birth are not present within it at all. When this is cleaned by removing the superficial stains, then, just like polishing the surface dross off gold and so on, the underlying condition, which is that the skandhas are empty of self but more than that, that there is wisdom present, is what is meditated on. I take refuge in that. The last section of verse, beginning with "Just as by polishing ..." is from the *Highest Continuum*.

[223] Take up the posture of the Seven Dharmas of Vairochana.

factor of your own mind—which is the lack of self of dharmas—and then also understand that mind and appearances are inseparable like waves and water are not different—which is the equal taste of grasped-grasping. Having aroused that understanding, do not be distracted outside; do not withdraw inside; do not grasp in between; and, not going astray into indeterminate states[224] or equanimity[225], rest in an empty way, like space. If your mind does not stay put but starts to have movement, given that whatever appearances of the sixfold group shine forth are empty, if you preserve[226] the meditation in self-pacification, self-liberation without engaging at all in acceptance and rejection, hope and fear, suppression and furtherance[227], the signs of an abiding mind will gradually occur. Then, by searching for mind as described in the instruction texts, a decision about the nature being primordially free from elaboration will be produced and, because there is no meditation to be done except only for the recognition of that actuality free from elaboration, you must rely simply on a mind that stays inseparable from it.

That has also been taught as "uncontrived freshness" and as "whatever arises, the innate". Thus, no matter how your own luminous, empty, free-from-grasping mind shines forth—abiding or moving, happy or sad, and so on—you preserve just that without alteration. Do not bind yourself up in the conceptual efforts that go with having things to be abandoned and antidotes for them! Instead, put yourself

---

[224] Tib. lung ma bstan. Indeterminate states are various blank states that can occur and which do not lead to liberation.

[225] Equanimity here means to be in a state of absorption on nothing in particular, in which you feel good in a mindless kind of way. It is a serious mistake of meditation.

[226] "To preserve" means to hold or keep or maintain the meditation.

[227] For suppression and furtherance, see the glossary.

in the non-meditation of supportless rigpa[228] and through that the
finalized śhamatha-vipaśhyanā of the Great Vehicle will happen.
While you are involved with such practice, a profound key point is
that, no matter what kind of temporary experiences or qualities of
the path might be produced, rather than attaching or clinging to
them, they should be self-recognized.

And with your speech, say this whilst remembering the meaning:

> The ground is emptiness.
> The path is characteristiclessness.
> The fruit is wishlessness.[229]

3. When some sort[230] of shamatha-vipashyana samadhi has arisen then, corresponding to the final wheel and to the Vajra Vehicle, the differentiations of existent and non-existent are precisely done and there is the introduction[231] as follows

If you have a coarse understanding of the excellent speech[232], texts,
and commentaries just that will suffice, but if not, you should at least
receive the reading transmission of *Mountain Dharma: An Ocean of
Definitive Meaning* and through that develop an understanding of the
view as much as you can. That will bring the understanding that,
although mind's entity—emptiness having the excellence of all

---

[228] For rigpa, see the glossary.

[229] These are the three doors of emancipation taught by the Buddha in
the *Prajñāpāramitā Sūtra*.

[230] ... good, poor, excellent, etcetera ...

[231] "Introduction" means introduction to the nature of mind; see the
glossary.

[232] The "excellent speech" is the words of the Buddha as written down
in the Buddhist canon.

superficies and the nature luminosity[233], the tathāgatagarbha—is taught under many different names—suchness, emptiness, mahāmudrī, AHAṂ, and so on—there is no fault of contradiction in that. That understanding frees you from fault that was expressed in these words:

> Everything the Buddha said taught emptiness and lack of self. Foolish ones who do not understand the meaning of emptiness and lack of self will degenerate.

And then, relying on the two truths and four reliances[234], the ultimate definitive meaning sūtras within the conqueror's excellent speech and your own experience of wisdom will meet and your practice of the path will become meaningful.

In that way, all the phenomena belonging to the adventitious, totally imaginary[235] mind, are empty like the image of gathered clouds, yet the dharmatā sugatagarbha, an uninterrupted stream of illumination and knowing[236] which has been introduced as self-arising wisdom, must be taken into practise. To do so, take refuge and arouse enlightenment mind as described above. Then, as is found in the excellent speech of Jetsun Tāranātha, meditate for one session on the recollection that the guru is buddha and at the end say:

---

[233] For "emptiness ..." and "the nature", see the glossary.

[234] To rely on the dharma (thing) being presented rather than the fame of the individual presenting it; to rely on the meaning in it rather than the words of it; to rely on the definitive meaning rather than the provisional meaning; and rely on wisdom rather than consciousness in order to ascertain the correct meaning of what was being taught.

[235] "Totally imaginary" is the name of the first of the three characters of the Mind Only system. It indicates that such things are only products of the conceptual mind.

[236] "Luminous knowing" is a term used in Mind Only to indicate the ultimate truth, which is a mind freed of the totally imaginary and other-controlled fictional truths. It emphasizes that there is an ultimate mind.

> The tathāgata is un-showable;
> It cannot be looked at with the eye.
> The dharma is in-expressible;
> It cannot be listened to with the ear.
> The saṅgha is un-compounded;
> It cannot be honoured with body or speech or mind.

and:

> Buddha nature is uncompounded thus is called "perma-
> nent". What is called "space" is buddha nature. Buddha
> nature is the tathāgata. The tathāgata is uncompounded.
> Uncompounded is permanent. Permanent is the dharma.
> The dharma is the saṅgha. The saṅgha is uncom-
> pounded. Uncompounded is permanent.

Saying that over and over, recollect that the superfactual Three
Jewels are permanent.

Then, as it says in the *Descent Into Laṅka*:

> When Mind Only has been taken as the reliance,
> There is no consideration of objects being external.
> Through relying on there being no appearances,
> Mind Only will be passed beyond.
> Through relying on a reference of the authentic[237],
> There being no appearances will be passed beyond.
> If the yogin remains in there being no appearances,
> The Great Vehicle will not be seen.

---

[237] Now, instead of taking as the reference point for practice something
which is close to reality but not quite it, one moves to taking a reference
point of the authentic itself and goes on from there. The Middle Way
references the authentic—which is a name for reality. In short, this is
saying that what is authentic requires both emptiness and appearance,
and the Mind Only system does not have the appearance part, so it has
to be left behind to reach the Middle Way.

This is saying that the realization of fictional confusion being Mind Only, the absence of appearances, must be torn down by the Middle Way and then, having passed beyond it, the non-mistaken way of suchness must be entered using the Middle Way which does have appearances with it[238].

What is "reference of the authentic" mentioned there? The answer is, "Just as none of the four elements are not pervaded by space, there is no knowable not pervaded by a buddha's dharmakāya. And, in the suchness of the buddha and oneself and all sentient beings, while there are none of the distinctions of good and bad, big and small, high and low, and so on, there is the ability to generate the buddha dharmas. It has time of being without beginning. That naturally present family or element[239] is obtained because the dharmatā exists in all migrators—the beings who have the breath of life—so every sentient being is one who has tathāgatagarbha"[240]. In order to make that clear, say this:

> Because the complete buddha's kāya radiates, and
> Because tathātā is undifferentiable, and
> Because they have the family, all bodied ones
> Always have the buddha garbha.

---

[238] ... as opposed to the Middle Way which does not have appearances with it, which would be the mistaken understanding of the Middle Way as known by those who insist on a negated emptiness of the second turning.

[239] Family is Skt. gotra, Tib. rigs. Element is Skt. dhātu, Tib. khams. These are key terms in tathāgatagarbha explanations.

[240] The answer here consists of a paraphrase of the meaning found in the *Descent Into Laṅka*. To clarify it, the relevant verse from the *Highest Continuum* is given next. The verse is very famous because of setting out the three reasons for the existence of tathāgatagarbha in all beings.

Then say this, while contemplating the meaning:[241]

> The pure ones' dharmakāya, the impure-and-pure ones'
> suchness, and the impure ones' family[242]—this way is how
> they have them.

> Just as there is a buddha in a bad lotus, honey in a honey
>   bee,
> Seed in a husk, gold inside impurity,
> Treasure in earth, bamboo and so on in small seeds,
> A king's body inside tattered clothing,
> A leader of humans in a bad woman's belly,
> And forms of jewels in the ground, likewise,
> In sentient beings obscured by the stains of
> Adventitious afflictions, this element is present.

Karma and cause and effect; full-ripening and afflictions; skandhas, dhātus, āyatanas, and interdependent origination; and so forth—everything having the aspect of complete separability has not only never existed in superfact but also is seated, without causing of contamination of that, in whatever has the fictional. And the self-arisen major and minor marks, the strengths, the fearlessnesses, the four close applications of mindfulnesses, love and great compassion, the Vajra-Like and other samādhis, the immeasurable wisdoms of the dharmadhātu, and so on[243], that is, the buddha dharmas having the aspect of being completely without separability more in number

---

[241] This next piece consists of a section of prose and of verse. The prose shows how the *Highest Continuum* states that there are three levels of beings and that each has the tathāgatagarbha in a certain way. The verse is taken directly from the first chapter of the *Highest Continuum*.

[242] Family here is the same as just mentioned above.

[243] "And so on" meaning "and the other wisdoms apart from dharma-dhātu".

than the grains of sand in the Ganges are primordially inherently present, and therefore not empty. That is made clear with:[244]

> Through trust in the basis as something that could be
>   separable from the stains
> And able to give rise to the good qualities,
> The element is empty of the adventitious,
> That which has the characteristic of being completely
>   separable,
> But is not empty of the unsurpassed dharmas,
> That which has the characteristic of being completely
>   inseparable.
> In luminosity what there is is what has not been made
> Which is not separable; it possesses all
> The buddha dharmas which exceed
> The sands of the River Ganges.

Furthermore, the śhrāvakas, pratyekas, and so on, viewing bliss as unsatisfactoriness, permanent as impermanent, self as lack of self, and clean as unclean, do not understand the meaning to be known from the words spoken by the conqueror. The meaning involved with those items is thus. Lack of self is to be called "saṃsāra". What is called "self" is the tathāgata. What is impermanent is the śhrāvakas and pratyekabuddhas. What is permanent is the tathāgata's dharmakāya. Unsatisfactoriness is everything of the Tīrthikas. Bliss is total nirvāṇa. What is wholly impure is compounded phenomena. What is wholly pure is the buddhas' and bodhisatvas' dharma of the authentic; your own mindness[245], sugatagarbha which is the four dharmas of the authentic that is beyond any mistake. Thinking, "I possess this" make the matter clear with this:

---

[244] Again, he has paraphrased the meaning in the *Highest Continuum* and now provides the actual quotation, which is again from the first chapter.

[245] For mindness, see the glossary.

That, because its nature is pure and
Because the latencies[246] have been abandoned, is clean.
Pure of the elaborations of self and no self
It is the holy self of utter peace.
Because mentation's nature, the aggregates and
Their cause, are reversed, it is bliss itself.
Because saṃsāra and nirvāṇa are
Realized as equality[247], it is permanence.

The basis for such attributes, the sugatagarbha, together with the many good qualities that are the attributes connected with a buddha, is here and now the self-knowing wisdom whose luminosity is un-stopped[248], the innate, co-emergence. This wisdom which is to be experienced through the three of hearing, contemplating, and meditating is seated within you as the basis of purification. When what is to be purified out, the adventitious stains, have been removed, the result of purification is that the actuality that is seated in you will have become manifest. Having become manifest, it is given the name, "dharmakāya free from stains". At that point, all the superficies of the whole of saṃsāra and nirvāṇa shine forth but, having merely shone forth, there is no wavering from the ground and they appear as a variety of superficies which are the reflections of this stainless crystal ball ... Do the main part, which is equipoise in that wisdom-emptiness of the noble ones, meditating in as many sessions as you prefer.

---

[246] For latency, see the glossary.

[247] "Equality" is a synonym for emptiness.

[248] For un-stopped, see the glossary.

LIST OF TEXTS CITED

A Complete Commentary to the Great Vehicle Treatise "The Highest Continuum" which Connects to Heart Meaning using the Explanation System of the Path of Direct Perception, Called "The Lion's Roar of the Non-Regressing" by Jamgon Kongtrul Lodro Thaye. Available from his *Collected Works* and available as an electronic edition free from the PKTC web-site.

A Partial Commentary to "The Miraculous Key Which Opens A Door to The Treasury Of Knowledge and Sums Up The Reasonings in The Ocean Of Texts on Reasoning" by Khenpo Tsultrim Gyatso and available free from the PKTC web-site.

"A Lamp's Illumination", Condensed Advice on Great Completion Thorough Cut by Dodrupchen III, Tenpa'i Nyima. Published by Padma Karpo Translation Committee, authored by Tony Duff, revised edition January 2014, ISBN: 978-9937-8244-6-0.

A Short Discussion of The Rise of Other Emptiness Madhyamaka, "The Music of Talk on the Definitive Meaning" by Khenpo Tsultrim Gyatso, published in Delhi in the late 1900's in a text used for studies at Rumtek.

A Treasure Trove of The Intent of The Profound Meaning, "A Chariot of Establishment". By the second Drukchen, Gyalwang Je. From his *Collected Works*. Translated by Tony Duff and published by Padma Karpo Translation Committee.

265

Aṅgulīmālā; Skt. aṅgulimāla sūtra. The *Sūtra Taught for the Benefit of Aṅgulimāla* is one of the definitive-meaning, profound sūtras of the Other Emptiness system.

An Authentic Expression of the Middle Way; Tib. dbu ma yang dag par brjod pa, a song by Milarepa.

An Explanation of the Four Yogas Points a Finger at the Superfactual; rnal 'byor gzhi'i bshad pa don dam mdzub tshugs bstan pa by All-knowing Padma Karpo. Included in his *Collected Works*. Translated and published by Tony Duff, Padma Karpo Translation Committee.

Avataṃsaka Sūtra; a Great Vehicle sūtra of the third wheel regarded as one of the four main Mind Only sūtras.

Blaze of Reasoning; Skt. tarkajvala by Bhavaviveka.

Clarifier of the Three Main Systems of Madhyamaka, The Chariot that Accomplishes the Definitive Meaning. Tib. dbu ma gzhung lugs gsal bar byed pa nges don grub pa'i shing rta zhes bya ba. By Padma Karpo, a famous commentary on Milarepa's song *An Authentic Expression of the Middle Way*.

Clear Lamp; Skt. pradipoddyotana namaṭīka by Chandrakīrti, a commentary on Nāgārjuna's Root Prajñā.

Clear Words; Skt. prasannapadā by Chandrakīrti, a commentary on Nāgārjuna's Root Prajñā.

Cloud of Jewels Sūtra; a Great Vehicle Sūtra that is one of the definitive-meaning, profound sūtras of the Other Emptiness system.

Collection of Praises; a collection of works of Nāgārjuna that are categorized as praises.

Collection of Reasonings; a collection of six works of Nāgārjuna that are categorized as texts concerning reasoning.

Collection of Stories; a collection of six works of Nāgārjuna that are categorized as texts that tell stories.

Commentary to Resting up in Mindness. Tib. sems nyid ngal bso grel pa. By Longchen Rabjam; his own commentary to his own text Resting up in Mindness.

Compendium of Wisdom's Birthplace; Tib. ye shes snying po kun la btus pa, Mind Only school commentary.

Complete Explanation of Enlightenment Mind; Skt. bodhicittavivaraṇa, Tib. byang sems rnam bshad by Nāgārjuna.

Crying to the Guru from Afar; Tib. bla ma rgyang bod. A "crying to the guru from afar" type of text written by Dzogchen Paltrul.

Defeating Confusion. Tib. 'khrul 'joms.

Defeating Harm. Skt. bṛiharttīka, Tib. gnod 'joms by Vasubhandu, a commentary to the twenty-thousand plus verse Prajñāpāramitā sūtra.

Densely Arrayed with Ornaments Sūtra; Skt. ghanavyuha, a Great Vehicle sūtra of the third wheel regarded as one of the four main Mind Only sūtras.

Descent into Laṅka; Skt. laṅkāvatārasūtra; a Great Vehicle sūtra of the third wheel regarded as one of the four main Mind Only sūtras. Other Emptiness followers additionally classify it as one of the sūtras representing the profound view and meditation system of Maitreya. Included in the Kangyur. A translation into English is available.

Dharaṇeshvara Sūtra; see Sūtra Petitioned by King Dharaṇeshvara.

Distinguishing Dharmas and Dharmatā; Skt. dharmadharmatāvibhaṅga; one of the five dharmas of Maitreya.

Distinguishing Middle and Extremes; Skt. madhyāntavibhaṅga; one of the five dharmas of Maitreya.

Engaging the Three Kāyas; Skt. trikāyāvatāra by Āchārya Nagāmitra.

Enlightenment Mind commentary is the same as the *Complete Explanation of Enlightenment Mind* by Nagarjuna.

Entrance; see Entering the Middle Way.

Entering the Middle Way; Skt. madhyamakāvātara by Chandrakīrti. The famous Indian text that presents the ten bhumis of the bodhisatvas with a very long explanation of the Madhyamaka prāsaṅgika view according to Nāgārjuna's system. Included in the Tangyur. An electronic version of the whole text with reader software is available from Padma Karpo Translation Committee.

Entering the Bodhisatva's Conduct; Skt. bodhisatvacaryāvatāra by Shāntideva. The famous text that shows the path of a bodhisatva in ten chapters. Included in the Tangyur. Several translations into English are available. An electronic version of the whole text with reader software is available published the Padma Karpo Translation Committee.

Four Hundred, a Yogāchāra text.

Great Cloud Sūtra; a Great Vehicle Sūtra that is one of the definitive-meaning, profound sūtras of the Other Emptiness system.

Great Commentary; *The Stainless Light, The Great Commentary on Kālachakra* by Puṇḍarīka. This is the greatest of commentaries on the Kālachakra. Included in the Tangyur.

Great Drum Sūtra; a Great Vehicle Sūtra that is one of the definitive-meaning, profound sūtras of the Other Emptiness system.

Great Nirvāṇa Sūtra; Skt. mahāparinirvana sūtra, a Great Vehicle Sūtra that is one of the definitive-meaning, profound sūtras of the Other Emptiness system.

Heart Prajñāpāramitā Sūtra; a Great Vehicle Sūtra of the middle turning.

Hevajra Tantra; Skt. hevajratantrarāja. Available in Tibetan as *The Two Sections* which are the only two sections of the complete Hevajra tantra now available. Included in the Kangyur. A translation into English of the two parts is available from Motilal Barnasidass Publishers.

Hinting At Dzogchen, Teachings of Tsoknyi Rinpoche; by Lotsawa Tony Duff, published 2008 by Padma Karpo Translation Committee, ISBN 978-9937-2-0224-4.

Holy Golden Light; a Great Vehicle Sūtra that is one of the definitive-meaning, profound sūtras of the Other Emptiness system.

Illuminator Tibetan-English Dictionary by Tony Duff, published 2000 by Padma Karpo Translation Committee, P.O. Box 4957, Kathmandu.

In Praise of Mind's Vajra; by Nāgārjuna.

In Praise of the Dharmadhātu; Skt. dharmadhātustotra (some give as dharmadhātustava) by Nāgārjuna.

Instructions for Practising the View of the Other Emptiness Great Middle Way, "Light Rays of Stainless Vajra Moon" by Jamgon Kongtrul Yontan Gyatso. From the Treasury of Oral Instructions, Tib. dam ngag mdzod.

Jñānavajrasamucchaya Tantra; unknown.

Kālachakra Tantra; the root tantra of the Kālachakra system.

Lam Rim Yeshe Nyingpo by Jamgon Kongtrul Lodro Thaye on the practice of innermost Dzogchen.

Lamp of Certainty; Tib. nges shes gron me by Ju Mipham Namgyal, included in his *Collected Works*.

Lamp of the Three Modes; Skt. nayatrayapradīpa; by Tripiṭakamāla Āryadeva. Included in the Tangyur.

Middle and Extremes; see Distinguishing Middle and Extremes.

Middle Way Stages of Meditation; Skt. madhyamaka bhavanākrama by Nāgārjuna.

Mahānirvāṇa; See Great Nirvāṇa Sutra.

Meeting of Father and Son; a Great Vehicle Sūtra that is one of the definitive-meaning, profound sūtras of the Other Emptiness system.

Mother; one of the Prajñāpāramitā Sūtras.

Mountain Dharma: An Ocean of Definitive Meaning; Tib. ri chos nges don rgya mtsho by Dolpopa Sherab Gyaltsen.

Ocean of Texts on Reasoning and Pramāṇa; a major work by the seventh Karmapa Chodrag Gyatso, included in his *Collected Works*.

Ocean of the Definitive, a Garland of Tenets; Tib. nges don rgya mtsho grub mtha' phreng ba by Panchen Shākya Chogden of the Sakya tradition.

Ornament of Manifest Realizations of the Prajñāpāramitā; Skt. prajñāpāramitā abhisamayālaṃkara, one of the five dharmas of Maitreya.

Ornament of the Madhyamaka; Skt. madhyamakālaṅkāra by Shāntarakṣhita.

Ornament of the Sūtras; Skt. mahāyānasūtrālaṅkāra, one of the five dharmas of Maitreya.

Praise of the Mother; by Rāhula, son of the Buddha.

Prajñāpāramitā Sūtra; the main sūtra of the middle turning.

Profound Definitive Meaning Sung on the Snowy Range; a song of Milarepa.

Progressive Stages of Meditation on Emptiness; Khenpo Tsultrim Gyatso, translated by Susanne Schefczyk. Published 1995 by Marpa Translation Committee, Nepal.

Reciting the Names of Mañjushrī Tantra; Skt. mañjushrīnāmasaṅgīti, a text containing the various appellations of Mañjushrī that is used as a liturgy for recitation. Included in the Nyingma Tantra Collection (rnying ma rgyud 'bum). Available in English as "The Wisdom of Manjushri".

Root Prajñā; Skt. mūla prajñā by Nāgārjuna. Nagarjuna's seminal exposition of the Madhyamaka prāsaṅgika system. Included in the Tangyur.

Root Tantra of Mañjushrī; Skt. mūla mañjushrī tantra.

Samantabhadra's Conduct; the famous prayer of aspiration by Samantabhadra, one of the eight bodhisatva mahasatva heart sons of the Buddha, called *The King of Prayers, the Prayer for Excellent Conduct.*

Showing Great Compassion Sūtra; Skt. mahākaruna nirdeśha sūtra, a definitive meaning sūtra of the Great Vehicle.

Showing The Extra Thought Sūtra; a definitive meaning sūtra of the Great Vehicle.

Stack of Jewels; Skt. ratnakūṭa sūtra, a major sūtra of the Great Vehicle.

Sūtra Petitioned by Devaputra; a Great Vehicle Sutra.

Sūtra Petitioned by King Dharaṇeśhvara; one of the definitive-meaning, profound sūtras of the Other Emptiness system.

Sūtra Petitioned by Living Tree; one of the definitive-meaning, profound sūtras of the Other Emptiness system.

Sūtra Petitioned by Śhrī Mālā Devī; one of the definitive-meaning, profound sūtras of the Other Emptiness system.

Sūtra Taught by Inexhaustible Intellect; Skt. akṣhyamati nirdeśha sūtra.

The Complete Commentary on Pramāṇa; Skt. pramāṇavarttika; the extensive commentary on the subject of pramāṇa written by Dharmakīrti. Included in the Tangyur.

The Extensive Jewel; a Great Vehicle sūtra.

The Fourth Council; Tib. bka'i bsdu ba bzhi pa, one of the principal works of Dolpopa Sherab Gyaltsen on Other Emptiness.

The Great Vehicle Highest Continuum Treatise; Skt. mahāyānottaratantra śhāstra; one of the five dharmas of Maitreya. Some feel that the Sanskrit name given is an invention and that the text was actually called "ratnagotravibhaṅga", *Distinguishing The Precious Lineage*. The text is about tathāgatagarbha, which is referred to either as the continuum or the lineage in the names of the texts. A translation into English is available.

The Lion's Roar of the Non-Regressing Commentary to the Highest Continuum; a major commentary on the *Highest Continuum* by Jamgon Kongtrul Lodro Thaye.

The Lion's Roar that Proclaims of Zhantong; Tib. khas blang gzhan stong sengge nga ro by Ju Namgyal Mipham, available in his *Collected Works*. Translated by Tony Duff and published by Padma Karpo Translation Committee.

The Lion's Roar that is a Thousand Doses of Sugatagarbha; Tib. bde gshegs stong thun sengge nga ro by Ju Namgyal Mipham, available in his *Collected Works*. Translated by Tony Duff and published by Padma Karpo Translation Committee.

The Mahāmudrā Distinguishing Provisional and Definitive; a song of Milarepa.

The Noble One, Unravelling the Intent. See Unravelling the Intent.

The Seven Sections; the seminal work by Dignaga that lays out pramāṇa in a group of seven works.

The Three Characters of Mind Only; teachings of Khenpo Tsultrim Gyatso translated by Tony Duff. Published by Padma Karpo Translation Committee, Nepal, 2008.

The Three Nails of Meditation; a song of Milarepa.

The Treasury of Dharmadhātu; Skt. chos dbyings mdzod. One of Longchen Rabjam's seven treasuries.

The Treasury of Knowledge; see *The Treasury which is an Encyclopædia of Knowledge*.

The Treasury which is an Encyclopædia of Knowledge; Tib. shes bya kun khyab mdzod; one of the five great treasuries written by Jamgon Kongtrul Lodro Thaye. An electronic version of the whole text with reader software is available published by the Padma Karpo Translation Committee.

The Two Truths; Tib. bden gnyis la 'jug pa; Entering the Two Truths.

Twenty Thousand; a version of the Prajñāpāramitā within twenty to thirty thousand lines.

Volume on Accumulations for Samādhi; Skt. samādhisaṃbhavāparivarta; Tib. ting nge 'dzin tshogs kyi le'u; a text by Āchārya Bodhibhadra; an Indian text that gives the details of the practice of concentration and what is needed for it. Accumulations in the title refers to what needs to be brought together in order to develop samadhi.

White Lotus of the Holy Dharma Sūtra; Skt. satdharma puṇḍarīka sūtra, a definitive meaning sūtra of the Great Vehicle.

Ultimate View, Meditation, Conduct, and Fruition; a song of Milarepa.

Unravelling the Intent (of the Conqueror); Skt. the saṃdhinirmocanasūtra; a Great Vehicle sūtra of the third wheel regarded as one of the four main Mind Only sūtras. A translation into English is available.

Vijñaptisiddhi; by the Indian āchārya Dharmapāla.

Vyakhaya-yuktī; one of the eight prakaraṇa of Vasubhandu.

GLOSSARY OF TERMS

Actuality, Tib. gnas lugs: A key term in both sūtra and tantra and one of a pair of terms, the other being "apparent reality" (Tib. snang lugs). The two terms are used when determining the reality of a situation. The actuality of any given situation is how (lugs) the situation actuality sits or is present (gnas); the apparent reality is how (lugs) any given situation appears (snang) to an observer. Something could appear in many different ways, depending on the circumstances at the time and on the being perceiving it but, regardless of those circumstances, it will always have its own actuality of how it really is. This term is frequently used in Mahāmudrā and Great Completion teachings to mean the fundamental reality of any given phenomenon or situation before any deluded mind alters it and makes it appear differently.

Adventitious, Tib. glo bur: This term has the connotations of popping up on the surface of something and of not being part of that thing. Therefore, even though it is often translated as "sudden", that only conveys half of the meaning. In Buddhist literature, something adventitious comes up as a surface event and disappears again precisely because it is not actually part of the thing on whose surface it appeared. It is frequently used in relation to the afflictions because they pop up on the surface of the mind of buddha-nature but are not part of the buddha-nature itself.

Affliction, Skt. kleśha, Tib. nyon mongs: This term is usually translated as emotion or disturbing emotion, etcetera, but the Buddha was very specific about the meaning of this word. When the Buddha referred to the emotions, meaning a movement of mind, he did not refer to them as such but called them "kleśha" in Sanskrit, meaning exactly "affliction". It is a basic part of the Buddhist teaching that emotions afflict beings, giving them problems at the time and causing more problems in the future.

Alaya, Skt. ālaya, Tib. kun gzhi: This term, if translated, is usually translated as all-base or something similar. It is a Sanskrit term that means a range that underlies and forms a basis for something else. In Buddhist teaching, it means a particular level of mind that sits beneath all other levels of mind. However, it is used in several different ways in the Buddhist teaching and changes to a different meaning in each case. In the Great Completion teachings, an important distinction is made between ālaya alone and ālaya consciousness.

All-Knowing One, Tib. kun mkhyen: Every century in Tibet, there were just a few people who seemed to know everything so were given the title "All-Knowing One". One of them was Longchen Rabjam and throughout this text All-Knowing One always refers to him. Moreover, of all the All-Knowing ones, Longchenpa was regarded as the greatest, therefore, he is also frequently referred to as the "great" or "greatest" All-Knowing One. Note that "All-Knowing" does not mean "omniscient one" even though it is often translated that way.

Alteration, altered: Same as contrivance *q.v.*

Appropriation, Skt. upādāna, Tib. nye bar len pa: This is the name of the ninth of the twelve links of interdependent origination. Tsongkhapa gives a good treatment of all twelve links in his interdependent origination section of the *Great Stages of the Path to Enlightenment*, a translation of which is available for free download from the PKTC web-site. It is the crucial point in the process at which a karma that has been previously planted is selected and activated as the karma that will propel the being into its next existence. In other words, it is the key point in a being's existence when the next type of existence is selected. There is the further point that, at the time of death, the particular place that the wind-mind settles in the subtle body, a place related to the seed syllables mentioned in the tantras, also determines the next birth. The two points are not different. The selection of the karma that will propel the next life then affects how the wind-mind will operate at the time of death.

Attribute analysis, Tib. rnam dpyad: "Attribute analysis" and "overall analysis" are a pair of terms used to highlight a crucial difference between conceptual and non-conceptual approaches towards understanding something, for example, the view of emptiness.

Attribute analysis is an assessment done using rational mind; it examines (Tib. dpyad) the individual, surface attributes (Tib. rnam pa) of something to come to a rational understanding of what the thing is. It conceptually eliminates the attribute which something is not in order to establish the concept of what something is. Therefore, it could also be called an "eliminative analysis". It entails what is called "distinction-removal" which is the conceptual process of distinguishing something as being this rather than that and in doing so eliminating what "that" is from the understanding of the thing.

Awareness, Skt. jñā, Tib. shes pa: "Awareness" is always used in our translations to mean the basic knower of mind or, as Buddhist teaching itself defines it, "a general term for any registering mind", whether dualistic or non-dualistic. Hence, it is used for both samsaric and nirvanic situations; for example, consciousness (Tib. rnam par shes pa) is a dualistic form of awareness.

Becoming, Skt. bhāvanā, Tib. srid pa: This is another name for samsaric existence. Beings in saṃsāra have a samsaric existence but, more than that, they are constantly in a state of becoming—becoming this type of being or that type of being in this abode or that, as they are driven along without choice by the karmic process that drives samsaric existence.

Bliss, Skt. sukha, Tib. bde: The Sanskrit term and its Tibetan translation are usually translated as "bliss" but refer to the whole range of possibilities of everything on the side of good as opposed to bad. Thus, the term will mean pleasant, happy, good, nice, easy, comfortable, blissful, and so on, depending on context.

Bodhicitta, Tib. byang chub sems: See under enlightenment mind.

Bodhisatva, Tib. byang chub sems dpa': A bodhisatva is a person who has engendered the bodhichitta, enlightenment mind, and, with that as a basis, has undertaken the path to the enlightenment of a truly complete buddha specifically for the welfare of other beings. Note that, despite the common appearance of "bodhisattva" in Western books on Buddhism, the Tibetan tradition has steadfastly maintained since the time of the earliest translations that the correct spelling is bodhisatva; see under satva and sattva.

Bodhisatva mahasattva, Skt. bodhisatva mahāsattva, Tib. byang chub sems dpa' sems dpa' chen po: In general, "bodhisatva" refers to *satva*, a being, who is on the path to *bodhi*, truly complete enlightenment, and "mahāsattva" refers to a person who is *mahā* at a greater level of *sattva* being, a higher kind of person. Thus, the usual explanation of *bodhisatva mahāsattva* is that it means "a being on the path to truly complete enlightenment, one who is a great type of being because of his intention to reach truly complete enlightenment for the sake of all sentient beings".

However, there is also a second, less common explanation, in which "mahāsattva" does not mean a great being in general but has the specific meaning of those bodhisatvas who, amongst all bodhisatvas, have attained a very great level of being. In this case, it particularly refers to bodhisatvas who have achieved and are dwelling on the highest bodhisatva levels, the eighth to tenth bodhisatva levels. Unlike bodhisatvas at all levels below that, these bodhisatvas have attained such a high level of purity that they cannot regress to a lower level. Their level of attainment is enormous and with it, they have many qualities which are very similar to those of a buddha. It is important to know of this second understanding of "bodhisatva mahāsattva", because when it is used with that meaning, it says something about the bodhisatvas being mentioned. For example, when any of the eight heart-sons of the Buddha are mentioned, they are often referred to as bodhisatva mahāsattvas to indicate their extreme level of attainment. In that case, they specifically are the bodhisatvas above all other bodhisatvas, ones who are close to truly complete enlightenment.

Capable One, Skt. muni, Tib. thub pa: The term "muni" as for example in "Shakyamuni" has long been thought to mean "sage" because of an entry in Monier-Williams excellent Sanskrit-English dictionary. In fact, it has been used by many Indian religions since the times of ancient India to mean in general, a religious practitioner "one who could do it", one who has made progress on a spiritual path and thereby become able to restrain his three doors away from non-virtue and affliction.

Illumination, Skt. vara, Tib. gsal ba: This term should be understood as an abbreviation of the Tibetan term, "'od gsal ba", which is translated with luminosity *q.v.* It is not another factor of mind distinct from luminosity but merely a convenient abbreviation in both Indian and Tibetan dharma language for luminosity.

Clinging, Tib. zhen pa: In Buddhism, this term refers specifically to the twofold process of dualistic mind mis-taking things that are not true, not pure, as true, pure, etcetera and then, because of seeing them as highly desirable even though they are not, attaching itself to or clinging to those things. This type of clinging acts as a kind of glue that keeps a person joined to the unsatisfactory things of cyclic existence because of mistakenly seeing them as desirable.

Complete purity, rnam dag: This term refers to the quality of a buddha's mind, which is completely pure compared to a sentient being's mind. The mind of a being in saṃsāra has its primordially pure nature covered over by the muck of dualistic mind. If the being practises correctly, the impurity can be removed and mind can be returned to its original state of complete purity.

Conceived effort, Tib. rtsol ba: In Buddhism, this term usually does not merely mean effort but has the specific connotation of effort of dualistic mind. In that case, it is effort that is produced by and functions specifically within the context of dualistic concept. For example, the term "mindfulness with effort" specifically means "a type of mindfulness that is occurring within the context of dualistic mind and its various operations". The term "effortless" is often used in Mahāmudrā and Great Completion to mean a way of being in which dualistic mind has been abandoned and, therefore, in which there is none of the striving of ordinary people.

Concept labels, Tib. mtshan ma: This is the technical name for the structures or concepts which function as the words of conceptual mind's language. They are the very basis of operation of the third skandha and hence of the way that dualistic mind communicates with its world. For example, a table seen in direct visual perception will have no concept labels involved with knowing it. However, when thought becomes involved and there is the thought "table" in an inferential or conceptual perception of the table, the name-tag "table" will be used to reference the table and that name tag is the concept label.

Although we usually reference phenomena via these concepts, the phenomena are not the dualistically referenced things we think of them as being. The actual fact of the phenomena is quite different from the concept labels used to discursively think about them and is known by wisdom rather than concept-based mind. Therefore, this term is often used in Buddhist literature to signify that dualistic samsaric mind is involved rather than non-dualistic wisdom. ✓

Confusion, Tib. 'khrul pa: In Buddhism, this term mostly refers to the fundamental confusion of taking things the wrong way that happens because of fundamental ignorance, although it can also have the more general meaning of having lots of thoughts and being confused about it. In the first case, it is defined like this "Confusion is the appearance to rational mind of something being present when it is not" and refers, for example, to seeing an object, such as a table, as being truly present, when in fact it is present only as mere, inter-dependent appearance.

Consciousness, Skt. vijñāna, Tib. rnam shes: The term means "awareness of superficies". A consciousness is a dualistic (jñā) awareness which simply registers a certain type of (vi) superfice, for example, an eye consciousness by definition registers only the superficies of visual form. A very important point is that the addition of the "vi" to the basic term (jñā) for awareness conveys the sense of a less than perfect way of being aware. This is not a wisdom awareness which knows every superfice in an utterly uncomplicated way but a limited type of awareness which is restricted to knowing one kind of superfice or another and which is part of the complicated—and highly unsatisfactory process—called (dualistic) mind. Note that this definition, which is a crucial part of understanding the role of consciousness in samsaric being, is fully conveyed by the Sanskrit and Tibetan terms but not at all by the English term.

Contrivance, contrived, Tib. bcos pa: A term meaning that something has been altered from its native state.

Cyclic existence: See under saṃsāra.

Dharmadhatu, Skt. dharmadhātu, Tib. chos kyi dbyings: A *dhātu* is a place or basis from or within which something can come into being. In the case of a dharma dhātu, it is the place or space which is a basis from and in which all dharmas or phenomena, can and do come into being. If a flower bed is the place where flowers grow and are found, the dharmadhātu is the dharma or phenomena bed in which all phenomena come into being and are found. The term is used in all levels of Buddhist teaching with that general meaning but the explanation of it becomes more profound as the teaching becomes more profound. For example, in Great Completion and Mahā-mudrā, it is the all-pervading sphere of luminosity-wisdom, given that luminosity is where phenomena arise and luminosity is none other than wisdom.

Dharmakaya, Skt. dharmakāya, Tib. chos sku: In the general teachings of Buddhism, this refers to the mind of a buddha, with "dharma" meaning reality and "kāya" meaning body. In the Thorough Cut practice of Great Completion it additionally has the special meaning of being the means by which one rapidly imposes liberation on oneself.

Dharmata, Skt. dharmatā, Tib. chos nyid: This is a general term meaning the way that something is, and can be applied to anything at all; it is similar in meaning to "actuality" *q.v.* For example, the dharmatā of water is wetness and the dharmatā of the becoming bardo is a place where beings are in a samsaric, or becoming mode, prior to entering a nature bardo. It is used frequently in Tibetan Buddhism to mean "the dharmatā of reality" but that is a specific case of the much larger meaning of the term. To read texts which use this term successfully, one has to understand that the term has a general meaning and then see how that applies in context.

Dharmin, Tib. chos can: Generally speaking a dharmin is a conceived-of phenomenon, so by implication belongs to the world of saṃsāra.

It is not only a phenomenon in general, a dharma, but has become a conceptualized phenomenon because of the samsaric context. Padma Karpo defines it as "awareness possessing a phenomenon" which puts the emphasis on the samsaric awareness knowing the phenomenon. ✓

Dhatu, Skt. dhātu, Tib. dbyings, khams: This term is used with three distinct meanings in this book. The first is as the abbreviation of dharmadhātu (see above); in that case the Tibetan is "dbyings". The second is as dhātu of skandhas, āyatanas, and dhātus where it means a basis from which consciousness arises, in which case the Tibetan is "khams". The third is with the meaning of a basic element or constituent, referring to the tathāgatagarbha which is the element of enlightenment within mind, in which case the Tibetan is "khams".

Discursive thought, Skt. vikalpa, Tib. rnam rtog: This means more than just the superficial thought that is heard as a voice in the head. It includes the entirety of conceptual process that arises due to mind contacting any object of any of the senses. The Sanskrit and Tibetan literally mean "(dualistic) thought (that arises from the mind wandering among the) various (superficies q.v. perceived in the doors of the senses)".

Elaboration, Tib. spro ba: This is a general name for what is given off by dualistic mind as it goes about its conceptual business. The term is pejorative in that it implies that a story has been made up, unnecessarily, about something which is actually nothing, which is empty. Elaborations, because of what they are, prevent a person from seeing emptiness directly.

Freedom from elaboration or being elaboration-free implies direct sight of emptiness. It is important to understand that these words are used in a theoretical or philosophical way in the second turning sutra teachings but are used in an experiential way in the final teachings of the third turning sutras and in the tantras of Great Completion and Mahāmudrā. In the former, being free of elaborations is a definition of what could happen according to the tenets of the Middle Way, and so on; in the latter it is a description of a state of being, one which, because it is empty of all the elaborations of dualistic being, is the actual sphere of emptiness.

Emptiness having the excellence of all superficies, Tib. rnam kun mchog ldan gyi stong pa nyid: This term is taught in the *Kālachakra Tantra* to emphasize the fact that emptiness is always unified with appearance. The tantra teaches, in conjunction with this term, that emptiness always has the excellence of all superficies, that is, always has the fullness of appearance with it. The name is employed in philosophical writings to imply that emptiness is never the bare kind of emptiness that can come from mistakenly understanding the Prajñāpāramitā teachings on emptiness.

The term is usually mistakenly translated as "emptiness endowed with the supreme of all aspects" because of mistaking the Tibetan term "mchog" to mean the buddha qualities. However, the translation as given is the correct understanding of the term, an understanding which is standard throughout Tibetan literature. Furthermore, grammatically speaking, this is emptiness which is not "endowed with" anything but simply "has" or "possesses" something.

Enlightenment mind, Skt. bodhicitta, Tib. byang chub sems: This is a key term of the Great Vehicle. It is the type of mind that is connected not with the lesser enlightenment of an arhat but the enlightenment of a truly complete buddha. As such, it is a mind which is connected with the aim of bringing all sentient beings to that same level of buddhahood. A person who has this mind has entered the Great Vehicle and is either a bodhisatva or a buddha.

It is important to understand that "enlightenment mind" is used to refer equally to the minds of all levels of bodhisatva on the path to buddhahood and to the mind of a buddha who has completed the path. Therefore, it is not "mind striving for enlightenment" as is so often translated, but "enlightenment mind", meaning that kind of mind which is connected with the full enlightenment of a truly complete buddha and which is present in all those who belong to the Great Vehicle.

Entity, Tib. ngo bo: The entity of something is just exactly what that thing is. In English we would often simply say "thing" rather than entity. However, in Buddhism, "thing" has a very specific meaning rather than the general meaning that it has in English. It has become common to translate this term as "essence" *q.v.* However, in most cases "entity", meaning what a thing is rather than an essence of that thing, is the correct translation for this term.

Equipoise and post-attainment, Tib. mnyam bzhag and rjes thob: Although often called "meditation and post-meditation", the actual term is "equipoise and post-attainment". There is great meaning in the actual wording which is lost by the looser translation.

Essence, Tib. ngo bo: This is a key term used throughout Buddhist theory. The original in Sanskrit and the term in Tibetan, too, has both meanings of "essence" and "entity". In some situations the term has more the first meaning and in others, the second. For example, when speaking of mind and mind's essence, it is referring to the core or essential part within mind. On the other hand, when speaking of something such as fire, one can speak of the entity, fire, and its characteristics, such as heat, and so on; in this case, the term does not mean essence but means that thing, what it actually is. See also under entity.

Exaggeration, Tib. skur 'debs pa: In Buddhism, this term is used in two ways. Firstly, it is used in general to mean misunderstanding from the perspective that one has added more to one's understanding of something than needs to be there. Secondly, it is used specifically to indicate that dualistic mind always overstates or exaggerates whatever object it is examining. Dualistic mind always adds the ideas of solidity, permanence, singularity, and so on to everything it references via the concepts that it uses. Severing of exaggeration either means removal of these un-necessary understandings when trying to properly comprehend something or removal of the dualistic process altogether when trying to get to the non-dualistic reality of a phenomenon.

Fact, Skt. artha, Tib. don: "Fact" is that knowledge of an object that occurs to the surface of mind or wisdom. It is not the object but what the mind or wisdom understands as the object. Thus there are two usages of "fact": fact known to dualistic and non-dualistic minds. The higher tantras especially use "fact" to refer to the actual fact known in direct perception of actuality. Thus, there are phrases such as "in fact" which do not mean that the author is speaking truly about something but that whatever is about to be said is referring to actual fact as known to wisdom. A further complexity is that phrases such as "in fact" in those contexts are often abbreviations of "in superfact" *q.v.* This brings a further difficulty for the reader because "superfact" can be used in a general way to indicate directly perceived non-samsaric fact or can be used according to its specific definition (for which see superfact). In Buddhist tradition, problems like this are solved by having the text explained by one's teacher. That might not be possible for some readers, so uses of the word "fact" should be looked at carefully to see whether they are indicating fact in general or the factual situation of knowing reality in direct perception.

Fictional, Skt. saṃvṛtti, Tib. kun rdzob: This term is paired with the term "superfactual" *q.v.* In the past, these terms have been translated as "relative" and "absolute" respectively, but those translations are nothing like the original terms. These terms are extremely important in the Buddhist teaching so it is very important that they be corrected, but more than that, if the actual meaning of these terms is not presented, then the teaching connected with them cannot be understood.

The Sanskrit term saṃvṛtti means a deliberate invention, a fiction, a hoax. It refers to the mind of ignorance which, because of being obscured and so not seeing suchness, is not true but a fiction. The things that appear to that ignorance are therefore fictional. Nonetheless, the beings who live in this ignorance believe that the things that appear to them through the filter of ignorance are true, are real. Therefore, these beings live in fictional truth.

Fictional and superfactual: Fictional and superfactual are our greatly improved translations for "relative" and "absolute" respectively. Briefly, the original Sanskrit word for fiction means a deliberately produced *fiction* and refers to the world projected by a mind controlled by ignorance. The original word for superfact means "that *superior fact* that appears on the surface of the mind of a noble one who has transcended saṃsāra" and refers to reality seen as it actually is. Relative and absolute do not convey this meaning at all and, when they are used, the meaning being presented is simply lost.

Fictional truth, Skt. saṃvṛtisatya, Tib. kun rdzob bden pa: See under fictional.

Fictional truth enlightenment mind, Tib. kun rdzob bden pa'i byang chub sems: One of a pair of terms explained in the Great Vehicle; the other is Superfactual Truth Enlightenment Mind. See under fictional truth and superfactual truth for information about those terms. Enlightenment mind is defined as two types. The fictional type is the conventional type: it is explained as consisting of love and great compassion within the framework of an intention to obtain truly complete enlightenment for the sake of all sentient beings. The superfactual truth type is the ultimate type: it is explained as the enlightenment mind that is directly perceiving emptiness.

Field, Field realm, Tib. zhing, zhing khams: This term is often translated "buddha field" though there is no "buddha" in the term. There are many different types of "fields" in both saṃsāra and nirvāṇa. Thus there are fields that belong to enlightenment and ones that belong to ignorance. Moreover, just as there are "realms" of saṃsāra— desire, form, and formless—so there are realms of nirvāṇa—the fields of the dharmakāya, saṃbhogakāya, and nirmāṇakāya and these are therefore called "field realms".

Foremost instruction, Skt. upadeśha, Tib. man ngag: There are several types of instruction mentioned in Buddhist literature: there is the general level of instruction which is the meaning contained in the words of the texts of the tradition; on a more personal and direct level there is oral instruction which has been passed down from teacher to student from the time of the buddha; and on the most profound level there are foremost instructions which are not only oral instructions provided by one's guru but are special, core instructions that come out of personal experience and which convey the teaching concisely and with the full weight of personal experience. Foremost instructions or upadeśha are crucial to the Vajra Vehicle because these are the special way of passing on the profound instructions needed for the student's realization.

Formative, Skt. saṃskāra, Tib. 'du byed. This term is usually translated as "formations", but a formation is the product of that which caused its formation, whereas this term refers to the agent which will cause a formation. The formatives, which are the contents of the fourth of the five aggregates, cause the production of a future set of aggregates for the mindstream involved. There are two types of formatives, ones which are a type of mind and ones which are not. The former includes all of the afflictions.

Fortune, fortunate person, Tib. skal ldan: To meet with any given dharma teaching, a person must have accumulated the karmic fortune needed for such a rare opportunity, and this kind of person is then called "a fortunate one" or "fortunate person". This term is especially used in the Vajra Vehicle, whose teachings and practices are generally very hard to meet with.

Garbha, Skt. garbha, Tib. snying po: see under sugatagarbha.

Grasped-grasping, Tib. gzung 'dzin: When mind is turned outwardly as it is in the normal operation of dualistic mind, it has developed two faces that appear simultaneously. Special names are given to these two faces: mind appearing in the form of the external object being referenced is called "that which is grasped" and mind appearing in the form of the consciousness that is registering it is called the "grasper" or "grasping" of it. Thus, there is the pair of terms "grasped-grasper" or "grasped-grasping". When these two terms are used, it alerts one to the fact that a Mind Only style of presentation is being discussed. This pair of terms pervades Mind Only, Middle Way, and tantric writings and is exceptionally important in all of them.

Note that one could substitute the word "apprehended" for "grasped" and "apprehender" for "grasper" or "grasping" and that would reflect one connotation of the original Sanskrit terminology. The solidified duality of grasped and grasper is nothing but an invention of dualistic thought; it has that kind of character or characteristic.

Great Bliss, Skt. mahāsukha, Tib. bde ba chen po: Great bliss is a standard but inexact translation of this key term. The phrase actually means "the great state of satisfactoriness" that comes with entering an enlightened kind of existence. It is blissful in that it is totally satisfactory, a condition of perfect ease, in comparison to samsaric existence which is totally unsatisfactory and always with some kind of dis-ease. As Thrangu Rinpoche once observed, if saṃsāra is thought of as "great suffering" then this is better thought of as the "great ease". Similarly, if saṃsāra is "total unsatisfactoriness" then this is the "great satisfactoriness".

Great Vehicle, Skt. mahāyāna, Tib. theg pa chen po: The Buddha's teachings as a whole can be summed up into three vehicles where a vehicle is defined as that which can carry a person to a certain destination. The first vehicle, called the Lesser Vehicle, contains the teachings designed to get an individual moving on the spiritual path through showing the unsatisfactory state of cyclic existence and an emancipation from that. However, that path is only concerned with personal emancipation and fails to take account of all of the beings that there are in existence. There used to be eighteen schools of Lesser Vehicle in India but the only one surviving nowadays is the Theravāda of south-east Asia. The Greater Vehicle is a step up from that. The Buddha explained that it was great in comparison to the Lesser Vehicle for seven reasons. The first of those is that it is concerned with attaining the truly complete enlightenment of a truly complete buddha for the sake of every sentient being where the Lesser Vehicle is concerned only with a personal liberation that is not truly complete enlightenment and which is achieved only for the sake of that practitioner. The Great Vehicle has two divisions: a conventional form in which the path is taught in a logical, conventional way, and an unconventional form in which the path is taught in a very direct way. This latter vehicle is called the Vajra Vehicle because it takes the innermost, indestructible (vajra) fact of reality of one's own mind as the vehicle to enlightenment.

Ground, Tib. gzhi: This is the first member of the formulation of ground, path, and fruition. Ground, path, and fruition is the way that the teachings of the path of oral instruction belonging to the Vajra Vehicle are presented to students. Ground refers to the basic situation as it is.

Guardian, Skt. nātha, Tib. mgon po: This name is a respectful title reserved for the buddhas. It means that they both protect and nurture sentient beings who they oversee, like a child who, having no parents has been given or has found a guardian. It is often translated as "protector" but that correctly translates another Sanskrit term to start with and on top of that is insufficient because it does not include the aspect of nurturing. It is also given to other beings such as bodhisatvas who have a similar quality, for example, Guardian Nāgārjuna and Guardian Maitreya.

Intentional conduct, Tib. mos spyod: A name in the Great Vehicle for the path activities done at levels of both accumulation and connection. At this level, one is still intending to directly realize emptiness. Note that intention is the name of one of the fifty-one mental events. Thus this name implies that it is conduct still at the level of dualistic being, though it is a good mind because it intends to reach non-dualistic being. Also, by definition there is no real accomplishment until the path of seeing is reached, so there is no real accomplishment at the level of intentional conduct. Intentional conduct as non-accomplishment followed by the three paths which are levels of accomplishment is a general presentation contained in the common vehicle.

Introduction and To Introduce, Tib. ngos sprad and ngos sprod pa respectively: This pair of terms is usually mistakenly translated today as "pointing out" and "to point out". The terms are the standard terms used in day to day life for the situation in which one person introduces another person to someone or something. They are the exact same words as our English "introduction" and "to introduce".

In the Vajra Vehicle, these terms are specifically used for the situation in which one person introduces another person to the nature of his own mind. There is a term in Tibetan for "pointing out", but that term is never used for this purpose because in this case no one points out anything. Rather, a person is introduced by another person to a part of himself that he has forgotten about.

Kagyu, Tib. bka' brgyud: There are four main schools of Buddhism in Tibet—Nyingma, Kagyu, Sakya, and Gelug. Nyingma is the oldest school dating from about 800 C.E. Kagyu and Sakya both appeared in the 12th century C.E. Each of these three schools came directly from India. The Gelug school came later and did not come directly from India but came from the other three. The Nyingma school holds the tantric teachings called Great Completion (Dzogchen); the other three schools hold the tantric teachings called Mahāmudrā. Kagyu practitioners often join Nyingma practice with their Kagyu practice and Kagyu teachers often teach both, so it is common to hear about Kagyu and Nyingma together.

Knower, Tib. ha go ba: "Knower" is a generic term for that which knows. There are many types of knower, with each having its own qualities and name, too. For example, *wisdom* is a non-dualistic knower, *mind* is the dualistic samsaric version of it, *consciousness* refers to the individual "registers" of samsaric mind, and so on. Sometimes a term is needed which simply says "that which knows" without further implication of what kind of knowing it might be; *knower* is one of a few terms of that sort.

Latency, Skt. vāsanā, Tib. bag chags: The original Sanskrit has the meaning exactly of "latency". The Tibetan term translates that inexactly with "something sitting there (Tib. chags) within the environment of mind (Tib. bag)". Although it has become popular to translate this term into English with "habitual pattern", that is not its meaning. The term refers to a karmic seed that has been imprinted on the mindstream and is present there as a latency, ready and waiting to come into manifestation.

Lesser Vehicle, Skt. hīnayāna, Tib. theg pa dman pa: See under Great Vehicle.

Luminosity or illumination, Skt. prabhāsvara, Tib. 'od gsal ba: The core of mind has two aspects: an emptiness factor and a knowing factor. The Buddha and many Indian religious teachers used "luminosity" as a metaphor for the knowing quality of the core of mind. If in English we would say "Mind has a knowing quality", the teachers of ancient India would say, "Mind has an illuminative quality; it is like a source of light which illuminates what it knows".

This term has been translated as "clear light" but that is a mistake that comes from not understanding the etymology of the word. It does not refer to a light that has the quality of clearness (something that makes no sense, actually!) but to the illuminative property which is the nature of the empty mind.

Note also that in both Sanskrit and Tibetan Buddhist literature, this term is frequently abbreviated just to Skt. "vara" and Tib. "gsal ba" with no change of meaning. Unfortunately, this has been thought to be another word and it has then been translated with "clarity", when in fact it is just this term in abbreviation.

Mahamudra, Skt. mahāmudrā, Tib. phyag rgya chen po: Mahāmudrā is the name of a set of ultimate teachings on reality and also of the reality itself. This is explained at length in the book *Gampopa's Mahamudra: The Five-Part Mahamudra of the Kagyus* by Tony Duff, published by Padma Karpo Translation Committee, 2008, ISBN 978-9937-2-0607-5.

Mentation, Skt. manaskāra, Tib. yid la byed pa: Mentation is the act of using the mental mind in general and is also one of the omnipresent mental events q.v. Its use implies the presence of dualistic mind. Non-mentating could be simply not using the dualistic mind but is usually used to imply the absence of dualistic mind, that is, the presence of wisdom.

Migrator, Tib. 'gro ba: Migrator is one of several terms that were commonly used by the Buddha to mean "sentient being". It shows sentient beings from the perspective of their constantly being forced to go here and there from one rebirth to another by the power of karma. They are like flies caught in a jar, constantly buzzing back and forth. The term is often translated using "beings" which is another general term for sentient beings but doing so loses the meaning entirely: Buddhist authors who know the tradition do not use the word loosely but use it specifically to give the sense of beings who are constantly and helplessly going from one birth to another, and that is how the term should be read. The term "six migrators" refers to the six types of migrators within samsaric existence—hell-beings, pretas, animals, humans, demi-gods, and gods.

Mind, Skt. chitta, Tib. sems: There are several terms for mind in the Buddhist tradition, each with its own, specific meaning. This term is the most general term for the samsaric type of mind. It refers to the type of mind that is produced because of fundamental ignorance of enlightened mind. Whereas the wisdom of enlightened mind lacks all complexity and knows in a non-dualistic way, this mind of un-enlightenment is a very complicated apparatus that only ever knows in a dualistic way.

The Mahāmudrā and Great Completion teachings use the terms "entity of mind" and "mind's entity" to refer to what this complicated, samsaric mind is at core—the enlightened form of mind.

Mindfulness, Skt. smṛiti, Tib. dran pa: A particular mental event, one that has the ability to keep mind on its object. Together with alertness, it is one of the two causes of developing śhamatha. See under alertness for an explanation.

Mindness, Skt. chittatā, Tib. sems nyid: Mindness is a specific term of the tantras. It is one of many terms meaning the essence of mind or the nature of mind. It conveys the sense of "what mind is at its very core". It has sometimes been translated as "mind itself" but that is a misunderstanding of the Tibetan word "nyid". The term does not mean "that thing mind" where mind refers to dualistic mind. Rather, it means the very core of dualistic mind, what mind is at root, without all of the dualistic baggage.

Mindness is a path term. It refers to exactly the same thing as "actuality" or "actuality of mind" which is a ground term but does so from the practitioner's perspective. It conveys the sense to a practitioner that he has baggage of dualistic mind that has not yet been purified but that there is a core to that mind that he can work with.

Muni: See under capable one.

Noble one, Skt. ārya, Tib. 'phags pa: In Buddhism, a noble one is a being who has become spiritually advanced to the point that he has passed beyond cyclic existence. According to the Buddha, the beings in cyclic existence were ordinary beings, spiritual commoners, and the beings who had passed beyond it were special, the nobility.

Non-regressing, Tib. phyir mi ldogs pa: This is a standard term used to describe the ultimate teachings on emptiness of the third turning of the wheel of dharma, called Other Emptiness. When a person has heard and comprehended these teachings, he immediately understands that all other teachings of the second and third turnings of the wheel are not ultimate and assumes the position that he will never turn back from these teachings and regress to taking one of the lesser views as ultimate.

Not stopped, Tib. ma 'gags pa: An important path term in the teaching of both Mahāmudrā and Great Completion. There are two ways to explain this term: according to view and to practice. The following explanation is of the latter type. The core of mind has two parts—emptiness and luminosity—which are in fact unified so must come that way in practice. However, a practitioner who is still on the path will fall into one extreme or the other and that results in "stoppage" of the expression of the luminosity. When emptiness and luminosity are unified in practice, there is no stoppage of the expression of the luminosity that comes from having fallen into one extreme or the other. Thus "non-stopped luminosity" is a term that indicates that there is the luminosity with all of its appearance yet that luminosity, for the practitioner, is not mistaken, is not stopped off. "Stopped luminosity" is an experience like luminosity but in which the appearances have, at least to some extent, not been mixed with emptiness.

Outflow, Skt. āsrāva, Tib. zag pa: The Sanskrit term means a bad discharge, like pus coming out of a wound. Outflows occur when wisdom loses its footing and falls into the elaborations of dualistic mind. Therefore, anything with duality also has outflows. This is sometimes translated as "defiled" or "conditioned" but these fail to capture the meaning. The idea is that wisdom can remain self-contained in its own unique sphere but, when it loses its ability to stay within itself, it starts to have leakages into dualism that are defilements on the wisdom. See also under un-outflowed.

Overall analysis, Tib. yongs dpyod: "Attribute analysis" and "overall analysis" are a pair of terms; see under attribute analysis.

Poisons, Tib. dug: In Buddhism, poison is a general term for the afflictions. For samsaric beings, the afflictions are poisonous things which harm them. The Buddha most commonly spoke of the three poisons, which are the principal afflictions of desire, aggression, and ignorance. He also spoke of "the five poisons" which is a slightly longer enumeration of the principal afflictions: desire, aggression, delusion, pride, and jealousy.

Post-attainment, Tib. rjes thob: See under equipoise and post-attainment.

Prajna, Skt. prajñā, Tib. shes rab: The Sanskrit term, literally meaning "best type of mind" is defined as that which makes correct distinctions between this and that and hence which arrives at correct understanding. It has been translated as "wisdom" but that is not correct because it is, generally speaking, a mental event belonging to dualistic mind where "wisdom" is used to refer to the non-dualistic knower of a buddha. Moreover, the main feature of prajñā is its ability to distinguish correctly between one thing and another and hence to arrive at a correct understanding.

Provisional and definitive meaning, Skt. neyartha and nitartha, Tib. drangs don and nges don: This is a pair of terms used to distinguish which is an ultimate or final teaching and which is not. A teaching which guides a student along to a certain understanding where the understanding led to is not an ultimate understanding is called "provisional meaning". The teaching is not false even though it does not show the final meaning; it is a technique of skilful means used to lead a student in steps to the final meaning. A teaching which shows a student the final meaning directly is called "definitive meaning". The understanding presented cannot be refined or shown in a more precise way; it is the final and actual understanding to be understood. These terms are most often used in Buddhism when discussing the status of the three turnings of the wheel of dharma.

Rational mind, Tib. blo: Rational mind is one of several terms for mind in Buddhist terminology. It specifically refers to a mind that judges this against that. With rare exception it is used to refer to samsaric mind, given that samsaric mind only works in the dualistic mode of comparing this versus that. Because of this, the term is mostly used in a pejorative sense to point out samsaric mind as opposed to an enlightened type of mind.

The Gelugpa tradition does have a positive meaning for this term and their documents will sometimes use it in that way; they make the claim that a buddha has an enlightened type of this mind. That is not wrong; one could refer to the ability of a buddha's wisdom to make a distinction between this and that with the term "rational

mind". However, the Kagyu and Nyingma traditions in their Mahāmudrā and Great Completion teachings, reserve this term for the
dualistic mind. In their teachings, it is the villain, so to speak, which
needs to be removed from the practitioner's being in order to obtain
enlightenment.

This term has been commonly translated simply as "mind" but that
fails to identify this term properly and leaves it confused with the
many other words that are also translated simply as "mind". It is
not just another mind but is specifically the sort of mind that creates
the situation of this and that (*ratio* in Latin) and hence, at least in
the teachings of Kagyu and Nyingma, upholds the duality of
saṃsāra. In that case, it is the very opposite of the essence of mind.
Thus, this is a key term which should be noted and not just glossed
over as "mind".

Realization, Tib. rtogs pa: Realization has a very specific meaning: it
refers to correct knowledge that has been gained in such a way that
the knowledge does not abate. There are two important points
here. Firstly, realization is not absolute. It refers to the removal
of obscurations, one at a time. Each time that a practitioner
removes an obscuration, he gains a realization because of it.
Therefore, there are as many levels of realization as there are
obscurations. Maitreya, in the *Ornament of Manifest Realizations*,
shows how the removal of the various obscurations that go with each
of the three realms of samsaric existence produces realization.

Secondly, realization is stable or, as the Tibetan wording says, "unchanging". As Guru Rinpoche pointed out, "Intellectual knowledge
is like a patch, it drops away; experiences on the path are temporary,
they evaporate like mist; realization is unchanging".

A special usage of "realization" is found in the Essence Mahāmudrā
and Great Completion teachings. There, realization is the term
used to describe what happens at the moment when mindness is actually met during either introduction to or self-recognition of
mindness. It is called realization because, in that glimpse, one
actually directly sees the innate wisdom mind. The realization has
not been stabilized but it is realization.

Reference and Referencing, Tib. dmigs pa: Referencing is the name for the process in which dualistic mind references an actual object by using a conceptual label instead of the actual object. Whatever is referenced is then called a reference. Note that these terms imply the presence of dualistic mind and their opposites, non-referencing and being without reference imply the presence of non-dualistic wisdom.

Rigpa, Tib. rig pa: This is the singularly most important term in the whole of Great Completion and Mahāmudrā. In particular, it is the key word of all words in the Great Completion system of the Thorough Cut. Rigpa literally means to know in the sense of "I see!" It is used at all levels of meaning from the coarsest everyday sense of knowing something to the deepest sense of knowing something as presented in the system of Thorough Cut. The system of Thorough Cut uses this term in a very special sense, though it still retains its basic meaning of "to know". To translate it as "awareness" which is common practice these days is a poor practice; there are many kinds of awareness but there is only one rigpa and besides, rigpa is substantially more than just awareness. Since this is such an important term and since it lacks an equivalent in English, I choose not to translate it. However, it will be helpful when reading the text to understand the meaning as just given.

This is the term used to indicate enlightened mind as experienced by the practitioner on the path of these practices. The term itself specifically refers to the dynamic knowing quality of mind. It absolutely does not mean a simple registering, as implied by the word "awareness" which unfortunately is often used to translate this term. There is no word in English that exactly matches it, though the idea of "seeing" or "insight on the spot" is very close. Proof of this is found in the fact that the original Sanskrit term "vidyā" is actually the root of all words in English that start with "vid" and mean "to see", for example, "video", "vision", and so on. Chogyam Trungpa Rinpoche, who was particularly skilled at getting Tibetan words into English, also stated that this term rigpa really did not have a good equivalent in English, though he thought that "insight" was the closest. My own conclusion after hearing extensive teaching on it is that rigpa is just best left untranslated. However, it will be helpful when reading the text to understanding the meaning as just given.

Rishi, Skt. ṛiṣhi, Tib. drang srong: A rishi is a holy man. The Sanskrit itself means one who has a sufficient level of spiritual accomplishment and knowledge to bring others along the path of spirituality properly. It was a common appellation in ancient India where there were many rishis. The Buddha was often referred to as "the rishi" meaning the rishi of all rishis or as the "great ṛiṣhi" meaning the greatest of all rishis.

Samsara, Skt. saṃsāra, Tib. 'khor ba: This is the most general name for the type of existence in which sentient beings live. It refers to the fact that they continue on from one existence to another, always within the enclosure of births that are produced by ignorance and experienced as unsatisfactory. The original Sanskrit means to be constantly going about, here and there. The Tibetan term literally means "cycling", because of which it is frequently translated into English with "cyclic existence" though that is not quite the meaning of the term.

Satva and sattva: According to the Tibetan tradition established at the time of the great translation work done at Samye under the watch of Padmasambhava not to mention one hundred and sixty-three of the greatest Buddhist scholars of Sanskrit-speaking India, there is a difference of meaning between the Sanskrit terms "satva" and "sattva", with satva meaning "an heroic kind of being" and "sattva" meaning simply "a being". According to the Tibetan tradition established under the advice of the Indian scholars mentioned above, satva is correct for the words Vajrasatva and bodhisatva, whereas sattva is correct for the words samayasattva, samādhisattva, and jñānasattva, and is also used alone to refer to any or all of these three satvas.

All Tibetan texts produced since the time of the great translations conform to this system and all Tibetan experts agree that this is correct, but Western translators of Tibetan texts have for the last few hundred years claimed that they know better and have changed "satva" to "sattva" in every case, causing confusion amongst Westerners confronted by the correct spellings. Recently, publications by Western Sanskrit scholars have been appearing in which these great experts finally admit that they were wrong and that the Tibetan system is and always has been correct!

Secret Mantra, Skt. guhyamantra, Tib. gsang sngags: Another name for the Vajra Vehicle or the tantric teachings.

Shamatha, Skt. śhamatha, Tib. gzhi gnas: This is the name of one of the two main practices of meditation used in the Buddhist system to gain insight into reality. This practice creates a one-pointedness of mind which can then be used as a foundation for development of the insight of the other practice, vipaśhyanā. If the development of śhamatha is taken through to completion, the result is a mind that sits stably on its object without any effort and a body which is filled with ease. Altogether, this result of the practice is called "the creation of workability of body and mind".

Sugata, Tib. bde bar gshegs pa: This term is one of many names for a buddha. It has the twofold meaning of someone who has gone on a good, pleasant, easy journey and who has arrived at a place which is good, pleasant, and full of ease. The meaning in relation to buddhahood is explained at length in *Unending Auspiciousness, the Sutra of the Recollection of the Noble Three Jewels* by Tony Duff, published by Padma Karpo Translation Committee, 2010, ISBN: 978-9937-8386-1-0.

Sugatagarbha, Tib. bde bar gshegs pa'i snying po: This is one of a pair of terms for the potential existing in all sentient beings that makes the attainment of buddhahood possible, also called the buddha-nature. The other term is tathāgatagarbha. The sanskrit term "garbha" primarily means something which is potent but contained in an outer shell, like a seed, and is also used to mean a matrix or womb from which something can be produced. Both meanings are applicable. Tibetans translated garbha with "snying po" which has many meanings but in this case means "an essence or core", which was their take on the meaning of buddha-nature. The meaning altogether is a seed contained within the obscurations of samsaric being, which makes it possible to become a sugata or tathagatha, that is, a buddha.

Sugatagarbha has the same basic meaning as tathāgatagarbha but is a practical way of talking where tathagātagarbha is theoretical. Sugatagarbha is used when an author is talking about the practical realities of an essence that can be or is being developed into enlightened being. For example, in the sutras of the third turning of the wheel, the Buddha speaks of tathagatagarbha when laying out the theory of buddha-nature but switches to sugatagarbha when speaking of wisdom as what is to be actually attained. Similarly, the tantras, which are mainly concerned with the practical attainment of wisdom mainly, use the term sugatagarbha and rarely use the term tathāgatagarbha. See also under sugata.

Superfactual, Skt. paramārtha, Tib. don dam: This term is paired with the term "fictional" *q.v.* In the past, the terms have been translated as "relative" and "absolute" respectively, but those translations are nothing like the original terms. These terms are extremely important in the Buddhist teaching so it is very important that their translations be corrected but, more than that, if the actual meaning of these terms is not presented, the teaching connected with them cannot be understood.

The Sanskrit term literally means "the fact for that which is above all others, special, superior" and refers to the wisdom mind possessed by those who have developed themselves spiritually to the point of having transcended saṃsāra. That wisdom is *superior* to an ordinary, un-developed person's consciousness and the *facts* that appear on its surface are superior compared to the facts that appear on the ordinary person's consciousness. Therefore, it is superfact or the holy fact, more literally. What this wisdom knows is true for the beings who have it, therefore what the wisdom sees is superfactual truth.

Superfactual truth, Skt. paramārthasatya, Tib. don dam bden pa: See under superfactual.

Superfactual truth enlightenment mind, Tib. don dam bden pa'i byang chub sems: This is one of a pair of terms; the other is Fictional Truth Enlightenment Mind *q.v.* for explanation.

Superfice, superficies, Tib. rnam pa: In discussions of mind, a distinction is made between the entity of mind which is a mere knower and the superficial things that appear on its surface and which are known by it. In other words, the superficies are the various things which pass over the surface of mind but which are not mind. Superficies are all the specifics that constitute appearance—for example, the colour white within a moment of visual consciousness, the sound heard within an ear consciousness, and so on.

Suppression and furtherance, Tib. dgag sgrub: Suppression and furtherance is the term used to express the way that dualistic mind approaches the path to enlightenment. In that case, some states of mind are regarded as ones to be discarded, so the practitioner takes the approach of attempting to suppress or stop them, and some are regarded as ones to be developed, so the practitioner takes the approach of trying to go further with and develop them. These two poles represent the way that dualistic mind always works with itself. Thorough Cut practice goes beyond that duality.

Tathagatagarbha, Skt. tathāgatagarbha, Tib. de bzhin gshegs pa'i snying po: This means the garbha or seed of a tathāgata; see under sugatagarbha.

Temporary experience, Tib. nyams: The practice of meditation brings with it various experiences that happen simply because of doing meditation. These experiences are temporary experiences and not the final, unchanging experience, of realization.

The authentic, Tib. yang dag: A name for reality, that which is real. For example "the view of the authentic" means "the view of reality" not a correct view.

The element, Skt. dhātu, Tib. khams. The Sanskrit term has many meanings; the meaning here is "a fundamental substance from which something else can be produced". When the Buddha explained the tathāgatagarbha or buddha nature in the third turning of the wheel, he used several names for it, each one showing a specific aspect of it. He called it the element with the meaning "that basis substance from which buddhahood can be produced". He called it "the type" meaning that it was the same sort of thing as buddhahood and therefore could lead to buddhahood; this term is also translated as "family" and "lineage". He also called it "the seed" meaning the seed of enlightenment. He also called it "the garbha"; see under sugatagarbha for the meaning.

The nature, Tib. rang bzhin: The nature is one of the three characteristics—entity, nature, and un-stopped compassionate activity—of the core of mind. Using this term emphasizes that the empty entity does have a nature. In other words, its use explicitly shows that the core of mind is not merely empty. If you ask "Well, what is that nature like?" The answer is that it is luminosity, it is wisdom.

Third order thousandfold world system, Tib. stong gsum 'jig rten: Indian cosmology has for its smallest cosmic unit a single Mt. Meru with four continents type of world system; an analogy might be a single planetary system like our solar system. One thousand of those makes a first order thousandfold world system; an analogy might be a galaxy. One thousand of those makes a second order thousandfold world system; an analogy might be a region of space with many galaxies. One thousand of those makes a third order thousandfold world system (1000 raised to the power 3); an analogy would be one whole universe like ours. The Buddha said that there were countless numbers of third order thousandfold world systems, each of which would be roughly equivalent to a universe like ours.

Three Vehicles, theg pa gsum: The entire teachings of the Buddha can be summed up into three "vehicles". Each vehicle is a complete set of teachings that will take a person to a particular level of spiritual attainment. The first one, the Lesser Vehicle, is a set of teachings that will take a person out of cyclic existence but will not lead the person to full enlightenment. The second one, the Great Vehicle, is "great" relative to the Lesser Vehicle because it can lead a person to full enlightenment. The third vehicle, the Vajra Vehicle, also can lead a person to full enlightenment. The difference between the Great and Vajra Vehicles is that the first consists of exoteric teachings that are suitable for anyone whereas the second consists of esoteric teachings that are not. The Great Vehicle and the Vajra Vehicle both lead to the same attainment, but the first proceeds very gradually whereas the second is very fast. The Great Vehicle proceeds using the sūtra teachings of the Buddha whereas the Vajra Vehicle proceeds using the tantric teachings.

Tirthika, Skt. tīrthika, Tib. mu stegs pa: This is a very kind name adopted by the Buddha for those who did not follow him but who, because they followed some other spiritual path, had at least started on the path back to enlightenment. The Sanskrit name means "those who have arrived at the steps at the edge of the pool". A lengthy explanation is given in the *Illuminator Tibetan-English Dictionary* by Tony Duff and published by Padma Karpo Translation Committee.

Two Purities or Two Complete Purities, Tib. dag pa gnyis or rnam par dag pa gnyis: This refers to the fruitional state of buddhahood as something which is totally cleared of all samsaric aspects. It is defined in various ways. One is that buddhahood is the state in which the dharmakāya has been completely purified of the two obscurations. Another is that the dharmakāya and form kāyas are completely purified of all samsaric impurities.

Unaltered or uncontrived, Tib. ma bcos pa: This term is the opposite of altered and contrived. It refers to something which has not been altered from its native state; something which has been left just as it is.

Un-outflowed, Skt. anāśhrāva, Tib. zag pa med pa: Un-outflowed dharmas are ones that are connected with wisdom that has not lost its footing and leaked out into a defiled state; it is self-contained wisdom without any taint of dualistic mind and its apparatus. See also outflowed.

Unsatisfactoriness, Skt. duḥkha, Tib. sdug bngal: This term is usually translated into English with "suffering" but there are many problems with that. When the Buddha talked about the nature of samsaric existence, he said that it was unsatisfactory. He used the term "duḥkha", which includes actual suffering but means much more than that. Duḥkha is one of a pair of terms, the other being "sukha", which is usually translated as, but does not only mean, bliss. The real meaning of duḥkha is "everything on the side of bad"—not good, uncomfortable, unpleasant, not nice, and so on. Thus, it means "unsatisfactory in every possible way". The real meaning of its opposite, sukha, is "everything on the side of good"—not bad, comfortable, pleasant, nice, and so on. Therefore, that he is completely liberated from the sufferings actually means that he has completely liberated himself from the unsatisfactoriness of samsara, which includes all types of suffering and happiness, too.

Un-stopped, Tib. ma 'gags pa: An important path term in the teaching of both Mahāmudrā and Great Completion. The essence of mind has two parts: emptiness and luminosity. Both of these must come unified. However, when a practitioner does the practice, he will fall into one extreme or the other and that is called "stoppage". The aim of the practice is to get to the stage in which there is both emptiness and luminosity together. In that case, there is no stoppage of falling into one extreme or the other. Thus non-stopped luminosity is a term that indicates that there is the luminosity with all of its appearance yet that luminosity, for the practitioner, is not mistaken, is not stopped off. Stopped luminosity is an experience like luminosity but in which the appearances have, at least to some extent, not been mixed with emptiness.

Vajra Vehicle, Skt. vajrayāna, Tib. rdo rje'i theg pa: See under Great Vehicle.

Valid cognizer, valid cognition, Skt. pramāṇa, Tib. tshad ma: The Sanskrit term "pramāṇa" literally means "best type of mentality" and comes to mean "a valid cognizer". Its value is that is can be used to validate anything that can be known. The Tibetans translated this term with "tshad ma" meaning an "evaluator"—something which can be used to evaluate the truth or not of whatever it is given to know. It is the term used in logic to indicate a mind which is knowing validly and which therefore can be used to validate the object it is knowing.

Valid cognizers are named according to the kind of test they are employed to do. A valid cognizer of the conventional or a valid cognizer of the fictional tests within conventions, within the realm of rational, dualistic mind. A valid cognizer of the ultimate or valid cognizer of superfact tests for the superfactual level, beyond dualistic mind.

Vehicle of Characteristics, Tib. mtshan nyid theg pa: Another of many names for the conventional Great Vehicle; see under Great Vehicle. It is called the Vehicle of Characteristics because the teachings in it rely on a conventional approach in which logic is used to find reality and in doing so, the characteristics of phenomena are a key part of the explanations of the system.

View, meditation, and conduct, Tib. lta sgom spyod: This set of three is a formulation of the teachings that contains all of the meaning of the path.

Vipashyana, Skt. vipaśhyanā, Tib. lhag mthong: This is the Sanskrit name for one of the two main practices of meditation needed in the Buddhist system for gaining insight into reality. The other one, śhamatha, keeps the mind focussed while this one looks piercingly into the nature of things.

Wisdom, Skt. jñāna, Tib. ye shes: This is a fruition term that refers to the kind of mind—the kind of knower—possessed by a buddha. Sentient beings do have this kind of knower but it is covered over by a very complex apparatus for knowing, that is, dualistic mind. If they practise the path to buddhahood, they will leave behind their obscuration and return to having this kind of knower.

The Sanskrit term has the sense of knowing in the most simple and immediate way. This sort of knowing is present at the core of every being's mind. Therefore, the Tibetans called it "the particular type of awareness which is there primordially". Because of the Tibetan wording it has often been called "primordial wisdom" in English translations, but that goes too far; it is just "wisdom" in the sense of the most fundamental knowing possible.

Wisdom does not operate in the same way as samsaric mind; it comes about in and of itself without depending on cause and effect. Therefore it is frequently referred to as "self-arising wisdom" *q.v.*

ABOUT THE AUTHOR,
PADMA KARPO TRANSLATION COMMITTEE,
AND THEIR SUPPORTS FOR STUDY

I have been encouraged over the years by all of my teachers to pass on the knowledge I have accumulated in a lifetime dedicated to study and practice, primarily in the Tibetan tradition of Buddhism. On the one hand, they have encouraged me to teach. On the other, they are concerned that, while many general books on Buddhism have been and are being published, there are few books that present the actual texts of the tradition. Therefore they, together with a number of major figures in the Buddhist book publishing world, have also encouraged me to translate and publish high quality translations of individual texts of the tradition.

My teachers always remark with great appreciation on the extraordinary amount of teaching that I have heard in this life. It allows for highly informed, accurate translations of a sort not usually seen. Briefly, I spent the 1970's studying, practising, then teaching the Gelugpa system at Chenrezig Institute, Australia, where I was a founding member and also the first Australian to be ordained as a monk in the Tibetan Buddhist tradition. In 1980, I moved to the United States to study at the feet of the Vidyadhara Chogyam Trungpa Rinpoche. I stayed in his Vajradhatu community, now called Shambhala, where I studied and practised all the Karma Kagyu, Nyingma, and Shambhala teachings being presented there and was a senior member of the Nalanda Translation Committee. After the vidyadhara's nirvana, I moved in 1992 to Nepal, where I have been continuously involved with the study, practise, translation, and teaching of the Kagyu system and especially of the Nyingma system of Great Completion. In recent years, I have spent extended times in Tibet with the greatest living Tibetan masters of Great Completion, receiving very pure transmissions of the ultimate levels of this teaching directly in Tibetan and practising them there in retreat. In that way, I have studied and practised extensively not in one Tibetan tradition as is usually done, but in three of the four Tibetan traditions—Gelug, Kagyu, and Nyingma—and also in the Theravada tradition, too.

With that as a basis, I have taken a comprehensive and long term approach to the work of translation. For any language, one first must have the lettering needed to write the language. Therefore, as a member of the Nalanda Translation Committee, I spent some years in the 1980's making Tibetan word-processing software and high-quality Tibetan fonts. After that, reliable lexical works are needed. Therefore, during the 1990's I spent some years writing the *Illuminator Tibetan-English Dictionary* and a set of treatises on Tibetan grammar, preparing a variety of key Tibetan reference works needed for the study and translation of Tibetan Buddhist texts, and giving our Tibetan software the tools needed to translate and research Tibetan texts. During this time, I also translated full-time for various Tibetan gurus and ran the Drukpa Kagyu Heritage Project—at the time the largest project in Asia for the preservation of Tibetan Buddhist texts. With the dictionaries, grammar texts, and specialized software in place, and a wealth of knowledge, I turned my attention in the year 2000 to the translation and publication of important texts of Tibetan Buddhist literature.

Padma Karpo Translation Committee (PKTC) was set up to provide a home for the translation and publication work. The committee focusses on producing books containing the best of Tibetan literature, and, especially, books that meet the needs of practitioners. At the time of writing, PKTC has published a wide range of books that, collectively, make a complete program of study for those practising Tibetan Buddhism, and especially for those interested in the higher tantras. All in all, you will find many books both free and for sale on the PKTC web-site. Most are available both as paper editions and e-books.

It would take up too much space here to present an extensive guide to our books and how they can be used as the basis for a study program. However, a guide of that sort is available on the PKTC web-site, whose address is on the copyright page of this book and we recommend that you read it to see how this book fits into the overall scheme of PKTC publications. In short, given that this book is about Other Emptiness, other books of interest would be:

- *The Noble One Called "Point of Passage Wisdom", A Great Vehicle Sutra*, the root sūtra of the twenty sūtras of Other Emptiness of the third turning of the wheel;

- *Instructions for Practising the View of Other Emptiness*, a text by the first Jamgon Kongtrul showing the practice of Other Emptiness according to the Jonang tradition;

- *The Lion's Roar that Proclaims Zhantong*, a text by Ju Mipham which shows the view of Other Emptiness then goes through arguments raised by Tsongkhapa's followers against the Other Emptiness system;

- *Maitripa's Writings on the View*, a selection of important texts written by the Indian master Maitrīpa showing his understanding of the Other Emptiness approach;

- *A Juggernaut of the Non-Dual View, Ultimate Teachings of the Second Drukchen, Gyalwang Je*, a set of sixty-six teachings on the non-dual view of the tantras which shows clearly the Other Emptiness view of the Kagyus.

These texts on Kagyu Mahāmudrā indirectly show the meaning of Other Emptiness given that Other Emptiness is the view underlying Kagyu Mahāmudrā:

- *Drukchen Padma Karpo's Collected Works on Mahamudra*
- *Dusum Khyenpa's Songs and Teachings*
- *Gampopa's Mahamudra, The Five-Part Mahamudra of the Kagyus*

We make a point of including, where possible, the relevant Tibetan texts in Tibetan script in our books. We also make them available in electronic editions that can be downloaded free from our web-site, as discussed below. Unfortunately, it would have taken too much space to include the Tibetan texts for this book.

ELECTRONIC RESOURCES

PKTC has developed a complete range of electronic tools to facilitate the study and translation of Tibetan texts. For many years now, this software has been a prime resource for Tibetan Buddhist centres throughout the world, including in Tibet itself. It is available through the PKTC web-site.

The wordprocessor TibetDoc has the only complete set of tools for creating, correcting, and formatting Tibetan text according to the norms of the Tibetan language. It can also be used to make texts with mixed Tibetan and English or other languages. Extremely high quality Tibetan fonts, based on the forms of Tibetan calligraphy learned from old masters from pre-Communist-Chinese Tibet, are also available. Because of their excellence, these typefaces have achieved a legendary status amongst Tibetans.

TibetDoc is used to prepare electronic editions of Tibetan texts in the PKTC text input office in Asia. Tibetan texts are often corrupt so the input texts are carefully corrected prior to distribution. After that, they are made available through the PKTC web-site. These electronic texts are not careless productions like so many of the Tibetan texts found on the web, but are highly reliable editions useful to non-scholars and scholars alike. Some of the larger collections of these texts are for purchase, but most are available for free download.

The electronic texts can be read, searched, and even made into an electronic library using either TibetDoc or our other software, TibetD Reader. Like TibetDoc, TibetD Reader is advanced software with many capabilities made specifically to meet the needs of reading and researching Tibetan texts. PKTC software is for purchase but we make a free version of TibetD Reader available for free download on the PKTC web-site.

A key feature of TibetDoc and Tibet Reader is that Tibetan terms in texts can be looked up on the spot using PKTC's electronic dictionaries. PKTC also has several electronic dictionaries—some Tibetan-Tibetan and some Tibetan-English—and a number of other reference works. The *Illuminator Tibetan-English Dictionary* is renowned for its completeness and accuracy.

This combination of software, texts, reference works, and dictionaries that work together seamlessly has become famous over the years. It has been the basis of many, large publishing projects within the Tibetan Buddhist community around the world for over thirty years and is popular amongst all those needing to work with Tibetan language or deepen their understanding of Buddhism through Tibetan texts.

INDEX

311